All Creatures
Great and Small

All Creatures Great and Small

DANIEL P. MANNIX

ISBN: 979-8-3372-0090-3

This edition published in 2025 by Open Road Integrated Media, Inc.
180 Maiden Lane
New York, NY 10038
www.openroadmedia.com

To Jule: my dear wife,
who has stuck to me
through eagles, pythons,
tarantulas, and two children

Introduction

A Mexican friend of mine once remarked after reading my umpteenth article about my adventures with animals in Taxco and Acapulco, "You've made more money out of this country than Cortez did." This is a slight exaggeration, but I've been writing since I was eighteen and a lot of words have run through my typewriter since then. Aguila, my eagle, is top dog—or top bird—with articles about her in *The Saturday Evening Post, True, Coronet, Holiday,* and *Life.* Next would probably come the vampire bats, although plenty has been published about Rani, my cheetah, also. My first article (about my skunks) was published in the old *St. Nicholas* magazine in 1931 and other stories about them have appeared in *This Week, Collier's* and now *True.*

True magazine has published over sixty of my articles, mostly about my pets, and several of the stories in this book are about the same animals. Doug Kennedy (*True's* editor), Charlie Barnard, and my old friend Peter Barrett have struggled with me for many years over such problems as underwater photographs of a cormorant catching fish and close-ups of a tarantula's fangs (these were highly successful and so grisly that several lady readers indignantly cancelled their subscriptions).

In a mood that Thoreau defines as "quiet desperation," Jule Mannix, my wife, published a book about our adventures together which Ballantine Books has brought out under the title of *Eagle in the Bathtub*. Jule has recounted several of these same adventures; from the point of view of the innocent victim so to speak. Then, too, there's the story of the pets I had as a boy collected in *The Backyard Zoo*, published by Coward & McCann "way back in 1934 and now a 'collector's item'" (I've never known what that phrase meant but it sounds impressive).

Those of you who know about the Mannix Menagerie will meet a few old friends, and many new ones. To those of you who find the whole business coming as a fresh shock, I can only wish good luck. To the publishers and editors who have made it possible for me to support eagles, cheetahs, otters, cormorants, pythons, tarantulas, anteaters, and armadillos—plus a wife and two children—I can only say, "Thanks, pals."

All Creatures
Great and Small

One

Curled up in my lap while I write this is Macho, a tiny squirrel monkey who is one of the gentlest, most affectionate pets I have ever known. Macho does not belong to me; he is the property of my eighteen-year-old daughter Julie, but although for seven years Julie lavished endless attention on Jupo, a spider monkey who had the disposition of King Kong and the strength of Gargantua, Julie does not like Macho. The little fellow cries bitterly when left alone, so taking care of him has been relegated to me. As Julie sadly told me, "Daddy, I'm sorry about Macho, but he just doesn't have a real personality like Jupo."

Jupo certainly had a personality. She bit everyone in the household (except Julie); my son Danny still carries the scar where Jupo ripped open the side of his leg when he was playfully wrestling with his sister. Jupo ran loose about the farm in the summer and established a blockade of the house; no one was allowed in or out without bribing her with fruit. Deliverymen arrived at the house carrying their offerings like ancient priests assuaging the wrath of a vengeful deity. When some guests arrived one day with a little boy who attempted to bypass Jupo's outstretched paw and as a result had to have seven stitches taken in his forearm, Jupo went to the zoo—the first animal I have ever consigned to a life behind bars. Julie visits her there once a week with a present of fruit. Jupo now has a husband, a male spider monkey even bigger and tougher than she. It is amazing and somewhat pitiful to see the once all-powerful Jupo sitting humbly in one corner of the cage while Butch takes the fruit, selects the best pieces for himself, and passes on what is left to his meek consort. "But Jupo seems to admire him for it," Julie told me in bewilderment. "She won't come to me any more; she just goes and sits beside that horrid bully of a Butch whenever he'll let her."

Admittedly, after Jupo anything short of a tyrannosaurus would be an anticlimax, and Macho presents no problem. Poor gentle little Macho! Unlike Jupo, who went through the house like an unguided missile, Macho is perfectly willing to sit in my lap watching the typewriter keys clicking away, only occasionally putting out a hand to tug softly at my arm so I will stop long enough to stroke his head and convince him that he's not been forgotten. I must be getting old because, frankly, I prefer Macho to Jupo—but still I can see what Julie means. Macho is almost like a domestic kitten or puppy.

Domestic animals have been bred by man to accept a position of subservience. Wild animals are themselves. Astonishingly little is known about them—how they live, what they eat, above all how they think. Yet for thousands of years keeping wild animals was regarded as an invaluable skill, combining the extrasensory perception of the psychic with the practical knowledge of the scientist. Sir Henry Layard found a bas-relief in the ruins of Khorsabad carved three thousand years ago depicting Persian falconers with their hawks. Alexander the Great was astonished to find rajahs hunting with cheetahs that could outrun his fastest greyhounds; Friar Odoric, who went to China thirty years after Marco Polo, described fishing with trained cormorants; and in sixteenth-century Sweden an entire family would often be supported by a pet otter catching fish. Until recently it was a rare English youngster who didn't have a pet ferret or an American country boy without a pet 'coon. Today all this is fast becoming a lost art.

I have always had wild animal pets. My father was a captain in the Navy and during the many years he spent on active service, he and Mother were often away, so I was brought up in my grandparents' home on the Philadelphia Main Line—then largely open country. I didn't have many playmates; the estates were large and seemed inhabited mainly by regal dowagers and grim old gentlemen who lived in savage seclusion among their horses, formal gardens, and shooting preserves. We had only one car, a venerable Pierce Arrow which no one could drive except the chauffeur and which was only produced on formal occasions such as going to church or an occasional wedding. To employ this stately vehicle for such frivolous purposes as driving a boy to a friend's house was virtually unthinkable. Nor did the boy particularly want to be driven. By the time I was fourteen I was six feet two inches tall; gangling, a wretched athlete who had no interest in sports, and a nonconformist—or, as it was called in those days, "not regular." From the end of school in June until September I seldom saw another youngster my own age.

My grandparents never worried over my inability to "adjust to a group situation." It was part of the tradition of the Main Line to take eccentricities for granted—they were even considered a sign of good breeding. Across the street from us lived a happily married couple in an old Charles Addams mansion; as the lady was insane, her husband kept her locked in the attic when fits were upon her. As a child I saw nothing unusual in this—after all, Rochester in *Jane Eyre* kept his insane wife locked in a third-story room, and I regarded it fairly standard domestic practice.

Occasionally I would pass the lady's husband on my way to the little village of Bryn Mawr, where I occasionally went to get an ice-cream cone. I only spoke to him once; that was to tell him that his wife was running around our lower garden in her nightgown. He thanked me and said he'd attend to it after getting the morning paper.

Although my grandparents had strong ideas about interfering in other people's affairs, they did feel that a mild protest was in order this time. Grandfather prepared a note for the lady's husband suggesting that possibly he might exert more control "over the affected member of your family." Grandfather went over to deliver it and the door was opened by the lady in question, still in her nightgown, who snatched the note out of his hand and read it. She screamed "Affected yourself!" and burst into a string of profanity to which Grandfather listened politely while leaning on his silver-headed cane. When she had finished, Grandfather removed his hat and bowed; the lady curtsied. They parted with mutual expressions of esteem, and Grandfather returned and looked her up in the Social Register under *Married Maidens*. "Ah yes, she was Emma Gould," he remarked with satisfaction. "Very old family. Every member of it has either gone insane or committed suicide for the last hundred years."

Grandmother was not able to take quite such a broadminded view of our neighbors, but she never dreamed of questioning Grandfather's authority in such matters. After all, Grandfather was Old Philadelphia and Grandmother was not, although the money came from her side of the family. Grandmother's father had been an Irish immigrant who, according to Grandmother, had been the surveyor for the Pennsylvania Railroad when it ran its tracks to Altoona. Actually, from what I could gather it would have been more correct to say he had carried the implements of the actual surveyors—but he had unquestionably been an excellent businessman. When the railroad came to lay their tracks, it was discovered that the Irishman had quietly obtained a lien on most of the property along the right-of-way and was asking a substantial sum for it. As a result his daughter had been able to advance herself socially by marrying Grandfather who, as a distinguished Main Liner, had not the slightest intention of having to work for a living.

Unlike Grandfather, who was as slender as his cane, Grandmother was amply built, but she was so tall and carried herself so majestically she gave the impression of grandeur rather than plumpness. She always moved at a slow, dignified pace and I doubt if even the sudden appearance of a man-eating lion could have caused her to break her carefully paced stride.

Looking back, I realized that Grandmother must have been a very lonely woman even though she had a small coterie of friends, mainly elderly maiden ladies most of whom seemed to be selling homemade lace, hand-painted vases, or similar useful articles which Grandmother occasionally bought. Her household duties could not have been too irksome since we had a highly efficient housekeeper named Mary Clark, who ran the establishment with the authority of a Prussian drillmaster.

In these days when both parents and grandparents are "pals" to their children, it is hard to conceive of an era when children were not only not heard but also—as much as possible—not seen. I was brought up by a nurse until I was six and seldom saw my grandparents except in the evening, when I was taken to the "grown-ups' part of the house" to say good night, a solemn and somewhat scary ritual. The rest of the time I spent either in the nursery or in the garden. When I entered school, the nurse was dismissed in a tearful and hysterical scene I still vividly remember. It was thereafter my responsibility to get myself up at seven, dress, and go down stairs to the dining room where the maid served my breakfast. I then walked to the railroad station half a mile away and took the train to school, returning home just in time for supper (the school had an elaborate athletic program which lasted until dark). I saw my grandparents at supper and, after answering politely and formally some equally polite and formal inquiries as to how things had gone at school that day, ate my meal in silence. After supper, I did my homework and went to bed. It never occurred to either my grandparents or to me that any other sort of relationship was possible between us. We lived in different worlds and had nothing to say to each other. Of what possible interest could it be to me that Mary Clark had reported a napkin missing in the week's wash or that Grandfather had decided to read Anthony Trollope's *The Warden* for the third time? Or to my grandparents that I had been kept in at recess for not having been able to name the capital of Idaho?

I suppose most of my contemporaries grew up under much the same conditions except that—because their parents were at home, there was not the same gap in years between them and their elders. Certainly at school the other boys never mentioned their parents or even seemed conscious that they existed. But my schoolmates found their social contacts among each other while I was "not regular." For me, winter was a miserable time, endurable only because of the Saturdays and Sundays when I could get away from the strict routine of school and spend my time tramping through the country. But summer was heaven.

I would get up shortly after dawn and be out in the garden all day, returning reluctantly only for meals. As I grew older, I extended my explorations gradually year by year. I had plenty of territory to explore. My grandparents' place bordered on the Ashbridge farm, "Rosemont," which then covered over two hundred acres. At one time, the two Misses Ashbridge had owned the entire district which was—and still is—called Rosemont. They had sold the rights to lay tracks through the property to the Pennsylvania Railroad at the turn of the century, keeping only this small section. They still lived in their Colonial mansion on a hill near the old barn where Hessian troopers had stabled their horses during what the two old ladies always referred to when speaking to English visitors as "the late unpleasantness." Next to the Ashbridge farm was the Johnson estate, also covering several hundred acres and completely surrounded by an ornamental wrought-iron fence ten feet high. A convent has since purchased this property and the mother superior recently told me that it costs five thousand dollars a year just to keep this fence painted. But the fence was merely meant to shield the dozens of gardens—rose gardens, Japanese gardens, fruit gardens, Greek-temple gardens, swamp gardens, and many more. Each garden was surrounded by high boxwood hedges and connected by a series of waterfalls and fountains. It was magnificent—but it was a heck of a place to find a lost 10-foot alligator, as I'll explain later.

Bordering both the Ashbridge and Johnson estates was the Austin property, even larger and more elaborate. The Austins owned a tract of woods which I gradually came to know as well as I knew our own garden. Beyond the woods stretched out great lawns as green and smooth as billiard tables where flocks of peafowl wandered, the cocks spreading their incredible trains—displaying them not only for the hens but even to any small boy who stood in admiration of them. I swore then that I would someday own a peacock. There was also a game-keeper who had the habit of shooting at the same small boy with a shotgun loaded with rock salt. He only got me once, but that was enough; rock salt stings like a hive of hornets. I suppose that shooting small boys is illegal even when they are trespassing, but it never occurred to me to complain. In these more enlightened times, property owners must fence in farm pools to keep trespassing children from falling in, remove the doors of discarded refrigerators to prevent children from locking themselves inside, and take care to remove ladders in case a trespassing child should climb up one and fall off. But in those days it was taken for granted that if a child were caught trespassing he had to take the consequences.

On rainy days, I sat in our library and read. During their 200-year residence in Pennsylvania, my family had managed to build up a library containing at least one volume devoted to virtually any conceivable subject. By going over the shelves, I could trace the interests of my ancestors back to the time when the first of them had set foot in Mr. Penn's Woods, although I had no idea of their names. One had operated a forge, several had been ministers, another had been involved in the French Revolution (I did know about him; he'd been a member of the Swiss Guard who'd held the Tuileries against the mob), several had been sea captains (this was on my father's side), and one had had the happy thought of collecting pornography. I never knew who that one was, but his collection helped me to while away many a rainy afternoon—although it gave me an impression of the Facts of Life that would have fascinated Krafft-Ebing and outraged modern exponents of a sensible approach to this delicate subject. It never occurred to my grandparents to forbid me to look at these books. After all, they were part of The Library.

For many years, my favorite reading was fairy tales, from Thornton W. Burgess' "Quaddy" books to *The Arabian Nights* (Richard Burton translation with the famous Terminal Essay).

To me, and perhaps to the authors of the tales too, wild animals were the Little People; disliked, despised, but also feared and regarded with awe. True, not all wild animals were so regarded and for that reason I was more drawn toward animals capable of defending themselves against humans than those who are helpless. I was far more attracted to hawks than to pheasants, to snakes than to butterflies, to skunks rather than to rabbits. I had no interest in domestic animals. I never wanted to own a dog or a cat. The cows and workhorses on the Ashbridge farm, although I knew them well, were merely pleasant acquaintances but entirely lacking glamour.

If I had only known it, there were plenty of wild animals in the Austin woods and even on the Ashbridge farm—raccoon, opossum, woodchuck, skunk, weasels, and even a few white-tailed deer, but at eight I had never seen any of them and had no idea of their existence. Still, in that year I got my first pets.

One of the books in our library concerned the adventures of a Mr. du Chaillu on the West Coast of Africa (*circa* 1860) and his adventures with gorillas. When I was five years old, I was so fascinated by the pictures that my nurse read the book aloud to me. From that time on, I was determined to get a pet gorilla. I don't suppose I've ever wanted anything quite as much as I wanted that gorilla. When I was eight, I could read the book for myself and, since my birthday was coming up, I dared to ask my grandparents for a gorilla. They were mildly amused but promised me great things if I did well in school. I slaved over my books and spent my spare time arranging part of my room to accommodate the gorilla—my technique being to hang string from one chair to another so the gorilla would have something to swing on.

No gorilla arrived. Instead, I was given two Angora rabbits covered with long, white fur. I still think that my dear grandparents could have presented me with a monkey, but older people can't tell how much a seemingly inane desire can mean to a child. Nevertheless, the rabbits were alive and sufficiently exotic-looking to fascinate me.

The rabbits lived in a hutch with a wire runway that could be moved from one spot to another, and every evening I went out to move the hutch to a fresh, uncropped bit of lawn. Once I went out on a clear, warm spring evening with everything shining soft and silver instead of bright and golden as it does during the day. I followed the line of the privet hedge until I came on the rabbit hutch, There were two wild rabbits with their noses against the wire, talking to my pets.

They were only rabbits, but the contrast between the wild cottontails and the domestic rabbits was the contrast between a Mohawk—lean, alert, mysterious, and romantic—and a fat, uninteresting bourgeoise. As soon as they saw me, the wild rabbits were gone in two great bounds, but I never forgot them. It was not that I loved my own pets less; I simply loved the wild ones more. I determined that someday I would own wild animal pets.

The hutch was so constructed that it could not be opened, so I only saw the rabbits when they emerged for food or to hop around the wire runway. What went on inside the hutch remained a mystery—but I did notice that the female was growing progressively more nervous. After a while she would not leave the hutch until I had gone away, and if I returned while she was feeding, she would dart back in panic. Finally she seemed to disappear entirely and only the male; ever came out. I began to wonder if she had escaped, so one evening after putting in the food and walking off as usual, I doubled back behind the privet hedge and, lying on my stomach, watched to see what would happen.

The male was already busy with the lettuce leaves when I took up my position, but for a long time there was no sign of his wife. Then I saw her emerge cautiously. Behind her came six white balls of fluff. So far as I was concerned a miracle had happened.

I burst through the hedge shouting with excitement. The male gave a terrified thump with his hind legs—the traditional rabbit alarm signal—before bolting for the hutch. The female didn't bother thumping. She dove for the doorway with the babies after her. There was an instant's frantic congestion at the narrow opening with thrashing hind legs and writhing bodies. I stopped horrified at what I'd done; I was sure some of the babies would be crushed in the panic—as, indeed, might easily have happened—but all got through safely.

I couldn't believe that the rabbits would regard me as an enemy. I knelt down outside the runway and pleaded with them to come out. Like most children and even many adults, I was convinced that animals could understand human speech and would respond to logic. Unfortunately, the mother rabbit continued to cower inside the hutch and refused to let me see her babies. I was forced to admit that, Beatrix Potter notwithstanding, rabbits were not small human beings wearing fur coats. They were animals whose thought processes differed basically from mine.

This realization did not disillusion me with rabbits. Instead, it made them far more interesting than they had been before. Until then, the rabbits had been little more than attractive automata. They ate, moved about their runway, had to be cleaned—and that had been all. Now for the first time they were doing something interesting. Not only had they produced these incredibly wonderful little miniatures of themselves; but they had also suddenly developed personalities. The female was looking after her offspring, taking them out only when no danger threatened.

The male had stopped long enough to signal his family of danger before making a dash for safety himself.

I was utterly unable to understand why neither my grandparents nor the maids showed any interest in this marvelous event. They seemed to consider it only natural that rabbits should reproduce. The behavior of the male and the devotion of the mother, although I described both in detail, won only kindly smiles and "Yes, dear, I'm sure they're very cute little pets." Somewhat dampened, I returned to my own studies of the rabbit family.

The babies prospered. Grandmother, somewhat apprehensive that we would be overrun with rabbits, called the pet store to see if the proprietor would take the young off our hands and reported, considerably surprised, that the pet store owner would not only take them but pay five dollars each for them, Angora rabbits being rather rare and valuable. This meant that I was owner of thirty dollars' worth of rabbits, a fabulous sum. Even my grandparents now regarded the rabbits with more respect. After supper, Grandfather rummaged through the bookcases and produced a volume on rabbits. There I discovered the existence of such exotic varieties as the Old English Lop-eared, the New Zealand Red, and the Flemish Giant. I decided to go into the rabbit business.

The only trouble was that I would have to sell the babies to obtain capital. I would rather have parted with a couple of fingers—at least if the fingers could have been amputated painlessly. So in spite of my grandparents' arguments, I decided to keep the babies.

One morning I went out to the pen with the usual offering of lettuce, carrots, and rolled oats. As the babies had grown older the mother had lost much of her protective nervousness and the family had grown quite tame. I would start calling to them when I left the house, and by the time I rounded the privet hedge they would all be standing with their forepaws against the wire, waiting for breakfast. I called as usual, but there was no answering fury of excitement as the family hurried to take their position. Apprehensively I burst into a run.

The pen had been torn apart. Even the heavy hutch was broken open. Scattered on the grass were the dead bodies of the rabbits: the two parents lying side by side, the smaller corpses of the babies flung around the lawn.

I picked the babies up one after another—it was the first time I had ever handled them—still sure that they could not be really dead. Then I gathered up what was left of the parents. There were footprints of dogs everywhere in the soft earth of the pens—and I knew what dogs they were. One of our neighbors kept a pair of German shepherds and allowed them to run loose at night.

Still in a trance, I went to the garage, got a spade, and buried my first pets. Then I returned to the house. The routine of two years still lay heavy upon me and I sat down at table as I always did after feeding the rabbits. The maid brought me the usual two soft boiled eggs in a cup. I thanked her and put my spoon in the cup. Suddenly I was taken violently ill. Then I began to cry.

I remember Mary Clark putting me to bed and hearing Grandmother hurry from her bedroom, calling "What has happened, Mary? Has he been hurt?" For a while I must have been delirious. Later the doctor came. By that time, I was able to gasp out what had happened. Grandmother exclaimed, in exasperated relief, "Really, Danny, I thought it was something serious." Grandfather sat down on the bed and said gently "We'll get you some more rabbits, boy. Some of the ones we read about in the book." The doctor took a more practical view. He snapped, "Get out of that bed at once and get to school. You're not a baby any more."

Kennedy, our old Irish chauffeur, was notified that the Pierce Arrow had to be called into emergency service. Kennedy had been coachman before he was forced to abandon his beloved horses and associate with motor cars. He had been with us for years and the entire family trusted his judgment implicitly. I heard Grandmother say in despair, "But Thomas, if he behaves like this over the loss of a pair of rabbits, what will he ever do when he has to go out into the world?" Kennedy cleared his throat, a trick he had before answering an embarrassing question, and gently replied, "He's like the old gentleman, Ma'am." Kennedy always referred to Grandfather by that term. "Very sensitive. Real gentlemen, both of them. Thank God neither will ever have to work for a living."

Before leaving for school, I managed to see Grandfather and begged him not to get me any more rabbits. "I'll never have another pet as long as I live," I told him. "I couldn't go through anything like this a second time." Grandfather said he understood.

Two

True to the traditions of the Main Line, it never occurred either to me or to my grandparents to request the dogs' owners to keep their pets under control. That would have been interfering with their personal affairs. Instead, after several private conferences of which I was dimly aware, my grandparents decided that I needed some playmates of my own age. Apparently the nearest suitable children were the Willcoxes, who lived in Wawa some twenty miles away. Although Wawa was not strictly speaking on the Main Line, some fairly respectable people had been living there since the early eighteenth century and even affected to look down on the Main Liners as parvenus—a sort of snobbery in reverse. My grandparents had known the Willcoxes for many years, and as they had three children (two boys and a girl) of about my age it was decided to make the supreme sacrifice and use the Pierce Arrow to transport me to Wawa two or three times a month during the summer.

"It will be nice for you to have some little friends your own age to play with," Grandmother told me hopefully. Personally, I was convinced that the Willcoxes could never take the place of my lost rabbits, but I dutifully said that I would go. As far as I was concerned, this was simply another boring social chore like dancing class, church, or having to take tea with Grandmother's friends. If I could have foreseen the future, I would have been delirious with joy. And if Grandmother could have predicted the result of my meeting the dear little Willcoxes, she would never have allowed me off the property.

I had been asked to supper, so Kennedy was to drop me off at the Willcoxes, returning late that evening to retrieve me. Dressed in a costume suitable for an afternoon of fun and games—starched linen collar, a blue serge suit, and patent leather pumps—I departed in a depressed state of mind. I had not the slightest doubt that the Willcox children had no more desire to meet me than I had to meet them.

The Willcoxes lived in a Victorian mansion deep in a woods. The children were lined up on the front porch to greet me under the watchful eye of Mrs. Willcox and had clearly been ordered to Be Nice to Your Little Guest or Else. The boys were dressed in costumes similar to mine, obviously equally uncomfortable, and regarded me with marked distaste. I didn't blame them. They were somewhat younger than I, but the girl was my own age. They offered to take me on a tour of the grounds; since there seemed to be nothing else to do, I accepted.

I saw the tennis court, the rock garden, and the Garden-Club-Prize-Winning rhododendrons—all equally uninteresting. Although I tried to be polite, my lack of enthusiasm communicated itself to the Willcoxes and we plodded in the direction of their barn in silence. There I stopped amazed. Around the corner of the barn came a procession of the most astonishing-looking chickens I had ever seen. They seemed to be covered with long white hair like my rabbits. There were a cock, a hen, and four chicks.

"What *are* they?" was all I could say.

"White silkies," one of the boys said. "They've got black skins. Look!"

He ran over and, grabbing the astonished and indignant cock, parted the coat which I could now see was composed of long, soft, white feathers like fur. The skin was ebony-black.

I was so fascinated that the Willcoxes began to regard me as virtually a human being. "Do you like animals?" asked the girl.

I remembered that I would never have any more pets. "I used to, but not any more," I said, looking wistfully at the white silkies who were marching off with indignant clucks.

But I was so obviously entranced by the chickens that the Willcoxes held a hurried parley. Then my young hostess asked, "Would you like two of the white silky chicks when they get old enough to leave their mother?"

It was a heartbreaking temptation, but I held to my resolve. "There's no use my trying to have pets. Our neighbors' dogs would kill them." Then I told of the tragedy of the rabbits.

The Willcoxes listened sympathetically. "Well, dogs don't come around here," said the girl. "They're afraid of the skunks. These woods are full of skunks."

"I'll bet our Wawa skunks are the biggest in the world," said the youngest boy proudly. "And can they *skunk!*"

"Could I see them?" I asked eagerly.

"You can this evening. They only come out after dark. Say!" he went on, his face lighting up with a brilliant inspiration. "Why don't you catch a couple of skunks and take them home with you? You can get them tame and then the dogs will be afraid to come around."

We looked at each other with wild surmise and then started an impromptu war dance. "We'll need sacks—and flashlights—and we'll borrow Aunty's Cairn terriers. They're genuine skunk hounds. They can always find skunks."

A sudden doubt struck me. "You don't think my grandparents will mind? Don't skunks smell bad?"

"They don't smell at all!" I was assured. "You smell after running into a skunk, but the skunk doesn't smell a bit!"

That made it all right. The girl was the only one who seemed a little doubtful, but all she said was "I wouldn't introduce them to your grandparents right away. Some people don't like the smell very much—at least not until they get used to it."

The younger Willcoxes explained to me the technique of skunk-catching. "One person gets the skunk's attention while somebody else sneaks up behind him and picks him up by the tail. A skunk can't squirt while you're holding him by the tail."

"How do you know?"

"Oh, we've done it often. On Hallowe'en we catch skunks and put them in people's bathtubs. The people can't get them out without being squirted."

I was more convinced than ever that the Willcoxes were an outstanding family.

"If you've done it so often, maybe you'd better do the picking-up part," I suggested.

"No, we can pick up skunks anytime, but you're company and Mother said we had to be nice to you," said the oldest boy firmly.

The Willcoxes explained that it would save an awful lot of unnecessary explaining if we didn't mention our plans, so we had supper with Mr. and Mrs. Willcox in polite silence. As soon as the meal was over, we collected our bags and a flashlight and started out, stopping on the way at their aunt's home to collect the Cairn terriers, who came along delightedly.

Although the Willcoxes had assured me that Wawa was teeming with skunks, it was some time before we heard the terriers begin to bark. I was carrying the flashlight and led the excited rush. The dogs were on the side of a railroad embankment; because they were black, it was nearly impossible to see them unless they moved. Between them, a white V seemed to be floating a few inches above the ground. As I came closer and concentrated the flashlight's ray on the object, I saw it was indeed a skunk.

Skunks are about the size of a large cat and completely black except for the forked white strip on their back and the white tip of their tail. According to one theory, skunks have their typically white marking as a sort of protective coloration in reverse, to enable predators to see them and realize what they are. Otherwise the slow-moving skunks would be forced to waste their time spraying every stray fox, dog, and raccoon that came along. This particular skunk was standing at bay between the terriers, his big bushy tail raised warningly.

In my excitement, I ran forward unheedingly. The Willcoxes shouted warnings and I stopped. At the sight of me the skunk turned and fled, humping his way along the ground somewhat like an overgrown inchworm. Skunks are actually weasels, and all the weasel family travel at this peculiar run.

The terriers quickly cut him off from cover and the skunk stopped again, this time obviously determined to make a stand. When a skunk decides to stand, nothing will move him. Indians on the warpath wore skunkskins wrapped around their ankles to show that, come what might, they would never run away.

The terriers were barking their heads off but keeping a respectful distance. I came in cautiously. The skunk had raised his tail straight up with only the white tip on the end hanging down. As I approached, he stamped with his forefeet.

One of the Willcoxes whispered to me, "That's the second signal that he means business. The first is when he raises his tail. The last is when the white tip stands up. After that he lets you have it."

I took another step forward. Instantly the white tip rose and spread out like a tiny fan. "*Stop!*" shouted the Willcoxes in chorus.

I stopped. "What do I do next?"

"Give me the flashlight and I'll stay here and hold his attention," said one of the boys. "You sneak around behind him and pick him up by the tail."

I handed over the flashlight and started to execute my rear attack. The skunk heard me stumbling over the tracks and whirled around, but the excited terriers and the yelling Willcoxes caused him to turn again. Quietly I stole up from behind. Then I made a rush and grabbed for the tail.

The skunk was quicker. He spun about and let me have it with both barrels. A skunk's musk is carried in two little sacs under the base of his tail; these sacs connect to a small tubelike organ which the skunk can protrude—and aim—at will. This apparatus has nothing to do with the animal's sexual organs; males and females possess the same equipment. All the rest of the weasel family have these glands too, but use the musk simply to mark their caches so other animals will not disturb them. The skunk, however, has developed his apparatus into a deadly effective weapon. The musk is actually a potent acid which can cause permanent blindness. A skunk can fire six or seven times, although once the glands are completely empty, replenishment takes several hours. The musk burns where it touches the skin and can produce nausea and convulsions. To describe skunk musk simply as a bad smell is as much an understatement as saying mustard gas has an unpleasant odor. The skunk throws the musk away from himself—he has a range of about ten feet— and so the skunk is never contaminated, any more than a man throwing a gas grenade is affected by the gas.

All this knowledge is the result of later observation. At the time, all I knew was that the skunk had spun around and twisted his body into a U shape. I saw a quick gleam in the moonlight, for the musk is faintly phosphorescent, and felt something wet strike my cheek. Then I had the skunk by the tail.

Almost instantly my cheek began to burn as though scalding water had been thrown against it, and I fought for breath as if against tear gas. I managed to lift the skunk clear of the ground; he swung back and forth like a pendulum, trying to reach me with his teeth and claws. I tried to shout to the Willcoxes to bring the sack, but I couldn't speak. The skunk was getting heavy—a full-grown skunk will weigh about 10 pounds—and holding him at arm's length was getting trying for an eight-year-old. And the pain in my cheek, nose, lungs, and eyes was rapidly becoming unbearable. Luckily the skunk hadn't gotten me full in the face, or I'd have been seriously sick.

After what seemed to me an eternity, the Willcoxes finally got the mouth of the sack spread open and the flashlight turned on the opening, and I was able to drop my captive inside.

"My, he really did get you, didn't he?" asked one of my hosts, sniffing. "One good thing about it, from now on you can just walk up to any skunk and pick him up. You've got nothing to lose."

There was a stream nearby and I was conducted to it. I washed my face and, as the Willcoxes suggested, put some wet mud on my cheek. It helped some. After rinsing out my mouth and eyes time after time, I was ready to go on.

We got four more skunks that evening. By the time we were finished, everyone was thoroughly skunked because in the excitement the indignant animals were apt to spray the entire ensemble impartially, including the two terriers. I'm inclined to think that the Willcoxes were right in their theory that a skunk can't use his ammunition while suspended by the tail, but we never really had a chance to find out. All but one were too quick for us. I *think* I was able to pick up the last skunk before he was able to fire, but by that time we all smelled so much of the musk it was difficult to tell. Whether I did or not, my skill did me no good: while I was trying to angle him into the sack, his dangling feet managed to make contact with my trouser leg. He promptly braced himself and fired up my sleeve. The yellow liquid dripping down my hand got into an open cut and made me dance with pain.

Mrs. Willcox was standing on the porch calling for us when we got back. "What have you been doing?" she called indignantly. "Kennedy's here with the car for Dan and—oh *no!*"

We had gotten in range. Mrs. Willcox retreated inside. "Not one of you comes near this house until you've changed your clothes and washed off with the hose!" she shouted through the closed door.

I was so big and gangling that none of the junior Willcoxes' clothes would fit me; I would have to go home in my musk-drenched suit. We agreed that I could keep two skunks, a male and female (they are no more difficult to sex than cats), and the Willcoxes kept the other two as a surprise for some of their friends. I explained to Kennedy that since the skunks had already exhausted their ammunition, carrying them home in the car would present no problems. "Perhaps so, Master Dan, but I can only say the Pierce Arrow will never be the same again," said Kennedy grimly.

My grandparents had already gone to bed when I returned. Following the Willcoxes' suggestion, I put the skunks in my bathtub overnight. My clothes I threw down the back stairs, where the maids found them in the morning. For weeks afterward on damp days there was still a strong odor of skunk about those stairs. So far as I was personally concerned, after several washings with a good grade of strong carbolic soap I was as good as new—except for my hair. That had to be clipped.

I was so proud of my new acquisitions that my grandparents hadn't the heart to object. I think they rightly judged that to deprive me of the skunks after the rabbit tragedy would be too cruel. Grandmother did throw out a few hints about the supplanting the skunks with another pair of rabbits, but when I pointed out that the dogs would surely kill them she said no more. Even Kennedy—who had been forced to spend long hours washing out the car with benzine—realized how much the pair meant to me and helped build a pen for the new arrivals. Because skunks can dig, climb, and force their way through an amazingly small opening, constructing a skunkproof pen was a considerable task, but it was finally accomplished; my grandparents generously released Kennedy from his other duties when they learned that the skunks would have to remain in my bathtub until the pen was finished. Getting the skunks out of the tub without rendering the house unsuitable for human habitation presented certain difficulties, but I solved the problem by popping a box suddenly over the couple, slipping a thin board under it, and carrying them off without giving them a target for their scent-guns. Then I happily sat down to watch my first wild-animal pets parade around their new quarters.

Skunks are really extremely handsome animals. Their black fur is as rich and soft as silver fox (commercially it goes under the proud title "Alaskan sable") and their white markings are as pure as those of ermine. Only the brush of a really fine fox in prime condition can compare with the magnificent tails they carry in a graceful curve unless alarmed. Although they are a little too low-slung to be called graceful, they march around in an impressively determined manner and bear a strong resemblance to Sir Winston Churchill without the cigar.

In response to my pleas, Grandfather called the zoo to find out about the care and feeding of skunks, when they might be expected to breed, how many would be in a litter (a subject in which Grandmother was particularly interested), and how they could be tamed. In my innocence, I expected the zoo officials to have all this information at their fingertips. I learned then how little is actually known about even the commonest of wild animals. Although the Philadelphia Zoo has since worked out carefully balanced diets for wild animals, at that time the keeper of the small-mammal house could only tell us that so far as he knew skunks ate meat—the extent of his information.

I read everything I could find about skunks, which wasn't very much. I did discover that the Indian word for skunk was *sauteux* and that Chicago means "skunkland." Skunks played an important part in the development of America; their fur was in such demand that trappers were constantly opening new areas in search of the valuable pelts. Their musk was considered so precious that I hated to think how much of it had been wasted on me. According to a Mr. C. H. Merriam, it cured "asthma, whooping cough and croup," the theory apparently being that after a good whiff of skunk musk the patient forgot about all his other ailments. It was also used as a base for certain perfumes to give them a clinging quality. That I could understand. If there's any ingredient in which skunk musk is rich, it's a clinging quality. What the books didn't explain was how the perfume manufacturers deodorized the musk first. Nevertheless, I was confident that by operating a skunk dairy I would soon make my fortune.

I worked out my own diet for the skunks. They did eat meat but Mr. Lewis, the Ashbridge farmer, assured me that skunks were also fond of young corn—in fact, he spoke about the matter with deep feeling, having had cornfields virtually denuded by them. In addition, they were not above taking little chicks and robbing hen nests. I gathered that Mr. Lewis didn't like skunks, but I treasured his information. The Willcoxes had already told me that skunks frequently raided their garbage pails for table scraps. On the basis of this information, I fed my pair a mixed diet of meat, bread and milk, fruit, and vegetables. I discovered that, like humans, they would quickly grow tired of any one food so I tried to vary their meals as much as possible.

When I set about taming the skunks I discovered a principle that has stood me in good stead ever since: It is virtually impossible to tame an animal kept in a cage, especially if it has a box into which it can retire if hard pressed. The animal must be kept in a room with you or on a collar and chain.

Broad-minded as my grandparents were on the subject of skunks, I suspected that there would be difficulty about keeping the skunks in the house. So I had to equip them with collar and chain, first putting on a rubber bathing cap to protect my hair and goggles to save my eyes. Getting a collar on a skunk presents considerable difficulties besides the obvious one. Skunks have no chin and little forehead. Also, they bite. But I could not have selected a better subject than a skunk to start my career as a wild-animal trainer. Skunks are naturally so fearless and have such phlegmatic natures that they soon quieted down. For three days the couple refused to eat from my hands, but finally the male took a milk-soaked roll. After examining it suspiciously he took an experimental nibble and then settled down to make up for his three-day fast. The female hurried up and started on the other end of the roll. Her husband objected with squeals and whines and at last I ventured to put another roll a few inches in front of them. Both eyed me with mistrust, but finally the male abandoned the roll to his mate and walked over to take the fresh offering. An hour later both of them were readily taking bits of meat from my fingers.

In a few days the couple became so tame that I could take off their chains and put them back in their pen. The male, always the more friendly, would run out of his house when he heard me coming and stand up with his feet against the wire, grunting to be taken out and played with. The female was more decorous and—although she liked to be scratched back of the ears—she'd only come to me when I was playing with the male and she'd begun to get jealous.

Much to my surprise, I found that both were playful, especially the male. He soon discovered that people were afraid of him; whenever he saw a stranger he would dash at him and do a handstand on his forefeet with his tail bent forward in a highly suggestive manner, prepared to fire over his own head (as I learned in the early days of my training, he could do this very skillfully). If the stranger ran—and most people did not stay on the order of their going but went at once—he would give chase as long as his short legs could keep up with them. If, on the other hand, they stood still, he'd stop his war dance and waddle up to make friends. He never actually threw his musk on these occasions, but it was pretty hard to persuade visitors that he was only playing. I called him Nikki, after a clown who was famous for walking on his hand.

Skunks aren't generally considered intelligent; Nikki was exceptional. He would play like a kitten with an empty spool on the end of a string—crouching, jumping, and standing on his hind legs to grab the spool. Sometimes I think he did it to amuse me more than to amuse himself. He quickly learned which of the maids were afraid of him and which were not. One maid had no time for Nikki and would shoo him away with a broom as though he were a cat, but Nikki never sprayed her. On the other hand, the parlor maid was terrified of him and Nikki would lay in wait for her behind the garbage cans, rushing out and doing his handstand whenever she appeared.

Mr. and Mrs. Nikki had a surprising vocabulary. Talking together, they made a "churring" noise with definite inflections that obviously meant something to them. Sometimes I would try to imitate it and both Nikkies would stop and stare at me for a few seconds as though wondering what I thought I was saying, then resume their conversation. When angry, they made a chattering sound much like that of an angry squirrel. Once Mrs. Nikki growled at me like a dog when I tried to pick her up. When really angry, they would give shrill screeches. While hunting for grubs in the garden, one would occasionally give a birdlike twittering sound, apparently to inform the other that a supply of food had been located. They loved yellow jackets' nests. These yellow-and-black-striped wasps had underground hives on the lawn and during the day a steady stream could be seen going in and out like a column of yellow smoke. They were a real menace to Bounds, the gardener, when he cut the grass. I would sometimes steal up on a hive, clap a quart milk bottle over the hole, and then watch from a respectful distance while the yellow jackets fizzed in it like soda water, but it was a tricky business because some of the wasps were always trapped outside and eager to avenge the indignity to their home. Although the Nikkies avoided the hives during the day, at night they would fearlessly dig them up and eat the grubs, the wasps being apparently asleep and helpless. It was while hunting out yellow-jacket nests that the Nikkies often signaled to each other by twittering. I thought their wasp-eating trait would endear them to Bounds, but he said that having to fill in the holes afterward was worse than being stung by yellow jackets.

Although I'm sure that I would have loved the Nikkies for their own sakes, an incident occurred which a psychologist might claim as the explanation of much of my subsequent passion for wild-animal pets.

Exclusive as the Main Line supposedly might be, there was a little community a few miles from our home composed entirely of Italian and Negro families. These two groups lived amiably together for many years—indeed until Mussolini invaded Abyssinia, when such a serious riot occurred among these long-time friendly neighbors that the police reserves had to be called out to suppress it. (However, that was long afterward.) During my youth, the youngsters from this village roamed the countryside as a sort of wolf pack and I lived in terror of them.

One evening while I was walking the Nikkies around the lower garden I heard a faint noise among the shrubbery and, looking up, saw half a dozen of the village boys staring at me. They had never before dared attack me on my own property; although I was frightened, I didn't run—mainly because flight would have left the Nikkies at their mercy. While I was trying to think what to do, one of the boys asked in an awed voice, "Ain't them things *skunks?*"

I admitted that they were.

The boys stared in open-eyed astonishment. Then one asked, "You got 'em tame? They won't stink you?"

"Only if I tell them to," I lied.

This pronouncement was greeted with a flow of respectful profanity. Gradually I began to realize that to these boys skunks were dangerous wild animals; they regarded them with almost supernatural fear. (Years later, I saw a gang of stevedores run in terror from a harmless black snake and had the disconcerting experience of causing panic in a lecture hall by releasing a trained falcon. Many people are more afraid of a wild animal than of a loaded revolver. It is the unknown that terrifies.)

Until now, these village boys had regarded me with contempt as a rich sissy and abject coward. Now they clearly looked on me with respect as a powerful magician. The sudden sense of power went to my head. Running toward them, I called "Here, Nikki!"—hoping that he would do his handstand. Nikki only looked up curiously and went on with his search for grubs, but the boys didn't wait. They turned and ran. One little fellow who couldn't keep up burst into tears. For some time I could hear his sobs as he stumbled after the others.

From then on, I never had any trouble with the village boys. If I met them on the back roads or in the fields, they carefully avoided me. Once when I passed a group, one who was obviously a newcomer to the neighborhood asked in an indignant and puzzled voice, "What's so special about him? What you guys scared of?" He was promptly hushed and I heard an awed voice whisper, "He's got trained skunks that'll go for you if he tells 'em to." It was one of the proudest moments of my life (even though, of course, I had absolutely no control over the Nikkies, and they were actually quite shy; Nikki did his celebrated handstand only when he was in a very special playful mood).

One day in April Mrs. Nikki collected a pair of my trousers which a maid had thoughtlessly left hanging on the clothesline and made a beautiful nest with them in one corner of her pen. Since I had several pairs of trousers, I saw no reason why I should take them back and Mary Clark thought my grandparents would probably share this point of view, as Mrs. Nikki had been housekeeping in the trousers for some time before the loss was discovered. Even so, the incident struck me as curious. Mrs. Nikki had never shown any nest-making proclivities before.

A few weeks later I found Nikki sitting unhappily outside the trousers. I thought he and his wife had had a fight and urged him to go in and make up. He tried to crawl down a leg, his usual entrance, only to be met by violent chattering. He hastily backed out and I lifted up the trouser legs and peered down it. There lay Mrs. Nikki with six squirming newborn babies beside her in an orderly row. Although they were hairless, the white stripes already showed clearly on their bare backs. Not even the arrival of the rabbit family had so thrilled me, but I had by now developed a certain amount of caution and said nothing to my grandparents.

With the babies slowing them down, I no longer made any attempt to keep the Nikkies confined. Then one evening as the babies grew older, I met the whole family out walking among the flower beds. Few wild animals are as soft, furry, and wholly delightful as skunk kittens. They were all parading in single file after their mother, trying to manage their huge, bushy tails and keep them curled over their backs in true skunk fashion. Every now and then a baby's tail would drop down and he would step on it by mistake, only to fall on his stumpy nose. Then he would give a twist of his hindquarters and hoist it up again with the gesture of a dowager switching her train into place. They were intensely solemn and obviously on their dignity so when I rushed at them, wild with excitement, the whole family was outraged; Mrs. Nikki even stamped at me.

I grabbed the nearest kitten and he stood on the palm of my hand instinctively trying to give the traditional skunk signals, but every time he stamped he nearly fell off and I had to balance him with my thumb so he could go through his routine. It turned out that he was too young to have any ammunition and after a while he became discouraged and allowed me to stroke him.

When the babies found that their parents accepted me, they took to following me around just as they did their mother. Bounds had a small mongrel named Rags who was about the size of a mop and spent most of his time hunting field mice. The baby skunks obviously considered this great sport and took to following Rags. Poor Rags began to behave like a small boy trying to get rid of a set of determined younger brothers while six devoted baby skunks tagged determinedly after him whenever he set out for the pasture.

Rags soon discovered that it was easy to ditch the babies because they were very near-sighted. He had only to make a quick jump to one side and the little flock would go marching past, following the scent of his footprints with their noses. When they came to the end of the trail, they would be completely lost and run around crying miserably until their mother or I came out and collected them.

The babies were remarkably individualistic. Two of them never tamed at all, refusing even to come to me for food, although they would not threaten to spray me unless I tried to pick them up. Three were about like Mrs. Nikki—they would feed from my hand and even allow me to pick them up, although occasionally for no apparent reason they would lose their tempers and bite. They never skunked me, but their teeth were sharp and the bites always infected. I had a hard time hiding my swollen fingers from my grandparents. When the babies fought among themselves, which they did frequently, they never used their spray guns, always relying on their teeth. I suppose they regarded me as another skunk.

But a little male was one of the nicest pets I was ever to have. He would play endlessly with me, darting out from ambush under the rhododendrons to grab one of my bare toes and worry it with mimic growls like a puppy. If I refused to play with him, he'd pull insistently at my trouser cuff until I picked him up. He'd leave the rest of the family at any time to be with me. Often after long hours of play, he'd climb into my lap and go to sleep and I'd have to carry him to his trouser-nest and put him to bed, still fast asleep. He was the most curious of all the skunks: everything new had to be investigated and, if possible, taken apart. Usually the only way to get rid of him was to give him some small object (it made no difference what) wrapped up in a piece of cloth and securely tied. Nikki Junior, as I called him, would work ceaselessly until he got the cloth open and then proudly bring me the hidden treasure.

My grandparents seldom went into the lower garden where the skunks lived, especially in the evenings when the Nikkies were abroad, so the babies were half-grown before their existence was discovered. It was the parlor maid who betrayed me. She saw the Nikki family marching in procession across the clothes drying yard one evening and went to Grandmother. Her position was that having Nikki harry her around was bad enough but if she was to be pursued by a posse of skunks, she would have to give notice. I was summoned before the family tribunal.

Grandfather presented no trouble. I had a photograph of the baby skunks feeding from a long dish which I felt sure would melt anyone's heart. Grandfather accepted it politely, remarking "Sady, sady, so the skunks have had all these babies, eh?" and went back to reading *The Newcomes. Sady* was an old term meaning "thank you" as applied to a small child. Grandmother, however, was not so easily appeased. Only after a long argument and a solemn oath never to allow any of the Nikki family near the maids' part of the establishment (which included the drying ground, a tiny garden with an arbor, and the back porch) was I allowed to keep the babies on sufferance.

As the skunks wandered about pretty much at their own sweet will I had no idea how I was to maintain my part of the contract, but fortune favored me. Going unexpectedly one afternoon through the maids' dining room, I found the parlor maid having a tea party for the local chapter of the Daughters of the Sinn Fein, the *pièce de résistance* being a large layer cake which I knew Grandmother had intended to last the entire household for several days. I said nothing, merely stopped and looked long and eloquently at the cake before going on. Before I could get out the back door, the parlor maid had hurried after me to express her passionate love for skunks of all ages, sizes, and description and to assure me that she would never trouble Grandmother again over such a minor matter. I accepted her assurance.

As the babies grew older they became increasingly nocturnal, but Rags and I used to take them for walks in the evenings. The walks were leisurely affairs; the skunks stopped every few feet to dig up grubs. Grubs seemed to be their main diet—grubs were about the only living things that couldn't outrun them. Occasionally in a burst of speed they'd run down a snail, and once the biggest baby actually caught a field mouse. They were death on Japanese beetles. The whole flock would collect under the apple trees and I would shake the beetles down to them. The crunching of the beetles' hard carapaces sounded like the crackling of tiny firecrackers.

We hadn't been troubled much by the German shepherds that summer because their owner had gone to Maine and had put the dogs in a kennel. So it was not until autumn, when the skunks were going to the orchard in the evenings in search of fallen apples, that the two met. I was some distance away when I saw the shepherds streaking through the trees, evidently thinking they had discovered a perfect bonanza of cats. I started running and shouting, but the Nikki family didn't need me.

The skunks were so used to playing with Rags that they showed absolutely no fear of the oncoming dogs, but as the leading shepherd came closer, Nikki Junior turned toward him with a weary expression as though to say he didn't want to be rude but was too busy to play. He made a polite handstand and then prepared to turn away, but the dog would have none of it. He charged and somehow the adolescent skunk suddenly seemed to realize that this was the real thing.

Instantly he stiffened and gave his warning stamps, but the dogs were almost on him. The next two signals were given almost simultaneously. I saw Nikki Junior twist himself into a perfect U and as the leading dog opened his mouth to grab his quarry, the skunk fired full into his enemy's face.

The dog leaped into the air as though he'd been shot. He fell over on his back, got up, fell down again, and then went around the garden in a series of great circles at full speed. The second shepherd, undeterred by his friend's fate, rushed in to be met by a broadside from all six youngsters. The dog turned a complete somersault and went into convulsions. Then he staggered off, stopping occasionally to rub his eyes against his forelegs. I subsequently had the satisfaction of hearing that he made a straight line for his owner's living-room sofa. The skunks waited with their tails raised until both dogs had disappeared and then trundled off after apples.

Not even when the Nikkies forced the village boys to regard me with respect had I felt such supreme fulfillment. From then on I was completely wedded to wild-animal pets.

Three

I was twelve before I acquired my next pets. My grandparents had a town house which they rented; that year it was leased to a family with a boy about my age who shared my interest in animals. This family spent their summers in Nova Scotia and I was invited to accompany them. I was delighted to go—and my grandparents were equally delighted to have me do something besides "make a hermit of myself," as Grandmother expressed it. The Nikkies and their descendants presented no difficulties; they were perfectly capable of shifting for themselves.

While I was in Nova Scotia, I picked up a pair of porcupines, later to be named Claude and Claudette. I was interested in porcupines not only because they were wild animals but also because, like the skunks, they were dog-proof. Porcupines are not popular with lumbermen because they strip trees of their bark. I was horrified when one lumberman told me profanely that he killed every quill pig he found. I begged to be allowed to ransom the next two, and a few days later the man presented me with two indignant porcupines. Getting them back to Rosemont was quite a problem—the pair quietly and systematically ate their way out of every box I put them in. I finally solved the dilemma by putting them in a wire cage, but this had the disadvantage that the porcupines could reach you with their quilly tails through the wire if you weren't careful. Finding a porter who would help carry them through the Pennsylvania Station wasn't any too easy either, but I finally got them home.

I encountered no trouble from my grandparents about the porcupines. Grandmother was perhaps a little disappointed that I hadn't returned a normal, healthy boy evincing a keen interest in baseball, hopscotch, rolling a hoop, or whatever it was that normal, healthy boys did—she was rather vague on the subject. Grandfather, so far as I could tell, didn't even know that the porcupines existed. The place was fairly large, and I could have raised Bengal tigers as long as I kept them out of his way. So I was able to install the porcupines in a new pen without opposition.

Knowing something about skunks, I had taken for granted that I was an authority on all wild animals and that porcupines would behave like quilled skunks. I soon found out that there was no more similarity between the porcupines and the Nikkies than between the Nikkies and a domestic cat or dog. Claude and Claudette had no sense of humor, no desire to play, and very little intelligence. Solid, unimaginative bourgeoise, they cared about nothing save eating and sleeping. Taming them was even less of a task than taming the Nikkies. Born invincible, the nervous apprehension that tortures most newly caught wild animals was simply not in their make-up. Before the week was out, both were lumbering over me for apples, carrots, and the salted peanuts of which they were especially fond. Their regular diet was rolled oats, bread, beets, turnips, potatoes, and such bark as they could strip from our trees before Bounds caught them. Removing a porcupine from a tree is a fairly difficult task; they cling like limpets and there is obviously no way you can grab them. Bounds solved the problem by forcing the end of a clothes pole between the porky and the limb and then using the full leverage of the pole to pry him loose. Luckily a porcupine can drop almost any distance from a tree to the ground without hurting himself. At least, mine never got hurt, and Bounds pried them off some mighty high fruit trees.

Although Claude and Claudette did not have the types of personality that would have endeared them to most people, I was fascinated by their foolproof method of defense. They were covered with a beautiful coat of thick, black hair that made them look more like teddy bears than dangerous animals. So far as one could tell by looking at them, they did not have a quill to their names except for the tip of a white spear or two that showed in the black brush of the tail. But when Rags or one of the Nikkies approached them, the porcupines would turn their backs, raise their tails, and with a quick movement hunch their shoulders like a man pulling up his coat collar on a cold day. Instantly, their fur coats folded forward to reveal a veritable briar patch of long black and white quills pointing in all directions.

Porcupines do not stand entirely on the defensive. Although they cannot throw their quills, their stumpy, powerful tails are covered with the terrible miniature spears; touching a porcupine's tail is equivalent to pulling the wire attached to the trigger of a set-gun. Immediately the tail lashes back and forth with astonishing rapidity, and at each blow half a dozen or so quills are driven into your hand. These quills are terrible objects. They are barbed, not like a fishhook, but with innumerable little scales that lie flat when the quill enters the flesh but open out when you try to remove it. A dog or a wildcat is condemned to death if he ever gets a mouthful of porcupine quills. He cannot extract the quills and they will work their way deeper and deeper into his flesh, festering as they go. Not even a skunk has such an efficient means of defense.

Perhaps I am being unfair to the quill pigs when I say that they had absolutely no intelligence or desire to play. Sometimes when I was feeding Claude, he would rear up on his hind legs, brace himself with his stubby tail, and, grabbing my hand with his forepaws, try to wrestle. I was never quite sure whether he was just trying to get the piece of apple or handful of salted peanuts away from me or whether he really wanted to play. Probably it was a combination of the two. The play of most wild animals is actually mimic combat—like Nikki's handstand and threatening gestures. This is why playing with a wild animal is a tricky business. The dividing line between play and attack is a fine one. Usually the owner and the animal work out an understanding as to how far the animal can go, but when a stranger comes along the animal does not draw a line. The stranger gets hurt, whereupon the pet-owner says condescendingly "Oh, don't worry—he's only playing." Actually, the animal himself probably doesn't know whether he's playing or attacking; the stranger does not automatically give him the cues he needs to know when he's gone too far.

Just as the Nikkies never tried to spray me once they had grown tame, so Claude and Claudette never used their quill-studded tails on me once we had come to an understanding. But the Nikkies would bite when annoyed, and so would the porcupines. When quarreling over food, they would often bite each other—although they never struck at each other with their tails. They treated me like one of the family.

But with strangers, they were prepared to use their full armament. The porcupines moved at a heavy, dignified pace that strongly reminded me of Grandmother's majestic stride. Also like Grandmother, they turned aside for no one, magnificently confident that everyone would give way for them. For a long time I wondered what would happen if Claude and Claudette ever encountered Grandmother head-on; it would be the meeting of an unmovable object and an irresistible force. Although Grandmother seldom went into the lower garden where the quill pigs lived, this historic confrontation did finally occur.

Grandmother was Walking through the rose arbor just as Claude and Claudette started through from the other side. They met halfway. Claude and Claudette were walking side by side and neither broke stride for an instant. Grandmother swept down on them imperiously, but the porcupines kept on. Just when a clash seemed inevitable, Claude raised his tail studded with long, daggerlike quills and shook it suggestively.

Grandmother paused and said "*Shoo!*," but she said it uncertainly. The porcupines tramped on, looking neither to the right nor to the left. Then Grandmother gave way. Forcing herself painfully into the rose vines, she cowered there while the porcupines paraded past—icily regular, splendidly null, without bothering to cast another look at her.

Curiously enough, Grandmother never objected to the porcupines. She clearly recognized in Claude and Claudette aristocrats of the old regime; not very intelligent and even perhaps on the dull side, but dignified and determined. Nikki with his handstand was equally clearly an irresponsible subversive influence and Grandmother only tolerated him because of me. If Nikki had been human, he would have been a slapstick comedian. Claude and Claudette, on the other hand, could have marched into the Union League Club and been instantly identified as members of long standing.

I got my next wild-animal pet by accident. The apple orchard on the Ashbridge farm covered some five acres; here the trees were carefully trimmed and the grass kept mowed, but half a mile away three apple trees had seeded themselves and grown wild not far from a dirt road that bordered the farm. I regarded these three trees as my own personal property, Ismaels of the orchard neglected by Mr. Lewis (the Ashbridge farmer), allowed to grow as they liked.

One afternoon as I was heading for the trees with a book under my arm, a flock of crows rose from the nearby cornfield. I had never been particularly interested in crows, mainly because they kept together in flocks instead of being rugged individualists, but they are dramatic birds seen at close hand—a big crow may have a wingspread of a couple of feet. I stopped to watch them and as I did so there came the stunning crack of a gun.

The leader of the flock swerved in flight, then pitched sideways with an almost-human cry. He fell heavily, beating the air desperately with one wing while the other hung limp. For a moment he succeeded in righting himself and floated downward in a long glide, but the crippled wing bent under him and he plunged heavily into the tall grass.

Now I saw that a car was stopped on the dirt road. A man was leaning out of it with a gun. Another man was in the seat beside him and I heard them laugh together. Then the car drove off.

It is terrible to see a wild creature shot. At one moment it is full of life, the next instant it is a bloody, worthless corpse. It is like seeing someone smash an exquisite vase or fling mud on a noble painting. I stood paralyzed, wondering "Why? But *why* do such a thing?"

Then I thought of the wounded crow and ran toward the spot where he had fallen. There was no sign of him except a few black breast feathers. I stood looking around and saw a slight motion in the tall grass a few feet away. Unable to fly, he was trying to escape on foot. I ran over to him and the bird turned on me, hissing and spreading his great sable wings, one dabbled with blood.

Bending over, I picked him up, taking care not to injure his wounded wing further. Most birds in such a situation will struggle hysterically. Not so the crow. He eyed my hands expertly, picked a good spot, and then struck with his pile-driver beak. The first blow broke the skin, the next made a considerable wound. Then the bird grabbed the edges of the cut and tore at it until I was forced to drop him.

This time I took off my sweater and wrapped him in that, holding his beak shut with one hand. Then I hurried home.

I kept the bird in the loft of our garage. The garage had formerly been the carriage house in which my grandparents kept their horses and, although the Pierce Arrow now stood where the Victoria once had, the stalls were still in place and the loft, once used to store hay and grain, remained untouched. I didn't know how to set the broken wing and never thought of asking my grandparents to call a veterinarian. All I could do was provide the bird with food and water—and wait.

The wing healed, although my new pet was never able to use it as well as before; he always flew with a limp. When the wing was healed I set about taming him, taking the precaution of wearing heavy leather gloves.

The first time I tried picking him up, he began an attack on the gloves with his powerful beak and became so interested in trying to break through that I was able to let go of him completely. He perched on my fist and tore away at the gloves until I tried to touch him with my other hand. Then he gave an outraged squawk and jumped down. But the gloves fascinated him. He kept coming back to have another go at them, and even after he became tame he continued to regard the gloves as his special toy. If I left one lying around he would find it, pull it over to me, and wait solemnly until I put it on. Once the glove was in place, he'd jump on my hand and start worrying the leather like a puppy with a slipper. His other specialty was untying shoelaces. He did this as a joke. If I was watching him, he never paid my laces any attention but if I was busy he would steal up from behind almost literally on tiptoe, quietly stretch out his long beak, neatly untie the laces and then go bounding off chuckling to himself. When I turned around he would squawk with delight and execute a war dance of triumph.

When I took him outside, he rode around on my shoulder, giving me an occasional friendly nip on the ear just to make sure that I hadn't forgotten about him, and making short, clumsy flights to low branches. In the house he developed a passionate interest in small objects, especially shiny ones, that he could pick up and hide. He was never interested in anything given him—but if he saw a workbasket, he would stroll toward it in a deceptively innocent way, looking everywhere except toward the basket, until he was standing beside it. Then after a quick glance right and left, he would study the contents for a few seconds. Down would go the beak and come up with a thimble or small pair of scissors. He'd hurry with his prize to the nearest sofa cushion and stuff the object underneath. Then he'd hurry away from the scene of the crime and perch on the back of a chair, preening his feathers with a particularly innocent expression. If I came along and retrieved the stolen article, he'd go into a full-color Donald Duck fury, bounding up and down on the chair back and screaming with indignation. This pilfering got to be so serious that I called him Jesse James, usually shortened to just Jesse.

Keeping Jesse in the house soon turned out to be impossible. Deprived of the daily challenges of the wild, Jesse invented his own challenges much as a child with a high IQ who finds ordinary schoolwork too dull for him and amuses himself tormenting his teachers. He made life miserable for the maids, hiding behind drapes and nipping them on the ankles as they went by or snatching pieces of food off the plates, flying off chuckling happily with his loot and then dropping it if no one chased him. Grandfather had a special chair near a long windowseat where he sat to read; Jesse would walk quietly along the window-seat, reach out and tear a page of Grandfather's book, ducking away before Grandfather could slap him. It was Grandmother, however, who finally decreed that the house would have to be out of bounds for Jesse. Grandmother did not have a pronounced sense of humor, and the first time Jesse bit her on the ankle she was not amused. In fact, she kicked him. Jesse never forgave her. Usually his ankle nips were nothing more than a light dab with his beak, but after recovering from the kick, he waylaid Grandmother in the dark hallway and really let her have it on the shin. Instead of running off chuckling in his usual fashion, he marched away muttering to himself. After Grandmother had finished rubbing her ankle and straightened up, he stole back and stabbed her in the other ankle. Grandmother sent for me and pronounced sentence: "That bird must go!"

So Jesse was exiled to the garden. At first he spent most of his time standing by the back door, ready to slip in the instant one of the maids opened it. But finally he learned that the house was forbidden to him. This was quite a blow for Jesse—he hated being left alone. He devoted his talents to annoying Rags. Whenever Rags went to sleep under a shady tree, Jesse would steal up on him, give the dog's long hair a quick tweak, and fly off before Rags could snap at him. Poor Rags slowly began to acquire a haunted look and I sympathized with him, but nothing I could do would break Jesse of this trick.

Until I acquired Jesse, it had never occurred to me that birds had any particular personalities or even that they were intelligent. Jesse was considerably smarter than the Nikkies, to say nothing of Claude and Claudette, and had an unlimited repertoire. In fact, I don't think I have ever owned a creature who had a more active mind. Jesse never seemed to rest. He was always thinking up some new game and seemed physically incapable of sitting still a minute. All the Corvidae (so-called because of their cone-shaped beaks) seem remarkably clever birds—crows, jays, ravens, and magpies. I have no idea why this family should depend so much more on their wits than do other birds, but all of them are great thieves and cause so much trouble that they are ruthlessly persecuted by humans. Although every man's hand is against them, they still survive. I can only say that I know of none of the beautifully colored songbirds possessing the brains and personality of a crow.

By the time I was fourteen, I had developed the collector's passion that seems to strike all youngsters and many adults. I wanted to own a private zoo and was eager to obtain any sort of wild animal—regardless of size, habits, or rarity. I would have accepted a meadow mouse or a moose with equal enthusiasm. Fortunately no one offered me a moose; the patience of even my grandparents would have come to an end. My parents were due to return shortly, and from then on the responsibility of raising me would be up to them, so I was allowed to keep any reasonably small animal I could find.

Simply collecting animals at random for no reason except to say that you own them is not a good plan for anyone, especially a youngster. Animals are not postage stamps; they are living creatures who need constant care and understanding. Because nearly all children take at least a cursory interest in animals, there is a popular impression that they are simply animated toys, created to be used as children's playthings. Actually, animals are mechanisms far too complicated to be handled by most children, just as Lewis Carrol's Alice books and the *Wind in the Willows* are really adult reading. However, some children show a marked mechanical bent and others an unusual appreciation of literature. I liked animals, and I was fortunately situated. With plenty of room, no other interests, and able to call on Kennedy or Bounds for help in the matter of pens and enclosures, I was able to maintain what eventually became a backyard zoo without too great injustice to my pets.

Gradually I acquired a great horned owl, a macaw, a green monkey, a Turkey buzzard named Susse, any number of snakes, and even a Chinese walking fish—who, unhappily, went for a walk on Montgomery Avenue and was run over by a car. From my point of view, at least, there was a definite advantage in such a miscellaneous collection. I got to know at least a little about a number of very different creatures. I discovered that although there were general rules governing the habits of separate species, each animal had his own individuality. John Masters, in *Bugles and a Tiger,* says (after making certain general statements about the Gurkas), "We can say that the snow is wet or frozen or dry-powdered, but every snowflake is different from every other snowflake." The same is true not only of groups of humans but also of animals.

Since those days, I have often received phone calls from anxious mothers asking "Johnny wants a pet raccoon. Do raccoons make good pets?" I can only answer: "That depends on the individual raccoon." I could add "It also depends on Johnny. If he won't work with the 'coon or is afraid of getting bitten, get him an opossum." Opossums seldom bite; in fact, they seldom do much of anything. Raccoons are a lot of fun, but they are also quick-tempered and difficult to handle. In general, the more intelligent and active an animal, the more difficult and potentially dangerous he can be. The most intelligent and responsive of all animals are the great apes, but virtually no one can handle them once they are full-grown.

An animal doesn't have to be a bundle of cute tricks or a master mind to be a good pet—as I had already discovered with Claude and Claudette. His habits may be so interesting that they compensate for his lack of vivacity. He may not even particularly like you, although this is naturally discouraging. One animal with whom I never did succeed in making friends was Snarlyeow, the opossum.

The name *Snarlyeow* is perhaps unkind. I found her while sawing down a dead tree where she had been living and took her home with me. Like all opossums, she played dead, keeping her face fixed in a frozen snarl, her legs stiff and her body limp. (Opossums have found this trick so effective that they even have changed their appearance to resemble a long-dead corpse.) Snarlyeow's coat was a coarse, dry, motheaten gray without any of the rich glossy sheer of a living beast. Her long, naked, ratlike tail looked as though it had once been covered with hair now rotted off. But in spite of her bad appearance Snarly was philosophical, and when she found that her trick of playing dead wouldn't work, she came to life and settled down in our home.

Snarly never took to me. But for some reason or other, she got along well with the cook. The cook explained that it was because Snarly looked like a baby pig she had had when a little girl in Ireland and Snarly spent most of her time in the kitchen where, not being particularly active, she caused little trouble.

Snarly's sleeping quarters were a considerable problem. She hated sleeping in a box or on a chair and never considered herself safe unless she was in the highest possible part of a room. She would rather swing from the chandelier by one foot and her tail all day than use the model doghouse stuffed with hay I had provided. Snarly's tail was her most remarkable feature. Opossums are the only animals in North America with prehensile tails. Snarly could use hers like a hand. Not only could she swing from it; she also used it as a sort of anchor to windward when moving along difficult terrain, such as traversing from the top of the cupboard to the stovepipe over the kitchen range. Being rather clumsy, she never completely trusted her hands, and even after getting a firm hold on the stovepipe she would not let go with her tail until the last possible second. The tail also made a convenient handle for carrying Snarly from one spot to another, although if she remained suspended by it too long, Snarly would start crawling up her own body until she reached your hand. On such occasions, she was known to bite—although she never bit the cook who could pick her up like a pet cat and park Snarly on her shoulder while shelling peas or peeling potatoes.

For some curious reason, Snarly finally settled on the top of a bookcase in the living room for her permanent quarters. I was afraid that Grandmother might object to this arrangement, but she never paid any attention to Snarly—possibly because Snarly, like most wild animals, was mainly nocturnal and seldom got up until evening, when Grandmother had retired. However, any unusual event, especially if it concerned food, woke Snarly. She had a habit of leaving her tail hanging over the edge of the bookcase and when a tea party was in progress and the tea and cakes were brought in, the tail would begin to sway back and forth. Then a long nose with a twitching, pink end and nervous whiskers would appear. At last Snarly would start down, hanging by her tail until her forepaws could find a hold, then hanging by her hands until her tail could grip a book still farther down. Grandmother sat with her back to the bookcase while pouring tea and often wondered what the guests were staring at until she turned around and saw Snarly preparing to join the party.

At last Grandmother grew tired of having guests scream, "Emma, there's a giant rat behind you!" Not wishing to order me to remove Snarly, she quietly gave a carpenter orders to build the bookcases up to the ceiling. Snarly had to find other sleeping quarters and settled on the water tank over the stove. She spent all one day moving up there, carrying her bedding wrapped up in her tail so as to have both feet and hands free to climb.

Since she always used the hot-water pipe to climb up, it was fortunate for her that the furnace was not used in the kitchen until midwinter. I fitted up a wooden trellis which Snarly refused to use except until the cook carried her over to it; then she would climb up only as a courtesy. When the fatal day came and the pipes grew hot, Snarly got a bad burn. After that, she carefully patted all pipes before climbing them.

In February, Snarly became increasingly secretive, hiding in the rear of her shelf and seldom appearing. Even her friend the cook couldn't coax her out and had to put her meals on the shelf. The meals would disappear when no one was looking. Remembering Mrs. Nikki's behavior, I guessed that Snarly was about to become a mother and I eagerly awaited the blessed event.

After a week's retirement Snarly reappeared, but to my great disappointment without babies. I decided that either she had simply been sick or had eaten them, a miserable habit many captive wild-animal mothers have. But a week later while I was carrying Snarly by the tail from an expedition she had made to check her old, lost home over the bookcase, I noticed that a long slit had appeared down her belly and within this slit were a number of tiny tails. My knowledge of the facts of life, especially the opossum facts of life, was rudimentary, and although I could recognize the tails as belonging to baby opossums I could only suppose that somehow Snarly had split up the middle due to my rough handling, exposing the babies inside her. Hurriedly putting Snarly down, I ran for the cook, who rushed in to help. She didn't know any more about the situation than I did, but as Snarly seemed perfectly well and—when we carefully spread the slit—the tiny babies inside seemed equally well, we decided that all was not lost.

The answer turned out to be that opossums are marsupials, the only marsupials in this hemisphere. They are among the oldest living mammals—really a prehistoric remnant. When the young are born, although they are not much bigger than bees, they manage to crawl through the mother's hair to her pouch, where they fix themselves on the teats. They grow remarkably quickly and by the end of a week are as big as mice.

Although Snarly continued to be very restless, she finally settled down on the shelf in the kitchen. A month later the babies emerged and rode around on her back, holding on with their tails. There were ten of them, and poor Snarly was worn to skin and bones nursing the litter. As they grew bigger and began to take short expeditions on their own, even the indulgent cook decided that there wasn't room in the kitchen for eleven opossums. So I took Snarly and her family to the loft over the garage barn. As the double door through which hay bales used to be hoisted up was open, she could leave whenever she wished, but she stayed on for another month. I left food there every day but seldom saw anything of Snarly or her children except for a long, pink, piggy snout peering down from a rafter and occasionally a few small snouts with it. When spring came Snarly vanished, taking her children with her. Interesting as she was, I had to admit that as an affectionate pet Snarly was a failure.

Although Snarly was hardly intelligent, she did have one great attribute—a youngster could handle her. Shortly after Snarly had returned to the wild, I got another pet: Wayatcha, a raccoon. The trouble with Wayatcha was that he had more brains than I did, and quickly found it out. By the time he reached his full weight of 25 pounds he was running the household and everyone—including me—lived in mortal terror of him. A big male raccoon is a formidable animal. A famous bull terrier in Toronto who had defeated every dog put into the pit with him was considered to have reached the apex of fighting ability when he killed a boar 'coon half his weight.

The idea of disciplining an animal had never occurred to me. It had never been necessary with my other pets, and I took for granted that all wild animals responded to love and kindness. Not that Wayatcha was vicious; he was simply determined and saw no more reason why he shouldn't always have his own way than would any other spoiled child.

I got Wayatcha when he was still a baby from a grocer who found him one morning in the storeroom. Wayatcha had gotten his head stuck in a jar of applesauce and couldn't get it out again. I took the baby to the loft of our garage-barn and tried to get the jar loose. There has been a great deal written about the marvelous manner in which animals know when you are trying to help them. I've never noticed it. I have yet to see one you didn't have to hogtie before lancing an abscess or washing out a cut, and Wayatcha was no exception. After struggling with him for half an hour and getting badly scratched, I finally had to break the jar. Wayatcha suffered no ill effects from his experience except a terrible bellyache from eating too much applesauce. I spent the next week trying to overcome the little wild creature's timid nature and another two years trying to put the fear of God into him.

Wayatcha tamed quickly—partly because he was young, but mainly because he was lonely. Raccoons stay with their mothers for a year at least after they are born, and I can only suppose that Wayatcha's mother had been killed, forcing the baby to shift for himself. At first he had a hard time understanding how anyone who had treated him so badly (he clearly regarded my efforts to get the jar off his head a brutal attack) should now be bringing him food. After much mental agony, he managed to take cookies from my hand, although he snarled and ran if I tried to touch him. But he didn't really lose his fear of me until I tried to play a joke on him.

One afternoon while Wayatcha was sitting on the barn floor beside me eating cookies, I held out a handful of raisins with my fist closed. Wayatcha finished the cookies and waddled over to inspect my fist. He smelled it, located the raisins, and then tried to pry my fingers open with his little black paws. When this did not work, he patted my hand and looked up questioningly. I chuckled to myself and said nothing. Then Wayatcha sat down with my fist in his lap to think it over.

Raccoons are very fond of clams; they open them by a sharp bite at the joint. I had forgotten this trick but Wayatcha had not. A few minutes later he had the raisins and I was getting first aid from a bottle of iodine. That was the end of Wayatcha's backwardness. After that he thought nothing of taking a flying leap at me as soon as I opened the cage door and hanging onto my necktie with one hand while he went through my pockets with the other. If I had known more about animals, I would then and there have begun to discipline Wayatcha. But there are few animals so appealing as a baby raccoon.

Even my grandparents, usually indifferent when not actually opposed to my pets, were delighted by Wayatcha. We were all fascinated at the wonderful manner in which he could use his hands. He was as clever as a monkey at opening doors and uncorking bottles. I honestly believe he could have threaded a needle had he wanted to. It was great fun to think up tricks for him and then see how long it would take him to open a box or drawer. We had a game like "find the thimble" played with a piece of candy. Wayatcha could use his nose instead of the usual "hot" and "cold" helps. Unfortunately, he got so expert at the game that he played it night and day, even opening drawers and kicking out the clothes just in case somebody had hidden some candy there by mistake.

Then the cook made a serious error. Wayatcha, like all raccoons, had a tidy habit of washing his food before eating it, and he selected the kitchen sink for this purpose. As he ate at all hours he was a nuisance, whining and pulling at the cook's skirts to turn the water on for him. At last in desperation she took fifteen minutes off and taught him the trick of the spigots. He learned at once, but nobody was ever able to teach him how to turn them off again. The natural result was that we had to keep all the bathroom doors locked. Simply closing them did no good, for Wayatcha could handle the doorknobs as well as any human.

I think Wayatcha's greatest pleasure was to go wading in the creek that ran through the Ashbridge farm in search of frogs and crayfish. Wayatcha would walk daintily along the bank until a frog dived into the soft mud. Then he would wade out to where the frog had disappeared and suddenly make a grab in the slime on the bottom. He always washed the frogs carefully; perhaps 'coons have developed their neat habit of washing their food because most of their hunting is done along the banks of streams.

As Wayatcha grew bigger, he became increasingly difficult to control. For a long time he never bit. I would be playing with him in the living room when Wayatcha would decide it was time to go to the kitchen for a light snack. He would start off at a trundling gait which looked clumsy but was surprisingly fast.

He was perfectly capable of opening the icebox and going off with the evening's roast; I therefore had to catch him. Wayatcha would not turn on me, but neither would he desist from his purpose. If I could catch him on the open floor, I could pick him up, put him out of the house, and lock the door. But if Wayatcha managed to get hold of a table leg or one of the water pipes, it was impossible to dislodge him. Even when I was carrying him off, Wayatcha's long arms were reaching out to grab any passing object. Once, while we were passing through the maids' dining room in which the table had been set for supper Wayatcha managed to clutch a corner of the tablecloth with results terrible to behold. When he reached his full weight and girth after two years, even picking him up wasn't too easy. The Indians call the raccoon "Little Cousin of the Bear" (the name we use comes from the Indian *Arocoun),* and Wayatcha was very much like a sawed-off grizzly. He was low-slung, powerful, and determined. He didn't exactly struggle when I tried to pick him up—he just kept right on going, and lifting him clean off the floor was a major operation.

When Wayatcha had been a cute baby, my grandparents and even the maids had been willing to forgive him a multitude of sins. Now, as a big boar 'coon, he wasn't nearly so charming. Still, perhaps surprisingly, the decision to forbid Wayatcha the house was mine, not my grandparents'. I had frankly grown tired of wrestling with this junior bruin and cleaning up after him. Not that Wayatcha wasn't perfectly housebroken—like all 'coons, he was very tidy in that respect, but he labored under the delusion that somebody might have hidden food behind the books in the bookcase, concealed something fascinating under the rugs, or left an article of great interest on top of the highest table in a room. By the time Wayatcha had satisfied his curiosity, repairing the damage was a good hour's hard work.

Wayatcha had no intention of being kept outside. He patrolled the house like a sentry, and as soon as anyone opened a door or a maid leaned out a window to shake a mop, Wayatcha was on the spot in a matter of seconds. From then on he was in; no one could close a door or window against Wayatcha when he wanted to exert his full strength.

About this time I began to have an uneasy feeling that instead of Wayatcha's being my pet, I was becoming his. Wayatcha believed in discipline. He wasn't cruel with me, only firm. When I tried to get a collar and chain on him, Wayatcha did not bite; he merely jerked the collar off each time I fitted it around his neck. When I grew more insistent, Wayatcha walked away and—as I couldn't hold him and put on the collar at the same time—I had to let him go.

Wayatcha was two years old before he ever bit me, and then because he was frightened and confused.

One afternoon I missed Wayatcha. Since finding him was usually no problem (it was avoiding him that presented difficulties), I was fearful that someone had shot him or the village boys had killed him with a club. Supper-time came and still no Wayatcha. After supper, I went out again, this time taking Rags with me. Rags was no friend of Wayatcha's—they had played together when Wayatcha was a baby, but when he got big he was too rough for the little dog—but I still hoped he might be of some help.

It was almost dark when I saw Rags sniffing at the mouth of a big drainpipe that ran from the garage-barn to the compost pile. I got on my hands and knees and looked up the pipe. I couldn't see anything, but I heard a curious, frightened whining. It didn't sound like any noise Wayatcha usually made. He had a conversational *chur-chur* when we were playing together, a plaintive *er-er-er* when he wanted something, and occasionally at night I would hear him give the typical 'coon's whicker, an almost bird-like note apparently used as a mating call. I couldn't believe that this was Wayatcha, nor could I understand what he was doing up that pipe. Nevertheless, I crawled in to see.

The pipe was so small that I was barely able to worm my way along. I had gotten some ten feet up it when the whining started again, this time running up the scale until it became a shrill scream. It didn't sound frightened any more, only furious. I said *"Wayatcha?"* doubtfully and put out my hand. I touched Wayatcha's bristly fur neck; as I did so, he sank his teeth into my hand.

The pain was excruciating and I screamed in agony. Then I tried to wriggle backward out of the pipe, but I could only go inches at a time—and meanwhile Wayatcha was following me, biting as he came. I was afraid he'd get me by the face and kept putting up my hands to push him away. Each time I did so, Wayatcha would seize my hand and worry it, growling and hissing.

By the time I finally got out of the pipe, I was crying with pain and my hands looked as though I'd run them through a meat grinder. Rags was bouncing around outside, barking hysterically. Wayatcha followed me out. He started for me again and I ran. Then he turned on Rags, who promptly and sensibly fled like a leaf on the wind. After looking around him Wayatcha marched off, muttering to himself.

I staggered to the back door, leaving a trail of blood behind me. The cook screamed when she saw me and shouted for Mary Clark. Mary took one look at me, cried "Holy Saints, Master Dan!," and led me to the bathroom. While she washed my hands, she called to the upstairs maid: "Telephone Dr. Griggs and tell him to come at once. Don't let the Madam know, she'd be that upset!" I sat weeping and watching the blood run out of my mutilated hands until Dr. Griggs arrived. He cauterized the cuts with iodine and then sewed them. Those were the days before Novocain, and I shall never forget the pain. I remember screaming and Mary holding my head while pleading, "Please, Master Dan, the Madam and the old gentleman will hear you!" At last she gave me a twisted washcloth to bite on. I don't know how many stitches the doctor took because toward the last I was delirious.

Of course, when my grandparents saw my hands the next morning they demanded an explanation. When they heard what had happened, Grandmother wanted to send for a vet and have Wayatcha put down. I begged for his life so passionately that Grandmother finally said "Well, we'll see," but I heard her stamping upstairs to the phone. Grandfather merely remarked "Your Cousin Kenneth used to feel that way about horses. One finally killed him. Let me see, was that in ninety-eight or ninety-nine?" and went to his file of *Social Registers* to see when Cousin Kenneth's name disappeared from the list. I rushed outside to find Wayatcha and hide him.

Wayatcha, however, had taken matters into his own paws and disappeared. He never returned.

Obviously, I should never have crawled up the pipe after Wayatcha, particularly when he was frightened and angry. I have no idea what he was doing up the pipe or why he refused to come out. Possibly dogs had chased him and he had taken refuge there. But my greatest mistake was allowing him to control me instead of controlling him. Once a powerful wild animal learns that he is stronger than his owner he becomes potentially dangerous—an unfortunate fact sentimentalists dislike to admit. Wild animals are frequently extremely rough with their own families. A male 'coon, once the breeding season is over, will half-kill his former mate if he finds her looking for frogs in his favorite pool, and the female will be equally rough with her own cubs once they become old enough to shift for themselves. It is unreasonable to suppose that they would put a human in a different category than their own species.

Disciplining wild animals is a complicated technique. For example, if I had tried to punish Wayatcha by using a whip I would only have infuriated him and forced him to turn on me. Also, raccoons have such thick coats that a blow has very little effect—except to enrage them. What I should have done was put a collar on Wayatcha when he was still fairly small and use a lead-pole. Lead-poles are equipped with a snap on one end which can be opened and closed by a wire leading to the handle. When Wayatcha was heading for the kitchen, I could have snapped the lead-pole to a ring on his collar and held him. If he proved stubborn, I could have kept him on the lead-pole for several days until he realized that he could neither reach me nor escape. Eventually a habit pattern would form and Wayatcha would have accepted the fact that he had to obey. Restraints of this nature are no more cruel than using a bridle and bit on a horse. If the animal is to live with you, he must learn that he cannot always do what he wants and cannot turn on you whenever he is thwarted or in a bad mood.

At considerable cost, I had learned three important lessons from Wayatcha. (1) Unless the animal is as happy-go-lucky as the Nikkies or as phlegmatic as Claude and Claudette, he cannot be allowed to run wild. He will grow too independent. This is especially unwise if the animal is large enough to be dangerous. He loses all natural fear of man but learns no respect for him. A prime example of such semi-wild animals are the bears in Yellowstone Park—bears that are a constant potential menace to careless motorists. (2) The animal must be kept under control, but a type of control the animal can understand. A simple "treat 'em rough" policy is no good whatsoever; the technique must be slanted to the species and the individual animal. (3) You must always be prepared to have a potentially dangerous animal turn on you; not in the sense that the animal is "vicious," but in the sense that a horseman must always be prepared to have a high-spirited horse do the unexpected: The rider can never relax.

I did not know what I was doing when I tried to make a pet of Wayatcha without proper experience. I paid for my ignorance and I fear Wayatcha also paid a higher price, for he had only contempt for humans. But perhaps he returned to the wild and adopted 'coon ways instead of staying near civilization. I certainly hope so.

Four

To what must have been the intense relief of my grandparents, Father and Mother returned that summer. Father had retired from the Navy with the rank of rear admiral and planned to spend the rest of his life at Rosemont except for frequent trips to France, which he regarded as his real home. Mother had always hated traveling and returning to the familiar life of the Main Line was to her an ascent from purgatory to heaven.

After being separated from me for so many years, my parents, not unnaturally, were extremely indulgent. Father considered it a foregone conclusion that I would go to the Naval Academy at Annapolis and enter the service. After all, I was Daniel Pratt Mannix IV, and every Daniel Pratt Mannix had been in the Navy. He dismissed my interest in animals as a passing phase. "I remember when I was a kid I used to keep pet snakes and turtles," he remarked. "But of course I soon outgrew it." To Father, it was incredible that any youngster wouldn't feel the lure of the service which had been his whole life. Mother viewed the matter somewhat more seriously, but was confident that by quietly developing the social side of my life I would soon be weaned away from animals. As a result, I was forced into a round of dancing classes, parties, and church socials.

I so rebelled against this regime that Father had to be called in several times to apply military discipline. The truth was that neither of my parents knew what to make of me. Mother had been an extremely pretty and popular young girl in the Gibson girl tradition and could no more conceive of anyone disliking society than father could conceive of anyone not being entranced by the idea of plebe year at Annapolis. Mother had no interest in animals. She tolerated them not only because of me but because the troubles we had with them gave her an almost unlimited fund of amusing stories to tell her friends. She was an excellent raconteur; even today I occasionally meet people who exclaim, "Why, you must be Polly Mannix's son. I remember so well how Polly kept us in stitches with the story of what happened when your pet skunks turned up at her garden party."

Father regarded the animals simply as a nuisance. He would probably have forbidden me to keep them, but he was basically a kindly man, and also he undoubtedly felt that if after returning from so many years' absence he began our relationship by denying me something that obviously was my only interest we would be permanently estranged. He therefore shrugged off my zoo as a temporary hobby and waited for the fad to pass. Father was an outstanding athlete, the first American to swim the Hellespont (two years before Richard Halliburton claimed to have accomplished this feat) and his name is still prominently displayed on the walls of the gymnasium at the Naval Academy as one of their great gymnasts. There was even a cartoon about his physical development in his old Lucky Bag, showing his roommate rushing out explaining, "Pratt Mannix is expanding his chest and I ran out to catch my breath." When Mother wasn't explaining to me that if I didn't make better social contacts I would never be able to join the Union League Club, Father was gloomily prophesying that unless I made more of an effort to get on my high school football team I would never qualify for the Army-Navy game.

So, though I loved my parents, it was with mixed feelings that I saw them depart the following summer for a three-month stay in France, Father having spent so much of his life abroad that he felt vaguely restless at "being cooped up in the United States," as he expressed it. However, they arranged an elaborate social program for me to follow while they were away, centering mainly around our swimming pool. At that time a private swimming pool was an almost unheard-of luxury and was a guaranteed attraction for young people. I was then sixteen and before she left Mother had called up all of her friends who had youngsters about my age—and urged them to use the pool as if it were their own. Shortly after my dear parents had departed, I solved the problem of my social career by putting a ten-foot alligator in the pool.

I still think I had some justification. Making our estate the social center of the Main Line had not proved a success. Every day I had to spend an hour or so cleaning up the collection of newspapers, magazines, chewing gum wrappers, broken bathing caps, cigarette packages, and other junk. Much of the stuff had been thrown into the pool, so I had to dive for it in the evening after my "guests" had gone. If left overnight, the papers disintegrated and the water was full of floating bits that went to pieces in your hands when you tried to get them out.

At first the guests simply ignored me; anyhow I was usually off playing with the Nikkies, the porcupines, or my other pets. Most of them seemed to regard the pool as their personal property. A girl would arrive with four or five boys in tow, thus giving herself an aura of popularity and indebting them to her so she would be sure of cut-ins at the next dance. The boys, realizing they were doing the girl a favor, took for granted that they were honoring me. They never bothered to thank me. One boy had developed the habit of coming regularly—always bringing a dozen or so friends with him, all of whom ignored me except one fellow. He asked me if I really thought I could make the pool pay. I asked him what he meant.

"Why, Dick has been charging people fifty cents each to go swimming here. I naturally thought you got a percentage."

I appealed to my grandparents but they told me that after a long conversation with my parents, it had been decided I was to be more normal and have friends. But a few days later, the bunch of hoodlums really had a ball. They started by throwing all the pillows from the porch into the pool and then one of the boys lay on the heap and was towed around yelling "I'm Cleopatra!" Some of the girls wandered into the house, lying on beds and couches and burning cigarette holes in the upholstery. Someone else backed a car through the double doors of the garage and broke them. Mary Clark went down to expostulate with the crowd and was nearly pushed into the pool. Then I tried my luck.

When I appeared, there was a general shout of "Here comes old Sour-Puss"—which, it seems, was my new name. I asked the girls if they would mind staying out of the house in wet suits. The girls assured me they would do as they pleased. I asked the boys if they would clean up some of the mess they had made. The boys told me I could handle that. As they were all sons of old family friends, my grandparents didn't like to call the police. The crowd left about nine o'clock that evening, having nearly wrecked the place.

I remembered a trapper in South Carolina had written me a few weeks before asking if I could use a ten-foot alligator. I'd reluctantly refused, knowing that there were limits to my family's indulgence. Now I felt this was a good time to invest in alligators.

I telegraphed the trapper and in due time a huge packing case arrived by express. A note was nailed to the case explaining that the trapper had named the 'gator Daisy after his wife. I thought then, and still think, this was a beautiful tribute. Few trappers are so sentimental. Daisy she remained.

I got Kennedy to help me carry the case down to the swimming pool. The pool was enclosed by an ornamental fence which I hoped would restrain Daisy if she tried to go for a walk. While I was preparing to open the case with a hammer and chisel, Kennedy asked me what was inside. I told him an alligator.

"And what may an alligator be, Master Dan?" Kennedy wanted to know.

"It's a reptile," I explained—and added, seeing the blank look on Kennedy's face, "like a snake."

Kennedy said nothing but wandered over to inspect the fence. He was back a few minutes later while I was getting the planks loose.

"Master Dan, those fence railings are a deal too far apart to hold a snake."

"Wait 'till you see this animal and then tell me what you think."

I got the top planks off. Even I was a little taken aback by the sight of Daisy. Ten feet is a lot of 'gator, although admittedly much of that is tail.

"Well, do you think she can get out through the fence railings?" I asked.

Kennedy said quietly, "Master Dan, that thing couldn't get out through the barn doors," and left me to my own devices.

Daisy didn't look particularly dangerous. Like all alligators, she wore a perpetual grin which gave her a rather innocent air; also she seemed fast asleep. I managed to dump her out of the box and then, with the aid of a rake handle, tried to head her toward the pool. Right then I got my first lesson in handling alligators.

Reptiles are curious creatures, very unlike the warm-blooded mammals. The great saurians are leftovers from the Mesozoic period, when they ruled the earth. Generally they are extremely sluggish, seldom moving unless they must, and giving the impression of being almost inanimate. Their metabolism is so low that they can go for long periods without eating and in captivity are apt to pass into a state of inertia, refuse to eat, and slowly die. Being coldblooded, their bodies take on the temperature of the surrounding atmosphere; in cool weather they become virtually paralyzed. After the long trip in a cool, dark box Daisy seemed almost dead and I began to lever her over the grass as though manipulating a log. That this insensate creature could show any animation seemed incredible.

It was a hot summer's day and we were in the broiling sun. Daisy and I were still a few feet from the edge of the pool when she suddenly came to life. In all my experience with animals I have never seen any that moved so quickly as Daisy. Suddenly twisting herself into a V, she struck me with her powerful tail, using it to knock me toward her open jaws, which were coming toward me from the other direction.

I went over backward, as much from astonishment as from the blow of the tail. Daisy's jaws came together with a stunning crack that sounded like a giant slapping two boards together. Holding her off with the rake handle, I scrambled backward. Daisy made no attempt to follow me. She whirled around and rising on her short legs made a rush for the pool. She went astonishingly fast, dove in head first, and vanished.

The whole business had been such a complete surprise that I was badly shaken, and the sight of those huge jaws clashing together only a few inches away had been a disturbing sight. Cautiously I went to the edge of the pool and looked in. There was Daisy swimming around like a seal. I had had no idea alligators were so graceful in the water, although anything that depends largely on catching fish for a living must be a good swimmer. Daisy swam entirely with her tail, her legs folded up under her, but when she came to the end of the pool and swung around for the return trip, I could see the flash of her white belly. I looked forward to Daisy's meeting with the Main Line younger set.

The next day shortly after lunch, three cars swung into the drive bearing a happy crowd. A few minutes later there were shrieks of laughter as the car tore through a hedge, followed by occasional outbursts of mirth as the party spread over the lawn.

I was carrying Dracula, my Great Horned Owl, around at the time and getting Dracula back on her perch took a few minutes. By the time I headed for the pool I could hear the sound of splashing, almost instantly followed by such a fearful scream that I broke into a dead run. I was suddenly cold with terror. Like many teen-agers, I did not possess enough judgment to foresee the consequences of an act which had seemed merely a good joke. Today, teenagers driving souped-up cars will have a drag race and tear over a hill side by side on a two-lane highway. This is nothing but a game. It is not until they reach the crest of the hill and see another car coming toward them that they realize the consequences of their stunt—and then it is too late. Racing for the pool, I was positive Daisy had killed somebody.

Fool's luck was on my side. "Bugs" Brigman ("He's the awfullest boy, my dear, he just doesn't care what he does!") was being pulled out of the pool, his pimply face dough-white. A group of terrified girls were climbing out at the far end while the rest looked on in horror. To my intense relief I saw Daisy was still lying in her accustomed place at the bottom. She had paid no attention to the swimmers. After a few had dived in, someone had seen her, screamed, and started to panic.

An indignant committee came over to see me.

"Say, listen," the spokesman began, "do you know there's an alligator in your pool?"

"Of course, I put her there."

"Well, get her out. How do you expect us to go swimming with an alligator?"

"Oh, she doesn't take up much room."

"Very funny. I'll tell my parents and they'll tell your parents and you'll wish you hadn't been so smart."

"Go ahead. My grandparents own this place."

After this brilliant exchange, the crowd left. The news spread rapidly. The reaction of these youngsters was interesting. They had grown so used to using the pool as though it were their own that any attempt to stop them seemed not only outrageous but vaguely illegal. One girl telephoned me that she was giving a house party and intended to bring over the guests that afternoon. "And see that you have that alligator out of the pool before we get there," she snapped as she hung up. The guests arrived to find Daisy sunning herself on the bank. I learned afterward that they had intended to "call my bluff," but it's difficult to call the bluff of a ten-foot alligator. The party left.

Others worked more tactfully, through their parents. I began to receive calls from ladies who assured me that although it was a shame to betray their daughters' confidence, I was Betty's or Ruth's ideal. It always turned out that Betty or Ruth was giving a swimming party. Sometimes I was asked to garden parties only to discover when I arrived that it was to be a "swimming party" and I was to furnish the pool. No one believed me when I explained that even if I wished, I could not move Daisy at an hour's notice.

Poor Mother had intended to launch me in society. Instead, she gave me a dislike and suspicion of society which lasted for years.

For the next few weeks, Daisy never left the pool except to sunbathe on the edge. Feeding her was no problem. She spent most of her time on the bottom of the pool; although alligators don't have gills they seem able to stay under water almost indefinitely as long as they don't move about and use up oxygen. When Daisy was hungry she would cruise around with only her nostrils and eyes above the surface looking for something to eat. Alligators are magnificently equipped for this type of hunting. Their nostrils are on the top of their snouts and their eyes are elevated on knobs. Only the nostrils and eyes show above the surface and in muddy or opaque water a hunting alligator is nearly invisible.

When I saw Daisy cruising around, I would throw her a fish. As soon as the fish hit the surface of the water, she would shoot toward it, her broad, oar-shaped snout making a little V-shaped ripple as she came. A few yards from the fish she would submerge and glide swiftly toward her quarry but the ripple would continue on the surface, marking her progress. I resolved then if I were ever swimming in tropical waters and saw a V-shaped ripple headed my way I would get to land—fast. When Daisy struck, the blow was almost too fast to see. A sudden swirl, a flash of Daisy's white, open jaws, and the fish would vanish. If she were still hungry she'd stick her head above the surface, grinning in traditional alligator fashion. Then I'd throw her another fish. Daisy would dive after it, catch it broadside, surface while she shifted the fish around in her mouth so she could swallow it head first, and give one gulp.

I was able to go in swimming with Daisy, even if the first few times were nerve-wracking. Alligators have a habit of holding large prey under water until it stops making bubbles and then stowing it in a hole until it decomposes enough to make it readily edible. I was sure that Daisy wouldn't try to eat me—she was quite tame, and would even take fish from my hand—but she might hold me under water for an hour or two while making up her mind, and that would have been an unpleasant experience.

Daisy followed me about for some time, sniffing at my legs doubtfully, but as soon as I splashed she went away and lay on the bottom. At the time I attributed Daisy's behavior more to her being well fed than to any real intelligence, but possibly I was wrong. Many years later I saw that remarkable woman Grace Wiley call six alligators and crocodiles, each animal recognizing his own name and coming when called. Grace's saurians were as tame as dogs and she treated them as friends. Quite possibly Daisy knew me and wouldn't have been as forbearing with a stranger.

Experts can't seem to agree on how dangerous alligators are. Today, very few are left and probably no really big ones except in zoos. For many years they were shot wholesale for their hides. Now they are protected; even the "baby alligators" sold in pet stores are really South American caimans, not true alligators. There have been records of 19-foot alligators weighing 600 pounds, and such an animal certainly could be dangerous. Big 'gators have been known to kill a three-year-old cow and swallow three pigs, one after the other. Their jaws are so powerful they can crush the bones of an ox. Humans have been attacked by 'gators. One big 'gator seized a swimming man by the arm and swung it off at the shoulder. When a 'gator fastens onto large prey, he twists rapidly and wrings off whatever is in his mouth. However, the man lived—the 'gator's jaws closed with such force that they crushed the blood vessels and prevented bleeding. Probably alligators seldom make an unprovoked attack on humans, but a female alligator guarding her nest is a dangerous animal. She builds a nest some three feet high, using brush and weeds, and then covers it with a cone of mud. The eggs in the nest hatch, incubated by the heat of the sun and the decomposing brush, while the mother either adds water to the nest or removes surplus moisture with her body so the humidity remains exactly right. She will attack anything, animal or human, approaching the nest. The alligators who attack humans are often females guarding their homes.

After several weeks, I took for granted that Daisy would never go far from the pool and began leaving the fence gate open. But one night there was a terrific thunderstorm. Possibly the thunder frightened Daisy or possibly the damp earth seemed to her ideal for a stroll. At all events, when I came down the next morning Daisy was gone.

I had no trouble following her trail through the flower beds and across the Ashbridge wheat field; it looked as though someone had been dragging a log along. But when Daisy reached the Johnson estate and managed to get under the iron fence, I could find no more trace of her.

An experienced trespasser, I always made it a point to keep out of sight—never crossing an open lawn when I could keep to the shrubbery and never going near a house. But this day I was desperate. Having searched the lower gardens and found nothing, I went to the rose garden which was in full view of the Johnson mansion itself. I was still looking about for traces of Daisy when a window opened and Mrs. Johnson herself leaned out. In a friendly voice she called, "My dear, what's the matter?"

I had no intention of telling Mrs. Johnson that a ten-foot alligator was loose on her estate. Thinking quickly, I called back, "I'm looking for a little lost puppy."

"How sweet of you, dear. I'll come down and help you look," and the window banged shut.

I hadn't counted on that. In a few minutes Mrs. Johnson appeared and went from flower bed to flower bed, parting the bushes and calling, "Here darling, here boy!" I had a horrible vision of Daisy suddenly sticking her head out from between two bushes and snapping her jaws in Mrs. Johnson's face, but luckily at that moment I found Daisy's spoor going through a hedge. Leaving Mrs. Johnson I followed it eagerly across a stretch of damp grass under the iron fence to the next property.

Here was a tennis court with wire backstops and there, wonder of wonders, was Daisy. She had crawled onto the court and found herself enclosed on three sides. Being tired from her long walk, Daisy had simply lain down and gone to sleep.

Now came the problem of getting her home. While I was pondering it, a boy about my age came running out of the house and shouted, "Is that your alligator?"

I admitted ownership. "She certainly gave us a surprise this morning," said the boy, wild with delight and excitement. "We just rented this place for the summer and this morning my sister and I came out to see if the court was dry enough for tennis. We saw that alligator and took for granted that she was a bronze lawn ornament someone had left there. We never thought that she might be real."

"She's real enough," I told him.

"That's what we found. She looked heavy so Sis and I got a couple of sticks to lever her off the court. We stood on one side of her, counted 'One—Two—Three!' and stuck the sticks under her. By golly, she can move fast! She let out the most terrible bellow and chased us both across the court."

I went back and got Mother's Chrysler two-seater runabout, which had a rumble seat. As there wasn't room for both me and

Daisy in front, she had to ride in the rumble. She sat in it like a person except that her tail hung over the edge. Driving back to the house was quite an experience. People would go by, glance at Daisy sitting in the rumble, do a double take, and then scream, "It's a crocodile!" Then in their excitement they'd lose control of the wheel and nearly swerve into the Chrysler. I barely made it back.

Daisy only bit me once, and then quite by accident. She was lying on the edge of the pool and I was feeding her fish by hand. Once when she didn't open her mouth I reached out to pat her on the head, a trick that usually made Daisy open her jaws. But this time Daisy grabbed my hand.

The sudden shock of the powerful jaws clamping shut paralyzed my left arm to the elbow and I was sure my hand was gone. I instantly threw myself down at full length so I could roll with Daisy to avoid having my arm wrung off at the shoulder. But Daisy didn't roll. Instead, she sat there for some time, obviously thinking the situation over. Then she slowly and carefully opened her mouth. I saw my hand lying on her tongue, still intact except that four of Daisy's long teeth had gone through it.

My arm was too numb for me to control the muscles, but with my right hand I slowly worked my left off the teeth while Daisy sat with her mouth obligingly open. I felt no pain all the way to the Bryn Mawr Hospital and when I walked into the accident ward—still in the pajamas which were my usual summer costume—I merely told the intern, "My pet alligator bit me."

The intern excused himself and left the room. I waited a long time. I afterward found that he considered me a dangerous mental patient and was asking for help. Finally he returned with an older doctor used to the Main Line who took one look at me, and said, "That's Polly Mannix's son. I know the family. They're the kind of people who probably would have pet alligators" and set about treating my hand.

Apparently my case became something of a legend at the hospital. Last year when I went there to be treated for a bug I'd picked up in India, the young nurse who took my name gave an excited squeal and cried, "You must be the person who came here years ago when his pet alligator bit him. Do you still have the alligator?"

Unfortunately I don't. When my parents returned that autumn, Daisy had to go to the zoo.

Five

Both my parents were very upset about Daisy. They began to regard me as a sort of changeling. As Mother remarked in desperation to Grandfather, who took the whole affair with his usual placidity, "But gentlemen don't put alligators in swimming pools!" Grandfather effectively silenced this objection by remarking, "Colonel Biddle kept his pet alligator in the living room." Mother had no answer to that; the Biddles were the highest of high society. Father was unable to understand how I could still feel affection for an animal who had nearly bitten off my left hand although if I had received an equally serious injury in football, he would have accepted it as a matter of course. Both, however, agreed that Daisy would have to go to the zoo. I had to admit that Daisy did present certain problems, since she and Father couldn't very well use the pool at the same time, and he spent most of his spare time there practicing swimming strokes. Also, I had no way to keep Daisy over the winter. So with the help of Bounds and Kennedy I loaded her into a borrowed station wagon and drove her to the Philadelphia Zoo, where she still lives.

Even though I had not been conscious of the lack, there was one great disadvantage with all the animal pets I had had; there was nothing I could do with them except keep them. To most people interested in wild animals, this would not have seemed to be a disadvantage. Wild animals are merely interesting curiosities and no one expects a captive skunk or raccoon to do anything except be on exhibition. But aside from my brief collecting mania, my interest in animals had always been of a different sort. I could not claim to be a true zoologist or even a naturalist in the great tradition of Gilbert White, Ernest Thompson Seton, or Thoreau. I was either too lazy or too stupid to be willing to spend hours in the field observing nature for its own sake. I wanted the animals to live with me as friends, but I wanted to see them do something. I wanted to go frogging with Wayatcha or even watch the Nikkies dig up grubs in the garden. If I had been interested in domestic animals, I would have been an enthusiastic horseman or trained bird dogs or bred homing pigeons. All these animals perform some function. But what can anyone do with crows or opossums, or, for that matter, with any wild animal kept in semi-captivity? I had no idea until the last summer I spent at home.

In our library was a collection of bound copies of the *National Geographic*. Leafing through them one rainy after-noon, I came on an issue (December 1920) containing an article on falconry by Louis Agassiz Fuertes. Fuertes was unquestion-ably the greatest painter of birds of prey who ever lived and his pictures of a gyrfalcon striking down a heron in full flight, a peregrine knocking over a grouse on the Scotch moors, and Arabs hunting bustard with lanner falcons, hit me as whiskey is supposed to hit an Indian. I determined to be a falconer. We had one other book on the subject, a volume in the Badminton Library *(circa* 1892), *Coursing and Falconry* by the Honorable Gerald Lascelles with illustrations by G. E. Lodge, second only to Fuertes as a bird artist.

By great good luck, I met another youngster—Mark Sands—

who was also interested in falconry. Like all amateur falconers our greatest problem was how to get a falcon, preferably a peregrine falcon (known in America as a duckhawk), which the books assured us was the perfect bird for the art. We knew that peregrines nested on the sides of cliffs and we spent weeks checking geodetic survey maps of Pennsylvania looking for suitable cliffs, talking to game wardens, and trying to squeeze information from members of the Delaware Valley Ornithological Society, a birdwatchers' club who quite rightly disapproved of boys robbing peregrines' eyries but would occasionally make a slip of the tongue that could serve as a clue.

After gathering all the information we could, we left on a trip through the mountains of northern Pennsylvania in Mark's old Chewy, stopping to study the side of every likely looking cliff through binoculars, hoping to see the whitewash streaks of mutes dropped by the parent birds as they stood guard beside the eyrie. We were fooled by white lichens, by veins of white limestone, and even by the sunlight turning tiny trickles of water into silver strips. We had taken along sleeping bags (there were *no* motels in those days and we couldn't afford hotels) and food from our families' kitchens, but even so at the end of a week we began to run out of money. The only item we couldn't economize on was gas. In 1928, that cost 12¢ a gallon and Mark's ancient Chewy ate the stuff.

We were pressed for time. It was almost Memorial Day and we had learned from the Delaware Valley Ornithologists that Memorial Day marked the deadline when young peregrines would be hard-summed—have lost their baby down and grown their flight feathers. Once the nestlings or eyesses, as falconers called them, could fly there would be no way to catch them.

We decided we had money enough for one last day. Judging from our geodetic map, there were three more cliffs to check.

With luck, we could visit these three cliffs before running out of gas.

Then we got lost.

At two o'clock that afternoon, we were still lost. We were driving along a wagon track so overhung by pines it seemed like a tunnel. The high center scraped the old car's differential and I kept wondering what would happen if we got stuck. The track was so narrow we could not turn around and it was getting worse all the time. It would probably end in a garbage dump—we'd followed out tracks like that several times already. Then the trees suddenly dropped away and we found ourselves looking out over a valley. Here were cultivated farms, graded dirt roads, and on the other side crawled the broad river. Beyond it, a cliff reared up. By great good luck, the sun was behind us and low enough so it struck the side of the cliff with perfectly flat lighting that made every detail stand out. If we had gotten there an hour sooner, the cliff face would have been in shadow.

"This cliff isn't on our map," said Mark. We got out of the car and Mark put his field glasses on the red, sandstone formation for traces of the white mutes which, we'd been told, were the only external evidence of an eyrie. Then it happened.

From a barn covered with brilliantly colored hex signs, a flock of pigeons suddenly took off, moved by one of those strange mob impulses that affect flocks of birds and herds of animals. Flying all together like an enormous particolored blanket they swept across the river and then, wheeling like one bird, started back toward the barn. One of them was never to reach it.

From the cliff, a peregrine burst out. With a few hard cuts of his long, sickle-shaped wings he towered up into the clear air. He seemed to ignore the pigeons. He went higher and higher, shooting always upward. Through the powerful glasses, I could see him turn his head to study us for a moment with his wonderful telescopic eyes. Deciding that we were harmless, he continued to mount, finally turning his attention to the pigeons.

At the first glimpse of the steel-blue, streamlined body, the flock had started at full speed for the shelter of the barn. I could hear the whistle of their wings as they put forth every ounce of speed. The great blanket of birds banked as they whirled around, trying to avoid the poised death that hung over them.

Then the peregrine stooped; that is, he half closed his wings and dropped head first through the air like a knife. At first he gave a few, hard flaps with his wings to add impetus to his fall, but after that he simply guided himself with wings and tail. No one knows how fast a plunging falcon travels, but aviators have nosedived their planes beside a falcon on the stoop and the bird passed them when they were doing 160 miles per hour. A penny thrown from the top of the Empire State Building will fall with such speed and force as to kill a man standing on the street below, but a peregrine can overtake a falling object and play around it as a greyhound would play around a plowhorse.

The pigeons must have been flying at fifty or sixty miles an hour, never breaking their blanket formation, although it twisted and spread as the flock swept into the wind. The hawk was coming down so fast he seemed to be dropping in a series of great bounds. Then he reached the pigeons.

Without a pause he tore through the living mass, the pigeons opening a hole that instantly closed again. I thought he had missed, for the hawk had nothing in his talons when he reappeared below the varicolored flock. He took no more interest in the pigeons, swinging away over the river in a long, easy curve, his tail opening like a fan as he gradually checked his forward speed. A second later, I saw the dead body of a pigeon hurtling downward from the flock, struck dead in midair by a single blow of the peregrine's short, stiletto-sharp hind talons. The hawk swung back and as the dead bird plummeted toward the earth, he swept past it, picking the pigeon out of the air as easily as a child would catch a tossed autumn leaf. Instead of returning to the cliff, the peregrine mounted with the pigeon in his talons. As he rose, he gave a rapid series of shrill cries, strident and insistent; all in the same key. He seemed to be calling but there was no response. Up and up he went, the cries growing shriller and more demanding.

A flash of movement; a gleam of white breast along the cliff face. The female had decided to leave the nesting ledge and join her mate. The mate had seemed the most magnificent flying device ever conceived, but as the female mounted up beside him he became small, weak, almost ineffectual; she was a good third larger and correspondingly stronger and swifter. She was the falcon. To ornithologists, the term *falcon* simply means a certain genus of hawks having long slim wings, brown eyes, and a curious V-shaped protuberance on the upper beak. But to a falconer, only the female deserves the noble title *the falcon,* the male being called *tiercel,* meaning "a third." With peregrines, as with all hawks, the female is always larger than the male.

But although the tiercel was smaller than his powerful consort, there was no question who was head of the household. The next minute he gave his tardy wife an eloquent tongue-lashing. The abashed falcon swung around beneath him in great circles, not daring to approach her lord until his fury had subsided. The French call a little husband who bosses a big wife "a marriage of hawks," and now I could see why.

Having given his wife a dressing down, the tiercel dropped the pigeon and, turning on his wing, flashed away down the river still clearly in a rage. The falcon watched him anxiously, paying no attention to the falling quarry. Now surely the dead pigeon must strike the river and be lost. It was falling like a stone, gathering momentum every second. Then as the tiercel disappeared, the falcon made an easy swing toward the dropping bird, casually collected it with one foot, and mounted toward the eyrie on hard-beating wings, hampered by the additional weight of the dead bird and having to rise almost vertically up the cliff face.

As she rose, we could hear a series of monotonous *"Eeek—eek—eek"* from the eyesses. The cries were toneless and as steady as the ticking of a metronome. Then the falcon seemed to vanish into the cliff as she joined the young birds in the hidden nesting ledge.

Neither Mark nor I spoke for a minute; we were too excited. That terrific stoop of the tiercel's, followed by the graceful swoop of the falcon as she seized the quarry, was the most thrilling sight we'd ever seen in nature. Falconry has fascinated man for over five thousand years, not because the use of trained hawks is a particularly efficient way to obtain quarry but because falconry is the sport of flight. Nothing in the world moves like a falcon. It is the graceful flight of a swallow with the power of a thunderbolt behind it. A wild horse at full gallop, a porpoise playing around the bows of a ship under full steam, the flashing charge of a cheetah after his quarry—all these are magnificent but are nothing to a falcon.

Mark said in an awed voice, "Dan, we've got our own, personal private eyrie. I'll bet neither the DVOC or the game department know about this place. We'll never tell anybody. This is a hidden valley and probably that road we came down is the only way in or out."

So enthusiastic were we that for some time neither of us considered how we were to get to the eyrie. It was about 50 feet from the top of the cliff; over 300 feet from the base. The simplest plan would be to lower someone (I hoped not me) from the top of the cliff by a rope, but there was an overhang that jutted out like the eaves of a house. The climber would be left dangling on the end of the rope some ten or fifteen feet from the eyrie. Climbing up from the bottom seemed impossible. The cliff was almost sheer.

"I know a guy named Brad Bradley," said Mark after a long pause. "He can climb anything. We'll get him to go up."

When I got home, I set about turning the loft of our garage-barn into a mews, a hawk house. According to the books, the young falcon should be kept in the loft until she was hard-summed and then the loft door was to be opened allowing her to fly free. She would return every evening for food and day by day grow in strength until she began to kill for herself. Then she could be "taken up" and trained.

I never discussed my animals with my parents but somehow, probably through Kennedy, Father learned that I had started on a new project. One evening he called me in for a heart-to-heart talk.

"I understand you're trying to get another pet—some sort of bird," he began reluctantly. "Don't you think you're getting a little too old for this sort of thing?"

I was seventeen. I could only say "Yes sir."

"You should be thinking about the Academy," Father went on. "I don't wish to force you to select any special profession, although the Navy is one of the few gentleman's jobs left. But what would you want to do? Would you like to go to college and study zoology?"

I had no desire to study zoology. I'd had a course of it in school and it seemed to me to be simply a form of organic chemistry. I made no answer.

After waiting, Father went on. "You must be able to make a living, as I think you realize. We'll help you in anything you wish to do as long as you sincerely wish to do it, but surely you realize that playing around with pet animals is childish. Is there anything you really want to do?"

"No," I said miserably.

"Then let's talk about preparing you for the Academy examinations," Father said briskly, happy at having the situation definite at last.

I still wasn't going to give up my falcon. The next day, Mark called to say that Brad Bradley was willing to help us. We were to supply the rope—¾-inch Samson Spot cord. It had to be stretched and tested by dragging a log of wood the weight of a 170-pound man behind a car. The rope was bought and tested. Mark and Brad picked me up at 2 A.M. for the assault on the cliff.

We reached the valley shortly after dawn by the same narrow, dirt track. "It's impossible to climb to that eyrie from below," announced Brad, after studying the cliff through binoculars. "We'll have to follow the cliff until we can find a scalable place and then you fellows can lower me down from the top with the rope."

A ten-minute walk brought us to a part of the cliff that was climbable. At least Brad said it was. I said nothing but I could feel my stomach turn over as I looked up.

"I'll take the rope and go first," said Brad swinging the coils over his shoulder. "Don't follow too closely, in case of falling rocks."

One after another we started up.

For a time I kept on well enough, taking care not to look down. Then we came to a solid wall of rock that rose perfectly sheer above us for fifty feet. It was not only sheer, it actually leaned outward at the top so that we would have to crawl underneath the belly of the overhang. Nothing but a monkey could do that but Brad started up it, crawling along the rock like a lizard on a window pane.

For the first time, I made the mistake of looking down. To anyone in a different position, it would have seemed a marvelous view. The entire valley, checkerboarded with green and brown fields, lay spread out below us. Miles away, shining in the sunlight, I could see a tiny cart drawn by mouse-size horses crawling along two threadlike ruts in one of the brown fields. Directly below lay the river, smooth as oil in the pools and, where the rapids glinted in the sun, wrinkled as an old man's skin. On a path by the river I could see the minute figures of two girls who had stopped and were looking up at us.

I turned my attention to the cliff. As I crawled up ward, a terrible tingling sensation started at the calves of my legs and ran up my back to my cheekbones. My eyes were burning with the stinging sweat that dripped into them for, using both hands, I was unable to wipe my forehead.

Once I thought I was caught. Spread out against the cliff face, I could see nothing above but perfectly smooth rock and I was unable to let go with either hand long enough to feel down for an outcrop that could give me a foothold. I hung on as long as I could and then felt my fingers beginning to give way under the weight of my body.

Slowly I began to slide down the face of the rock, only friction and my clinging fingers breaking my fall. Almost imperceptibly I felt myself sliding faster and faster. "I'm done for now," I thought. "I wonder what it feels like to die?" Just then one of my fingers caught in a crevice. For a second I hung there by one hand and then my kicking feet found footholds.

I was weak and dizzy and knew in a few minutes I would become helpless. I crawled frantically upward. Helped as much by my momentum as anything, I saw the top growing nearer and nearer. Thousands of black spots appeared and whirled in front of my eyes. My stomach was cold and there was no feeling in my arms and legs. Suddenly a shower of stones fell on my upturned face and I felt my arm grasped. In a moment, Brad had jerked me over the edge.

I crawled a few feet away from that awful drop and lay panting on the soft, cool grass. Some little trees were growing there and I grasped one with a feeling of comfort, although all danger of falling was over.

Even Brad admitted, "That was worse than I thought it was going to be."

As we approached the ledge over the eyries, the falcon exploded from underneath us and darted about like a huge swallow, giving her angry *chit-chit-chit* call. Brad tied a double bowline in the end of the rope and put one leg in each of the two loops, while Mark took a turn of the rope around a sturdy pine and braced himself. My job was to stand on the edge of the cliff and relay Brad's instructions to Mark. The acoustics of a cliff are curious, and often the man being lowered can shout his head off without being heard by the man lowering.

When he reached the edge, Brad lay on his belly and wriggled slowly backward, Mark slowly paying out the rope. For a few yards he was able to creep down the slope until he came to the overhang that had nearly finished me when climbing the cliff. When Brad came to this final drop, he called "I'm going to swing clear."

I shouted to Mark, who called back "Tell him to go ahead!" as he braced himself. Brad sank into space while the furious falcon swung closer and closer, screaming.

Almost at once one of the greatest dangers in rope work became apparent. The rope began to twist and Brad was spun around so rapidly that twice he struck against the cliff. But the twisting stopped as Mark continued to pay out the rope inch by inch. In a few minutes, Brad called up, "I'm opposite the eyrie. Stop lowering."

"Can he reach it?" Mark shouted. Obviously Brad couldn't. Because of the overhang, he was swinging ten feet away from the side of the cliff.

"Get me a long pole," Brad called to me.

I cut a long, light pole and lowered it down. Brad put it against the cliff face and pushed himself away. I saw his plan now. He intended to start himself swaying like a pendulum until he could swing in and grab an outjut ting of rock.

Abruptly a new danger developed. The rope was wearing against the edge of the overhang. I could see the strands part one after the other, each giving a little puff of dust as it snapped.

"The rope!" I shouted. "Watch the rope!"

Brad glanced up, far more unconcerned than I. Giving one more shove he swung in and managed to grab a shelf of rock. The next second he had pulled himself into the eyrie.

The falcon was now frantic. She dived repeatedly at Brad's head. He ducked but paid no other attention to her, although a slash from her talons might have caused him to lose his balance.

We had forgotten to provide Brad anything to hold the young birds, so he stuffed two inside his shirt. Then he called, "Get ready. I'm going to swing out."

The next second he sprang out into midair. The rope groaned and screamed as it tore into the bark of the tree while Mark paid it out as rapidly as he dared. Brad glided swiftly down until he reached the branches of a hemlock far below us. Once in the safety of its branches, he untied himself and climbed down. Rather than climb down the cliff, Mark and I followed it out to its end, a walk of nearly five miles, and then came back along the river.

Brad was sitting under the hemlock waiting for us and examining a network of scratches across his chest made by the talons of the young birds. The two little eyesses were beside him, wrapped in his shirt. They were twin powder-puffs of white down with huge beaks and brown eyes. The brown flight feathers were just beginning to force their way through the baby fuzz which frayed off like cotton in our fingers when we lifted them. Both babies instantly set up a furious *chit-chit-chit,* but there was no answer from the mother. She knew she could do no more and was back in the eyrie with her other three nestlings.

My baby falcon rode back to the Main Line cuddled against my coat. She was puzzled, frightened, belligerent, and home-sick all in about the same degree. Her stumpy tail was only about half-grown but whenever she could she reared back on it, striking at me with her talons. Her talons were still small but they were sharp as daggers and her "mailed fist," as the medieval falconers called the falcon's scale-covered foot, was surprisingly powerful. Once when she managed to clamp down on my bare wrist, the curved talons sank into my flesh like red-hot suture needles into butter, and it was almost impossible to open her fist without hurting her.

During that long ride, I began to sense that this young eyess was unlike any pet I had ever kept before. Even physically she was a mass of contradictions; a woolly ball of down like a child's toy yet, with a hooked piratical beak and curved scimitars for talons. Surely all hawks should have "fierce yellow eyes," but her eyes were a soft brown even if the expression in them was fierce enough. For the first time I began to think that here was a creature of almost magical potentialities—and I was right, for she was the bird that has given its name to the oldest field sport known to man; a sport which dominated all Europe and Arabia for over a thousand years and left an indelible impres-sion on the medieval mind.

Six

When I reached home, I put the eyess in the loft of our garage-barn where she would spend the next three weeks—until her long flight feathers had grown into place and she was ready to fly. I named her Tara, after a famous medieval falcon.

Most baby wild animals, after they recover from the first shock of capture, respond to the warmth of the human hand and desire for companionship. I expected Tara to behave in the same way and to show the cheerful friendliness of Jesse, the crow. But falcons are aristocrats. They are not merely born free, they remain so forever. No matter how long she remains in captivity, a falcon never develops any affection for a human. They are never tamed; instead they become "manned"—they grow accustomed to the presence of a human and learn to follow a certain routine in relation to him. The man is never the falcon's master; he becomes the falcon's servant. The hawk learns to tolerate him as a convenience. It is this distinctive association between man and bird (exactly the opposite relationship must exist between man and an earthbound mammal) that makes falconry unique not only as a sport but also in the entire realm of man's relationship with animals.

We all want to be loved. We keep dogs because theirs is the

only love that money can buy. Failing love, we want dominance. We can dominate a horse or a dog and force him to do what we wish. A falcon gives no love and cannot be dominated. Once released, no power on earth can make a free-flying hawk return except her own will. The falconer must accept a hawk on her own terms, but he must do more than that. He must know how her mind works, what instincts guide her, and how her basic metabolism controls her actions.

When Tara was hard-summed I started "manning" her. The basic device in controlling a hawk is the hood, a little leather cap which fits over the bird's head, blindfolding her. For some curious psychological reason, all birds become calm When plunged into darkness. Although I had obtained a hood from Adrian Mollen, the famous Dutch falconer who was the last of a long line of professional falconers stretching back to the Middle Ages, I did not use it. Learning how to slip the hood over a falcon's head without infuriating her is a difficult trick— medieval falconers spent three years studying this one move- ment—and besides I couldn't believe it necessary. I knew that putting a mammal's head in a bag would not quiet him, only send him into a hysterical rage. Also, I was sure that I could win Tara's affections as I had Jesse's. As a result of my inexperience Tara never became completely "manned."

I did, however, use other standard falconry equipment. I put light leather straps, called jesses, around her legs. Jesses are the badge of a trained hawk as a collar is of a pet dog. She wears them at all times, even when in flight. Through holes in the ends of the jesses I fastened a swivel, then passed a leash through the swivel. Thus equipped, I could either carry Tara on my gloved fist or tie her to a cylindrical wooden block on the lawn that served as a perch. Unlike a crow or indeed virtually any other bird, a hawk will sit on such a block contentedly for hours.

Raptors (birds of prey) do not have the nervous, active minds of the Corvidae; in fact, except when in pursuit of game they are rather stupid creatures. After all the effort I had gone to getting her and after the glowing accounts of the "noble falcons" I had read, it was disappointing to find that Tara had far less personality than Jesse or even Susie, my pet turkey buzzard.

To man Tara, I carried her for hours on my fist, keeping tight hold of her jesses. Without a hood, this was a long, discouraging process. Tara screamed, baited (jumped) off my fist, hung by her jesses, had to be put back, fell off, and would finally end by sitting crouched on my hand, panting wildly with open beak. It seemed to me I had never had an animal show so little intelligence or response as Tara.

But eventually Tara learned to take her meals while on my fist. A falcon cannot be starved into submission; that would make her weak and dispirited. I had to keep offering her bits of food, which I learned to pop into her open beak when she tried to bite me. For a long time, Tara simply spit the pieces out again or sat sullenly holding them in her beak. Finally I learned that the sticky, raw meat had a tendency to adhere to the inside of her mouth, making it difficult for her to swallow it. So I spat on the meat first and then Tara swallowed it more readily. At last I could give her a dead bird and she would pluck and eat it while riding around on my glove.

The next step was to induce Tara to jump to my fist from the block for food. When she learned this trick I tied a long, light line (called a creance) to her jesses and persuaded her to fly several yards. The last step was teaching her to fly to the lure. The long-winged falcons, because of their twisting, swallowlike manner of flight, cannot land readily on the falconer's fist when coming in from a distance. They are taught to return to the lure, a small leather bag ornamented with feathers and swung at the end of a long line, which they strike in midair as though it were a flying bird. A small piece of meat is tied to the lure as a reward. When Tara learned to hit the swinging lure, she was ready to be flown free.

I put off the fatal day as long as I could. Although Tara would come to the lure immediately, I well knew that she was not tamed like my other pets and once she was free there was no bond of affection to hold us together. But a falcon permanently tethered to a wooden block is not a falcon. As a captive bird, Tara was worse than useless to me. Finally, I decided to take the chance.

I had supposed that the instant Tara found herself free from the restraining influence of the creance she would immediately tower into the sky, wheeling and circling as I had seen the wild falcons do at the eyrie, after which exhibition she might or might not return to me. Instead, Tara behaved exactly as she had done before, making short flights to the lure and allowing herself to be picked up and returned to the block without seeming to realize that she was free. Greatly relieved, although a little disappointed, I continued her training, gradually lengthening the distance from her block to the lure.

Then one afternoon as she flashed in toward the lure, Tara for no apparent reason suddenly swung away and went zooming off over the trees. Perhaps being inexperienced in flying, she found herself going too fast to hit the swinging lure at the right angle; perhaps she wasn't particularly hungry that day; perhaps something frightened her at the last instant. At all events, she was gone and I stood wildly swinging the lure while trying to keep her in sight through the thick foliage.

Tara took a long swing over the Ashbridge pasture, and even in my anxiety I thrilled at the sight of her "hedgehopping" over the tall grass one moment and then shooting up into the sky to do a slow "wing-over" before gliding along easily on outstretched wings. The flight of a falcon makes the flight of all other birds seem clumsy. I ran into the pasture, shouting and swinging the lure but Tara paid no attention to me. She made no attempt to fly off but neither did she make any attempt to return.

There was a light breeze blowing and Tara drifted toward the Ashbridge barn and lighted on the roof. I crossed the field and hurried into the barnyard. As I did so, pigeons burst out from their roost under the overhang coming together to form a flock, and rushed away directly under the falcon. To my astonishment, Tara paid no attention to them.

I ran under the overhang and scared out the few remaining birds. This time Tara went into action. She had not been expecting the first flight and wasn't ready for them, but now she dove from the roof and, shooting after the birds, singled one out of the flock. Remembering the neat, clean kill of the tiercel at the eyrie, I stood waiting for her to knock down the pigeon with a single blow.

But Tara was a young falcon and this pigeon was an experienced old bird who knew all about hawks. As Tara plunged down on him, the pigeon executed a neat barrel-roll, closing one wing and spinning. Tara whistled past. She had been diving head-first with her wings close to her body and her tail closed to offer a minimum, of air resistance, but now she opened her wings, spread her tail like a fan, and—using the momentum of her dive—shot upward to be above the pigeon again. With one graceful movement she turned over in the air and came down at a slant to strike the pigeon sideways and forestall another roll.

This time, surely, she must hit the bird. But instead of repeating his former trick the pigeon closed his wings and dropped as though shot, falling almost as fast as the stopping falcon. Tara made a wild grab for him as she went past, but the unexpected maneuver had thrown her off balance. She recovered herself and made a straight rush at the pigeon. For a few seconds both birds whirled about in the air like dead leaves. Then the pigeon maneuvered himself on top. Instantly he began to mount. With his shorter wings, he could rise more directly than could Tara. She followed him upward a few hundred yards and then, discouraged, came swinging back to the barn and lighted on the roof. Now she consented to come down to the lure.

For the first time in my life I had seen a pet wild animal in action. Much as I loved the Nikkies, much as I admired the sterling qualities of Claude and Claudette, and though I enjoyed Jesse's pranks, this was something different. It was not only the excitement of the chase, it was the miracle of seeing both birds display such unexpected abilities. Pigeons had always seemed to me fat, stupid creatures, but this bird had shown himself not only a crack flier but also a very clever fellow. Tara had been suddenly metamorphosed into an entirely different creature. True, she had been both outwitted and outflown, but she had corrected her mistakes each time and would clearly learn from the encounter. What a change from the majestic but dull bird sitting stolidly on her wooden block or the hysterical, unreasonable creature wildly baiting from my fist!

I had taken for granted that hawks were such superior flying mechanisms that they could capture other birds without trouble. Clearly I was wrong. As I was to learn later, not only pigeons but all game birds are perfectly capable of protecting themselves from any except the most experienced hawk and even then the hawk must be in perfect physical condition. How do young hawks survive before they learn the skills necessary to capture their prey? For weeks they hunt with their parents, who train them by example and, in the case of falcons, carry prey up to great heights and then drop it to allow the eyesses practice in seizing the quarry in midair. Even so, few of the eyesses survive. The hawk population never increases except in ratio to the game available. Although a pair of peregrines may live for over thirty years, producing an average family of four eyesses every year, only enough of the eyesses ultimately survive to take the place of the parent birds.

From that day on, I became an enthusiastic falconer. I did not neglect my other animals; they were far too dear to me for that. But if they were the steak, peas, and potatoes of life, Tara was the champagne. Through her I began to see the marvelous possibilities inherent in animals which only appear when they are in action. True, among animals action nearly always means conflict—but much the same is true of humans. Without conflict, humans may be as lovable as the Nikkies or as dignified as Claude and Claudette, but they are seldom exciting.

Occasionally I was asked by a Boy Scout troop, a ladies' club, or a school to give a talk on animals. I had some rather amateurish home movies of my pets and always brought an animal or two with me. Once I tried bringing Nikki Junior, but he got excited when the children started shouting and there was a regrettable incident which resulted in the auditorium's having to be closed for a week. These talks were pleasant enough but never caused any particular stir and I never thought of charging for them. Then I added some pictures of Tara in action after pigeons and starlings and included them in my film, also taking along Tara and flying her in the auditoriums.

Instantly the whole attitude of the audiences changed. Tara made a sensational hit. Even sitting on my fist Tara was more dramatic than any of my other animals, and the spectacle of her wheeling and turning over the heads of the audience was more impressive than if I'd produced a lion. Tara was not a particularly big bird—she only weighed about two pounds and had a three-foot wing spread—but there is something about a falcon that fascinates people. I spoke at the Academy of Natural Sciences in Philadelphia, an honor I'd never dreamed of attaining, and received calls from New York and Boston. For the first time I was able to ask for a fee—at first only $10, then $25, and finally $50.

My parents watched my growing progress with increasing concern. Mother was positive that although gentlemen *might* put alligators in swimming pools, they definitely didn't speak in public for money. Father warned me that this sort of conduct might conceivably prejudice my appointment to the Naval Academy. "There was an officer who kept a pet monkey on one ship where I served," he cautioned me. "The monkey hit the captain with a ripe mango during inspection. Believe me, that officer never got anywhere in the service after that." Still, he did not forbid me to lecture, so I kept on.

Mark Sands had trained his bird, and having no compunctions about using a hood had done a much better job than I had. Mark had named his falcon Lucybelle and trained her to work with his setter, Jack. Nearly all our bird dogs were originally developed to work with hawks rather than with guns and although Jack made a few mistakes (on one occasion when Lucybelle had caught a pheasant, Jack rushed in and tried to retrieve the falcon) he and Lucybelle had reached an understanding.

Due to my mismanagement Tara was never a good game hawk but we often went out hawking with Mark, Lucybelle, and Jack. We seldom caught much, but that was not the idea. The thrill of hawking is in the chase, not the capture. Falconry is the sport of flight and it is no coincidence that in the last war both

Hermann Goering, commander of the Luftwaffe and Sir Charles Portal, commander of the RAF, were enthusiastic falconers.

My only function on these hunts was to restrain Jack while Mark unhooded Lucybelle, freed the swivel and leash from her jesses, and then released her. Lucybelle would begin by making a great circuit of the area, and then start to mount. No bird can fly straight upward and falcons especially do not attempt such a wearing feat. Instead, the bird rises in a series of great circles until she reaches her "point for pride," the highest pitch she can attain. The higher a falcon rises, the more area she can command and the more terrible her plunging swoop becomes. Lucybelle would go up until she looked no bigger than a butterfly. Then she would begin to ride the air currents with outstretched wings, "waiting on" in falconry parlance, for quarry to be put up for her.

When we saw that Lucybelle was ready, I would release Jack. The setter would go bounding off through the cover while Lucybelle followed him half a mile up as he went from field to field. Sometimes when the falcon became convinced that Jack wasn't doing his best or had lost interest, she would come down on the dog in an indignant swoop, striking angrily at the startled setter as she shot past him, and then return to her point of pride while the chastened dog hurriedly got back to work.

Often we could tell when Jack had come to a point by watching the falcon. Instead of drifting in great circles, Lucybelle would steady herself in one spot, knowing as well as we did what the motionless, rigid point implied. When we saw that she was in position, Mark and I would rush in to flush the quarry—usually a pheasant. The game bird would go rocketing up and then the hunt was on.

As soon as the pheasant was well in the air, Lucybelle would come plunging down. Falcons wear small metal bells tied on their feet so if the hawk becomes lost in thick cover the falconer can still trace her by the sound of the bells. Traditionally, one bell is pitched a semi-tone higher than the other, otherwise the ringing of the bells would cancel each other out at certain heights and speeds. When Lucybelle began her stoop, her bells would ring furiously. Then the ringing would stop and we could hear nothing but the scream of the wind across the mouths of the bells as the falcon's speed increased. As Lucybelle shot past the pheasant, she would try to deliver the falcon's terrible death blow. This fatal stroke is delivered so swiftly and when the bird is moving at such great speed that for centuries falconers were uncertain exactly what happened. Some thought a falcon killed her prey by striking it with her breast bone, and many of the old artists portray this grotesque scene. Others believed that the falcon must kill the quarry with a quick blow of her beak. We know now that the falcon kills with her mailed fist or rather with projecting short, curved hind talons that correspond to our thumbs while the rest of her toes are curled up out of the way. She is going too fast to seize her prey; the shock would tear her legs out of her body, just as a man who has jumped off the top of the Empire State Building could not check his fall by grabbing a flagstaff halfway down. She must strike and keep on going, turning her head as she goes to see the effect of her blow.

When a falcon's stroke goes home, the game bird is killed as completely as though he had received both barrels of a shotgun. Often the body is actually knocked upward by the force of the blow backed by the falcon's terrific speed. There is an explosion of feathers that remain drifting in the air as the dead bird starts to drop toward the ground. Sometimes the falcon turns on her wing and seizes the falling corpse before it can hit the earth. More often she takes her time, makes a wide swing and drifts into the quarry after it has fallen. Then the falconer comes in quietly, lifts the dead quarry with the falcon still on it, and rewards her with a few bites before hooding her. Hawks cannot be trained to retrieve. They kill for themselves, not for man. If they kill their quarry out of sight of the falconer, he must find the bird before she has gorged on the kill and left it. Because of this, falconers in the Middle Ages were always mounted and many were the breakneck dashes across country to keep a hawk in sight.

But a dramatic kill was seldom the climax of our hunts. Usually the quarry got away. If he could reach cover he was safe; Lucybelle's long wings made it impossible for her to fly among trees or bushes. Even if the quarry were able to drop to the ground, he would probably escape—Lucybelle considered it beneath her dignity to take ground game. Instead she would dive repeatedly at the pheasant, striking at him as she did at Jack to force him to rise, but most pheasants preferred to run for the nearest bramble bush.

Flying at crows was even more exciting than flying pheasants—and even less rewarding. I once saw a crow shake off Lucybelle by flying between two strands of barbed-wire fence. The falcon, right on his tail feathers, tried to follow but her long wings caught on the barbs and she was hung like a fly on flypaper. A crow, like a pigeon, can fly more nearly straight up than a falcon, so a crow caught in the open would generally try to mount above the hawk. Sometimes Lucybelle would leave the chase and fly off until she could pick up a strong thermal draft from a distant hillside. Then she would let it carry her up. The watching crow when he saw the falcon rising above him would shut his wings and try to drop into the nearest cover. Then Lucybelle would have to go into a quick stoop, streaking across sky at a sharp angle to cut him off. Because of Jesse I could never really enjoy crow-hawking, but then the crow was seldom killed. Even if Lucybelle was able to catch the crow, when the two birds hit the ground the crow with his long beak was usually able to beat the falcon off. Crows are determined fighters.

Later in the summer I obtained a young goshawk from a Canadian trapper. I called the bird Guy. Goshawks are accipters (or "short-winged" hawks) and do not possess the grace and style of falcons. They are forest hawks and their short wings and long tails (which serve as a rudder so the hawk can make quick turns) enable them to fly at great speed through thick cover. In the Middle Ages, the falcons were flown by the nobility but the accipters were the poor man's practical meat-getter. Robin Hood owned a "gay goshawke" which he could use in the tangles of Sherwood Forest.

I had thought Tara was difficult, but I didn't know what the word meant until I tried to man Guy. Temperamentally, goshawks are entirely different than the "noble" falcons. They are simply constitutional psychopaths, alternating between moods of hysterical fury and black despondency. In short, they are a breed of manic-depressives. At the top of their emotional cycle, they will attack any quarry. In Afghanistan, goshawks have been trained to fasten their talons in an antelope's forehead and hold on until the hunters arrive. At their low point, they will scream with terror at the sight of a mouse. Oriental falconers call the upswing of the cycle *yarak* and induce this state by wrapping the bird in cold clothes or by the use of drugs, a course of treatment that is used with emotionally unstable humans.

But if a goshawk is carried enough, he will automatically pass into *yarak* for some unknown reason. Then his whole attitude changes. Instead of clinging apprehensively to the falconer's fist, uttering an occasional nervous twittering cry and ready to bait at the slightest motion, the hawk becomes a disciplined hunting instrument. He grips the glove fiercely, bending over to study every motion in the grass ahead with his keen yellow eyes for possible quarry. Even if you kick a clod of earth so that it rolls, the hawk is off your fist and gripping the clod so savagely it's hard to force him to release it. A mouse, a pheasant, even a passing dog are all the same to him. He will make a dash at anything he sees.

The goshawk is flown at the bolt—that is, flown straight from the fist at the quarry. He hunts close to the ground and puts everything into one short, terrible dash. I spent many happy hours crawling through barbed-wire fences and wading icy brooks with Guy on my fist, hunting rabbits. He was amazingly strong; a hawk must be to hold a rabbit weighing half again as much as he. Sometimes he would give me examples of his strength that were astonishing.

One afternoon I took Guy rabbit hunting through the thick covers of a tree nursery. The nurseryman had told me that rabbits were killing his young stock by gnawing off the bark. With the hawk poised on my fist I walked out the cover bordering some young peach-tree plantings. The hawk knew what we were after and kept turning his head slightly, watching for the flash of a white tail. Finally it came. As so often happened, Guy saw the rabbit before I did and was after him like a brown flicker of light.

Twenty feet away was a hedge. The rabbit ducked through a familiar hole but the hawk was just at his heels. He was going so fast that I expected to see him smash against the hedge. Instead, Guy suddenly spread his wings and tail and zoomed straight up, shooting over the hedge and dropping down on the other side like a stone.

I ran along the hedgerow until I came to a gate. Vaulting over, I trotted back to the hole. There was no sign of either hawk or rabbit, but there was a patch of fur. It had been a close call. Then I heard Guy's bells again.

I raced through an apple orchard, following the sound. On the side of a little rise I saw the rabbit dashing from tree to tree with the hawk after him. The rabbit was dodging around the boles, the hawk banking around the trunks right behind him. Each time the hawk cut in closer and closer until his inner wing seemed to scrape the bark. Suddenly the rabbit found an old woodchuck hole and plunged in. Guy, in a spasm of blind fury, flung himself in after the quarry. When I came up, Guy was so deep in the burrow that I had to go to the nurseryman's house, borrow a shovel; and dig him out. Once his wings were free, Guy braced them against the sides of the hole and slowly backed out. He had the rabbit tightly held at the end of one of his long legs. Guy weighed a pound and three quarters, the rabbit two and a half pounds; but even with the purchase of his powerful hind legs against the sides of the hole, the rabbit could not break the goshawk's grip.

Many may wonder why, when the sight of a shot crow sickened me, I did not regard falconry as cruel. I can only say that when animals are hunting each other as they do in a state of nature, I feel differently. My interest in the hunter overcomes my sympathy for the hunted. I do not enjoy fishing with a rod or skindiving with a spear but I have gotten a great thrill out of fishing with trained cormorants or with a pet otter.

Guy made as big a hit on the lecture platform as had Tara, but there was one element lacking with both birds and in the motion pictures I took of them. Magnificent and complicated hunting machines though they were, they lacked the personalities of Jesse or Susie. Also, neither was big enough to be truly impressive. If only I could find a bird large enough to be really spectacular with the appeal of Jesse and the fierce, dramatic qualities of a hunting hawk, I could make a profession of lecturing. But I had no idea where such a bird could be obtained—if, indeed, one existed. It was a purely academic problem, however, for the next year I left for the Naval Academy.

Seven

It still remains a mystery to me why Father should have regarded going in swimming with alligators or handling rattlesnakes a dangerous procedure while considering plebe year at the Naval Academy a salutary experience. There were upperclassmen in my division who made Daisy look like the Good Samaritan. Admittedly, I was never cut out for a career in the armed services. I think that I first became conscious of the gap between me and my classmates when at the end of the summer we graduated from white works (comfortably pajama-like garments) to formal white uniforms with stiff collars and innumerable brass buttons. I must have been the only fourth-classman who didn't rush out to have his picture taken in this new glory. To me, my uniform was only something else to be kept clean and I regarded it as the ancient mariner regarded the albatross around his neck. Although I made a conscientious effort to conform, there was something about me that at first infuriated and finally baffled my superiors. Once after parade, the commandant himself called me out and had me march up and down in front of him. At last he gave up in despair. "I can't figure it out," he announced hopelessly. "His brace is correct, his rifle is correct, and his uniform is correct.

But somehow when the corps passes in review he always looks as though he's going duck hunting."

The only bright spot in the eight terrible months I spent trying to follow in the family tradition was the time a talented third-classman who roomed next to me nearly electrocuted the admiral's staff. The entire corps was to be inspected and we had to scrub our rooms until the boards were worn thin. In full dress and at rigid attention we stood outside our rooms waiting for the inspection party. My neighbor was an electrical genius who amused himself by making the electric clocks in Bancroft Hall run backward and had tapped the official telephone line so he could call his girl in Baltimore. In some fashion he had gotten control of the electric elevator in which the inspection party traveled from floor to floor. As my room was directly opposite the elevator, I was able to study the expression on the faces of the admiral and his staff as they went up and down. On the first trip, they were the picture of dignity, leaning on their dress swords and staring severely out in front of them. The next time they went by, they had begun to look at each other uncomfortably. On the third trip, they were feverishly pressing buttons. On the fourth trip, they were shaking the iron grill door and screaming for help. My neighbor finally stopped the elevator midway between floors and then blew all the fuses in the buildings. The admiral and his staff had to be taken out through a trapdoor in the elevator's roof. Unfortunately, my talented neighbor was discovered and expelled. In my opinion, the Navy never completely recovered from this loss.

My own separation from the Navy came about in a far less dramatic fashion. I had gone from 170 pounds to 90 pounds, sweated so heavily that I had to change my sheets at least twice every night, and had developed the habit of fainting when required to stand at attention for more than two or three minutes. For my father's sake, the authorities did everything possible to carry me through, but when I finally had what was then referred to as a nervous breakdown, it was decided, as the commandant wrote Father, that "he is definitely not officer material." So I returned home.

I spent the next two months in bed. During this period, everyone was very gentle with me—especially Father, although my failure to make the grade in Annapolis must have been one of the bitterest disappointments in his life. When I finally recovered, there still remained the difficult problem of what I was to do. I could go to college, but there seemed little reason for this since college was to prepare one for some definite business or profession and I had shown no aptitude for any.

Grandfather had always seemed to ignore my existence in the same benevolent manner he ignored the rest of the universe so I was mildly surprised when, one afternoon as I was passing the library door, he called me inside. Grandfather was sitting in his favorite Morris chair by the window reading Charles Lever's *Charles O'Malley: The Irish Dragon*. He continued to read it throughout our interview.

"Are you worried about making a living?" Grandfather asked, still intent on his book.

"Yes," I admitted.

"There's no need to be concerned about that. Financial arrangements have been made to support you."

I well knew that Grandmother heartily agreed with my parents that I should be able to stand on my own feet financially and I knew equally well who controlled the family finances.

"But Grandfather, you haven't any money."

Grandfather shifted his attention to the next page. "I didn't say I had money; I said arrangements would be made. Your Grandmother has a heart condition and will not live more than a year or two. She believes she has made a will leaving her money to your parents. However, I supervised the drawing up of the will and you will be provided for immediately after her death."

"Will there be enough to support me for good?"

"No, but of course you will make a suitable marriage and then you'll have your wife's money."

"Girls don't seem to like me ever since I put Daisy in the swimming pool."

"What about Abigail Strafford? I realize," Grandfather went on judicially, turning another page, "that she is ugly as pig tracks, otherwise she wouldn't marry you, but I imagine you won't have to see much of her. She raises hackney ponies and spends most of her time at horse shows."

I departed from this interview greatly comforted. Not that I Could imagine myself married to Abigail Strafford, but at least I had a respite. For a time at least I would be "provided for."

It was the headmaster of my old school who talked my parents into sending me to college and performed the far more amazing feat of talking the admissions board of the University of Pennsylvania into taking me. An enthusiastic naturalist, he had always been sympathetic with my love of animals and, having a grotesque sense of humor, had considered the alligator in the swimming pool hilarious. "Let this boy take zoology and you'll be astonished at what he can do," he assured the skeptical board. "He has a genius for it. He'll be a credit to the university."

On the basis of this promise, I was admitted to the university. Six months later I flunked zoology.

By now, everyone had given me up as hopeless—especially myself. I transferred to the English department. For one of my first compositions, I selected the subject of tropical fish. Years before, while visiting the Philadelphia Academy of Natural

Sciences, I had seen some small fish in a tank belonging to the secretaries. They told me these fish were called guppies and actually gave birth to live young. They even presented me with a pair. A few weeks later I saw the female guppy swimming frantically back and forth near the surface of the water, her mouth just protruding. While I watched, I saw the young being born. No one would believe me when I told them of the event—every sensible person knew that fish laid eggs—but I raised the young and later tried to sell them to the proprietor of a big-city pet shop. The proprietor refused to purchase any such exotic creature as a guppy. "I've heard about 'em," he explained. "There's some more of these fancy fish that a few crackpots play around with. Call 'em tropicals. But the public wants great big flashy fish that are easy to keep—like goldfish. These tropicals have to be kept warm, fed special food, and ain't big enough. Believe me, they'll never catch on."

Later, I had gotten some more of these strange exotics. By the time I'd entered college, there was enough general interest in tropicals to make me think it worthwhile to send my composition to the *Saturday Evening Post*. Much to my surprise, the *Post* paid me $500 for it.

A few weeks later, I had another triumph. My English professor read one of my themes aloud and then added, "Mannix, I think the college literary magazine might take this. What do you do with your old English themes?"

"I sell them to the *Saturday Evening Post*," I told him.

The professor gasped, "I've been trying to sell something to the *Post* for the last forty years. Tell me, how do you do it?"

Unfortunately, it was a long time before I was able to sell the *Post* another piece.

After graduating from college, I spent three years working in traveling carnivals, having learned the technique of sword-swallowing from a performer in the Hahnemann Hospital who was suffering from a bad case of peritonitis as the result of a misswallow. Later, this man died and I bought his set of swords from his widow. Meanwhile, both my grandparents had died and I found myself in possession of an extremely modest income—but an income.

That summer I met a pretty little girl named Jule Junker who was working as a model and did radio shows on the side. Jule and I were married and for a wedding present I gave her a little Cairn terrier named Wriggles, a direct descendant of the famous Wawa Cairns who had started me on my career as a wild-animal keeper.

My income wasn't large enough to support both of us—plus Wriggles—and no magazine would buy my articles, We'd heard that living abroad was cheaper and decided to move to some foreign country until I could develop a salable style. The question was, what country?

I'd never abandoned my interest in animals and one day Jule and I were talking to J. W. Johnson, a well-known animal dealer, who was complaining about the shortage of dragons. "We used to get in regular shipments of them from Mexico," he remarked. "But they're so fast and bite so hard the trappers nowadays don't like to go after them."

Jule said mildly, "I had no idea there really were dragons, Mr. Johnson." But she said it in the tone of one who, after being married three months to me, was ready to believe anything.

Mr. Johnson laughed. "To animal dealers, 'dragons' are the big South American iguanas. Some of them measure as much as six feet and stand as high as a small dog. They can run like rabbits and bite like bulldogs. The natives claim about the only thing that can outdistance them is a bird."

Immediately I thought of a trained hawk but at the same time

I knew that no hawk could hold one of these big reptiles, nearly the size of Daisy. There was only one bird capable of such a feat: a trained eagle.

I knew of someone who did have a captive eagle. Some months before, while on a birdwatching trip in New Jersey, a group of friends and I stopped at Salem. Mr. Thompson, the local game warden, had a large American bald eagle in a chicken house. The bird had come down during a sleet storm with her wings covered with sleet and Mr. Thompson had put her in the chicken house with the idea of releasing her afterward. He had turned her loose but the bird had refused to leave the vicinity. She had taken to raiding the farmers' hen coops and done so much damage that Mr. Thompson had been forced to recapture her. At that time (1939) the American bald eagle, although our national bird, was not protected by law so Mr. Thompson had kept the bird as a curiosity.

Eagles have been trained for falconry. The Mongolian horsemen used them—and possibly still do—to capture foxes and even wolves for the fur. In the Middle Ages, eagles were occasionally trained to take stag, two birds being flown together in a "cast." However, even in those days when falconry was a mania throughout Europe, manning an eagle was regarded as a difficult and even dangerous task and the birds used were always eyesses taken from the nest. Judging from her plumage, this eagle was at least two years old—a "haggard" in falconry parlance—and even with hawks, haggards are notoriously hard to handle.

There was another, even greater, problem. The eagles used in falconry were always golden eagles. The golden eagle is a hunter like the falconer or goshawk. According to all the best authorities, the bald eagle is a scavenger almost like the turkey buzzard. He was selected as our national bird by Congress in 1782 because of his impressive appearance—with his snow-white head and tail, a bald eagle is one of the handsomest of all birds of prey—and because he is peculiarly American, found nowhere else in the world. The golden eagle is ubiquitous and was already the national emblem of Prussia and Russia. The selection was made over the violent protests of Benjamin Franklin whose candidate for the honor was the wild turkey. "The bald eagle is a bird of bad moral character," Franklin protested. "He does not get his living honestly. Too lazy to fish for himself, the bald eagle pursues the fishinghawk [osprey] and takes his fish from him. Like men who live by robbing, he is generally poor and often lousy. Besides, he is a rank coward. He is therefore by no means a proper emblem for brave and honest America."

Later ornithologists have tended to agree with Franklin. Robert Cushman Murphy says of the bald eagle in his *Land Birds of America* "The feeding habits of these birds are hardly as dignified as their appearance for their fare often consists of dead fish washed up on the beach. The bald eagle sometimes robs the hardworking fishhawk of its prey; occasionally it catches fish for itself or seizes wounded and crippled waterfowl." Mr. Murphy was the chairman of the ornithology department of the American Museum of Natural History, and he should know.

Certainly there would be no use in taking a de luxe vulture to Mexico in order to fight giant iguanas. But did these men really know what a bald eagle could do? Had either of them ever owned a trained bald eagle—or, for that matter, had any other naturalist? To the best of my knowledge, no one ever had. The bald eagle appears on our currency, on our national seal, and perhaps no other bird is so famous a symbol. Yet no one actually knows how intelligent these majestic birds are, what they were capable of doing—whether like the great Horned Owl they were merely impressive-appearing idiots or whether they possessed definite personalities. I had already learned from my experiences with wild-animal pets how little even zoologists know about the innate capabilities of wild animals. Perhaps the bald eagle was not as worthless a creature as Benjamin Franklin and Robert Murphy believed. On my last trip to Salem, I hadn't been especially interested in the captive bird except to feel sorry for any wild animal penned up for life. Now I decided to have another look at her.

So Jule and I, taking Wriggles with us, drove to Salem in a station wagon in which we had recklessly invested $800. Salem is a lovely little town with sidewalks made of bricks mellowed a golden orange by age and overhung by great trees. Mr. Thompson was glad to show us the eagle. She didn't look particularly impressive sitting on a rail in the chicken house. She was a uniform brownish-black in color and her cere (the waxlike flesh at the base of the beak) and her legs were a dirty yellow. Bald eagles do not get their full white head and tail feathers until they are six or seven years old, a phenomenon that deceived even so great a naturalist as Audubon. He thought these immature birds were a different species and named them the Washington eagle.

The eagle's plumage was a secondary consideration to me. I wanted to know if she had any individuality. Even a smart bird will often go stir-crazy if kept in captivity too long, and this bird had been confined for over a year.

"I'll show you something funny about this bird," remarked Mr. Thompson. He picked up a corncob and, opening the door of the chicken house, tossed it inside. The cob was still in the air when the eagle shot from her perch and seized it. I was reminded of the way Guy, my goshawk, bolted from my fist and seized a kicked clod of earth when in perfect *yarak*. But this bird did something I had never seen either Tara or Guy do. She began to play with the cob as Jesse would with a bright bit of metal, tossing it in the air, leaping up to meet it as it came down, rolling it back and forth on the floor, snapping at it with her beak.

While we watched, Wriggles ran over and put her forepaws on the wire front of the house to look inside. Instantly the eagle dropped the cob and hit the wire with her full force. Wriggles fled yelping but the eagle continued to beat against the wire, twisting it in her talons in a savage effort to get at the fleeing dog.

Years before I had dreamed of the bird large enough to be impressive, with the hunting instinct of a falcon but with the intelligence and personality of Jesse. This was the bird.

Having since flown golden eagles and many other species of raptors, I can say that I believe the bald eagle is among the smartest of the birds of prey. The very attributes which so offended Benjamin Franklin and Robert Murphy are a tribute to her intelligence, if not to her morals. Like a crow, she is smart enough to steal whenever she gets the chance. Like a vulture, she doesn't strain herself hunting if she can pick up animals killed along a highway or strained fish. Unlike the hawks, she takes an active interest in the world around her. She will play with a ball, a spool of thread, or even a corncob. However, she is also perfectly capable of catching her own food and, when necessary, is a fierce and determined hunter.

Mr. Thompson was quite willing to dispose of the bird for $25, which covered the cost of the chickens she had killed during her brief period of liberty. Then I got my first experience in handling an eagle. The bird had a six-foot wing spread, talons two inches long, and strength enough in her mailed fist to kill a wolf. I had put on a heavy leather falconer's glove, more than adequate for handling even the most powerful hawk, but in my struggle to put jesses on the bird, she grabbed me by my gloved hand with all her strength. Her terrible rear talon went through the padded leather as though it were linen. I could feel the talon scrape along the bare bone. My arm went numb to the shoulder. When I finally broke away, there was a hole in the back of my hand as big as a ten-penny nail. It was so deep I could see the muscles moving and the bare bone. My hand swelled like an inflated rubber glove and my wrist turned black and blue from the pressure.

Because of the swollen hand, it was some time before I could begin manning the bird. Jule and I were living in an apartment in New York, so the eagle moved in with us. There was nothing to do but allow her to fly loose around the living room while Wriggles stayed with us in the bedroom. Instead of sitting dignifiedly on the back of a sofa or on the arm of a chair like a falcon, the eagle set about to investigate everything in the room, as Jesse would have done. Being more powerful than Jesse, her investigation was more in the nature of demolishment. She tore the stuffing out of the chairs, got in the bathroom and ripped open the toothpaste, amused herself jumping up and pulling the pictures off the walls. Then she collected the stuffing from the chairs in the middle of the room and played games with it, bouncing up and down on the heap as though on a trampoline, beating with her wings as she went up to add to her altitude, and snatching up clawfuls of the material on each downward trip which she scattered as she rose again. She could amuse herself for hours like that.

She had absolutely no fear of us. Wriggles she frankly regarded as something eatable and spent a considerable part of her time trying to pull him out from under the bed. When forcibly expelled from the bedroom, she would wait outside the door for another chance. When, in the interests of ventilation, Jule would open the door a crack and then brace a heavy bureau against it so it couldn't be forced open, we would see a yellow eye peering through the crack and occasionally a long beak would be stuck through the opening and pull hopefully at the door jamb.

I took for granted that we could never keep the dog and bird together and even began to have considerable doubts if I could ever man this monster even when my hand healed. But the eagle really manned herself. The long periods of constant carrying or even the use of a hood were never necessary with the eagle. She gradually became accustomed not only to us but to Wriggles, whom she came to recognize as a member of the family. Except during the struggle with the jesses, she never attacked either of us, although admittedly during the first few days we kept out of her way, nor did she make any attempt to avoid us. During the first week, I treated her as I had Claude and Claudette when they were fresh from the wilds of Nova Scotia. I simply went around her, neither coming so close as to frighten or anger her nor keeping so far away that she could ignore my presence. The eagle would cock her head on one side and study me as I went by. Then when I crossed behind her, she would turn her head around as though her neck were a swivel to keep me in sight. Although she could only make a 180-degree turn, it sometimes seemed as though she could turn her head through the whole 360 degrees, for if I continued walking around her, she would snap her head about so rapidly the eye could hardly follow the motion and continue to watch me as I came around.

By the end of a week she had grown so accustomed to us that Jule could sweep around her. When the time came to sweep the spot where the bird was standing, Jule would pat the arm of the nearest chair, call "Up here, girl!," and the eagle would gravely step up on it while Jule proceeded with her housecleaning. We also got to know her moods. When she was doing her war dance among the stuffing she was in what Jule called "her rambunctious mood" which a falconer would call *yarak*, although this was not the strange, murderous, concentrated dedication of the true hunting hawk. Then she would jump to the back of the sofa, puff out her feathers, and lift one leg under her. Now it was safe to let Wriggles run around the apartment. The eagle would watch the little dog in a way that Jule felt was unpleasantly reminiscent of the way a robin watches a worm but never made any attempt to attack. Of course, we always made sure that the bird was well fed at such times. We fed her steak from the butcher's shop and also unplucked chickens since, like a hawk, she needed the feathers for "casting." All birds of prey devour not only the flesh but also the fur or feathers of their quarry. The indigestible material remains in the hawk's crop and is later thrown up in the form of a oblong, tightly packed mass called a "casting." These castings serve to clean out the hawk's crop and without them the inside of crop becomes gradually coated with slime, which makes the bird listless and dispirited.

Although admittedly our eagle wouldn't have been everyone's dish of tea, I became increasingly more interested in her. She was obviously a capable individual, bored with being confined in the small apartment, and I looked forward to working with her. Like Wayatcha, she could easily get out of hand—and indeed did, so far as poor Jule was concerned—but I knew enough about hawks to be confident that I could control her. I had invested in a much heavier glove—an ice-hockey goalman's glove—and even strengthened that with a thin board down the back to take the force of her hind talon. Meanwhile, I read everything I could find about our national bird.

The bald eagle is found from Alaska to Florida, although in most parts of the United States they are rapidly becoming extinct, either from being shot or because they are no longer fertile. No one knows exactly why, but one theory is that the birds are eating fish which have fed on insects killed by the widespread use of DDT and this apparently renders the eagles sterile. Although bald eagles have no moral qualms about robbing ospreys, their domestic life would appear to be ideal. The birds mate for life, which often means for fifty years or more. Their nests are often huge affairs; one nest near Vermilion, Ohio, was twelve feet deep and eight and one half feet across. At least two carloads of sticks went into its construction, some six feet long and a couple of inches thick. Every stick was painstakingly carried up by the parents to the top of a seventy-foot tree and woven into a tight mass. Typical of the "unhawklike" mentality of the bald eagle, they often put purely ornamental material in the nest—bright pieces, of paper, shiny bits of tin, or colored stones. The inside of the nest is lined with soft grasses and here the mother lays her clutch of eggs, usually two but occasionally three and sometimes four.

The parents take turns brooding the eggs, never leaving them unguarded. Since bald eagles breed very early in the spring, they occasionally have to contend with unseasonable snowstorms or heavy sleet. In bad weather, one bird will stand on the edge of the nest and spread its huge wings as a windbreak for the other. The birds usually return, to the same nest year after year; in past times at least, they seldom migrated. However, in recent years most pairs seem to winter in Florida. Probably in the old days there was more small game around during the cold months but today the birds would starve so they've altered their habits to fit the times.

The parents spend about six months of each year in household duties. Even after the young leave the nest, the parents remain with them, bringing them food and teaching them the tricks of their trade. To what extent bald eagles depend

on robbing osprey and picking up dead animals along highways (in recent years pairs of bald eagles have set up regular
patrols along certain well-traveled stretches) is a moot point.
One difficulty in getting any exact records results from the fact
that sportsmen's groups in the past have been quick to demand
that any bird-killing game be exterminated. Many naturalists
have, therefore, deliberately minimized the bald eagle's ability
as a hunter. Later, I took a series of motion pictures of a pair
of eagles, bringing food in to their young with the cooperation
of the (then) Biological Survey. The pictures showed that the
eagles were catching mallard and black duck, apparently by
dropping down on the birds suddenly from a great height. The
Survey asked me to suppress these pictures as they might be
used as an excuse by gun clubs to kill the eagles. The bald eagle,
then, would seem to be in a difficult position. If he doesn't hunt
game, he's a despised scavenger. If he does, he's a predator to
be exterminated. Personally, I suspect that the bald eagle does
whatever is easiest. When he can rob ospreys or pick up freshly
killed game, he does. Otherwise, he hunts.

The name bald eagle is unfortunate. It creates the image of
a bird with a naked head, like a vulture. A hundred years ago
when the name was given, *bald* meant "white." A "bald-face
heifer" was a cow with a white face. Naturalists have tried to
change the name to the "white-headed" eagle but the old term
sticks.

The legend that eagles carry off children is so well established
that nothing can shake it. The origin of this story would seem to
be an old apocryphal tale of a mother who saw her baby seized
by an eagle and carried off by the bird to its eyrie on the side of a
cliff. The heroic mother climbed the cliff and retrieved her child.
An eagle weighs only about ten pounds, and since it cannot
possibly lift more than its own weight, it could carry only a

very small baby. My bird, I later found, could not lift more than six pounds. Still, there are a few seemingly well-authenticated records of eagles having attacked not only children but even adults. The best-known case of an attack on a child occurred in 1832 and was recorded by the great naturalist Wilson. Wilson wrote:

"A woman . . . weeding in the garden had set her child down to amuse itself while she was at work; when a sudden and extraordinary rushing sound and a shrill scream from the child alarmed her. Starting up she beheld the infant thrown down and dragged some feet and a large bald eagle bearing off a fragment of its frock, which being the only part seized and giving way providentially saved the life of the infant."

I see no reason to doubt this story. There are cases of owls, foxes, and even raccoons attacking humans, so I suppose an occasional eagle may do the same thing.

As it was impossible to train the bird in New York, Jule and I decided to leave for Mexico as my hand had healed. We had fitted a crossbar in the back of the station wagon and, considerably to my surprise, the eagle learned very quickly to ride around sitting on the bar. I think she was glad to get out of the apartment and enjoyed looking out the window at the passing traffic. I had gotten a hood made to her measurements from Mr. L. N. Wight of Bolster Mills, Maine, one of the few people in America who make falconry equipment, but had never used it. Unlike other hawks, the eagle disliked the hood and seemed unhappy when she had it on. She liked to look around her and when hooded sat hunched up in sullen silence. So I seldom used it.

To make sure that we wouldn't run into complications at the border, I went to see the Mexican consul and explained what we hoped to do with the eagle. He was most gracious and assured me he would attend to all details. So it was with confidence that we packed the car and started off one morning, planning to drop in on the consulate and pick up the necessary papers. The consul was as charming as ever but explained there had been a delay in obtaining the papers.

"But we're all ready to go," I protested. "Our car is outside with the eagle sitting in it."

The consul looked at me dumfounded. "Good heavens, I had no idea you were actually being serious!" he exclaimed. "I thought you were a practical joker."

Almost a week elapsed before the necessary papers could be put through.

Eight

Although there are doubtless many ways of manning a eagle, I'd recommend carrying one about with you in a car for a week. The medieval falconers were never separated from their birds, even putting their hawks on a perch by their beds at night and carrying them during the day. Since an eagle is too heavy to be carried constantly, the best substitute is the swaying motion of a car. Exactly why constant motion has a soothing effect on a hawk no one knows, but apparently it lulls the bird somewhat as the motion of a cradle lulls a baby. Then, too, being constantly confined with a human naturally tends to tame a hawk. We had trouble finding motels that would accept us, so we camped out and the eagle spent the night on a block in the tent with us. By the time we crossed the Rio Grande River into Mexico, our eagle was well manned.

At every village where we stopped, children would rush out calling *"un águila, un águila!"*—*águila* being the Spanish name for an eagle. We got so used to hearing the word we finally named our bird Águila—and Águila she has remained.

Following the list of instructions Mr. Johnson had written out for us, we traveled south from Mexico City and made our headquarters in the little mountain town of Taxco. Taxco is built on the side of a cliff and is a maze of little cobblestone streets, walled gardens, and jasmine-hung, iron-grilled balconies. In the center of town on the only level spot in Taxco stands the great cathedral, banked on every side by the little red-roofed houses, peering over each other's shoulders to get a glimpse of the huge mother church. Jule and I rented a house with a little garden caught up in the cleft of the hill that made us feel as though we were living in a penthouse.

From our garden we could look out over miles of mountain peaks. The nearer hills were covered with a fine tracery of white threads which, through a telescope, resolved themselves into ancient burro trails, old when Cortez conquered the land. The hills around Taxco are rich in silver and sometimes we would see the pack trains crawling down the terrible slopes, the little burros looking no bigger than mice. Each donkey carried his load of silver ore, just as his ancestors had carried it for the Spanish conquistadors four hundred years earlier.

We stopped many of these trains and asked the Indian drivers about iguanas. Yes, there were iguanas back in the hills. They were hard to catch. They were *muy bravo,* very fierce. But none of the drivers seemed to know where to find them.

Then one day while wandering over a mountain slope near Taxco, Jule and I met Chon. Chon was twelve years old and stood some four feet high on bare, brown legs. When we met him, he and another boy were herding goats on the almost perpendicular slope of the cliff. Yes, Chon knew where there were iguanas and would lead us to the place when we had the *águila* trained. We promptly hired Chon as houseboy for the magnificent sum of fifty cents a week. Then I set about training *Aguila.*

The first step in training was to get Águila to fly short distances to my glove for meat. Águila had no objection to coming for the meat—but she preferred to walk. I could stand a hundred yards away and Águila would walk the entire distance. She found it easier than flying.

I'd never encountered this difficulty with my hawks and didn't know what to do about it. Finally, I found out the trouble. Águila was so big it was difficult for her to take off, just as a big bombing plane has more trouble leaving the ground than a light pursuit ship. She had to beat the air constantly with her wings to rise, and after two years in a chickenhouse and two months in an apartment, Águila was badly out of condition. A falcon in a similar predicament would have simply sat on the block until she starved to death. Águila had no intention of doing that. Instead, she walked.

I finally hit on the idea of putting Águila on top of a hill, going down to the valley below, and calling to her. With the force of gravity in her favor, I believed, Águila could make the flight easily enough.

I had determined to train Águila to come to my fist like an accipter rather than to a lure like a falcon because I thought she was too big and clumsy to catch a swinging lure. Going downhill Águila had no trouble taking off. With her great wings spread to the uttermost, she came sweeping down the side of the hill like a glider, picking up momentum every second. Unfortunately, she didn't know how to stop herself. A bird's wing is divided into two parts, roughly corresponding to the human arm. On the tip of what might be called the bird's forearm grow the long, thin primary feathers which can be open or closed like the human fingers. The principal purpose of these feathers is to give speed. Along the inner portion of the wing are the secondaries, all the same length and thicker than the slender primaries. These secondaries correspond to an airplane's flaps; the bird can raise or lower them as a unit and they operate independently of the primaries. To stop, a bird must drop her secondaries to serve as an air brake, at the same time lowering her tail so it is at right angles to her body and spreading it like a fan for further wind resistance. The primaries are meanwhile closed and turned crossways to the direction of the bird's flight. As she begins to "heave to" in terms of a sailing ship or "zooms into a stall" in aircraft terms, she must then reverse her wingbeat as though backing water for the landing. An experienced bird can so check her forward speed that she hangs almost motionless in the air for a second or two before drifting onto a perch. With small birds who do not have enough wingspread or weight to build up much momentum, this maneuver is quite simple. With a big bird, it is extremely complicated.

When Águila started down toward me, neither of us had any idea of the aeronautical problems involved. I was so delighted to see her flying and Águila was so intent on the meat in my hand that not until the bird was some ten feet away did it occur to us that she couldn't stop. Both of us realized the problem at almost the same instant. Águila began screaming with anger and apprehension and I tried to get out of her way. I was too late. The eagle hit me full on and knocked me sprawling, making a crash landing on top of me.

Although neither of us were hurt, Águila clearly considered the whole business my fault. She went into one of the hysterical tantrums which we were later to know so well. Bounding up and down on me as she had on the chair stuffings, she buffeted me with her wings at the same time making convulsive grabs at my chest with her talons. Luckily I had on a heavy leather jacket, for if the bird had been able to clamp her talons into my flesh, she would have locked her claws like a bulldog locking its jaws—and once a hawk does that, she is physically unable to release her grip as long as the frenzy is on her. Her grip under these conditions can only be compared to the grip of a drowning man; even he cannot release his hold and must be knocked senseless to avoid drowning his rescuer.

Instead of clamping to me, Águila clamped onto my jacket. Once her talons went through the leather and locked, she was fastened to it. I feel sure that Águila realized what had happened but she could not relax her grip Instead, still screaming with rage, she struck at me with her wings while trying to tear her talons loose. I managed to get the jacket off over my head, and even then Águila thrashed around still clinging to the jacket while trying to get at me. Hampered as she was, I was easily able to keep out of her way until she stopped exhausted, panting with open beak and outstretched wings.

I waited until she had quieted down and then walked over to her, holding out the meat on my gloved fist saying, "Well, old girl, it was all a mistake. Up you get!" Without any hesitation Águila stepped up on my fist, taking the jacket with her. She sat there still panting while I carried her back to Taxco. I put her on her block under the mango tree and went for her bathtub. This bathtub was a coffin we had purchased from the local undertaker. Águila liked to take a daily bath and as we could find nothing in Taxco big enough to hold her, I had purchased a coffin. I filled it with water and Águila instantly jumped in, still carrying the jacket clutched in one foot. She began to bathe in her usual manner, first ducking her head under the water, then plunging one shoulder in, catching a bowlful of water in the hollow of her wing and stretching up to allow it to run down her back. Finally she crouched down in the bottom of the coffin, fluffed out her feathers, and shook herself all over like a sparrow taking a bath in a saucer. Águila's baths took about half an hour and only when she was completely cooled off and relaxed did she relinquish her grip on the jacket. She left it in the coffin when she jumped out to dry herself.

I didn't try flying Águila directly to my fist again for several days. Instead, I flew her to the lure which I left on the ground. This method cost me several lures as Águila couldn't alight on the lure any better than she could alight on my fist and when she went head over tail, she took it out on the lure. However, lures were cheaper than leather jackets. In two weeks' time, Águila had learned how to alight.

She had not only learned how to land; she had also strengthened her wings so she could take off on the level. She was able to make short flights to my fist now. Mindful of my experience when Tara checked off and went soaring over the Ashbridge farm, I kept Águila on a creance during this period. Instead of the light string suitable for a falcon, I had to use a clothesline for Águila. Unable to handle both the creance and the eagle simultaneously, I turned the creance over to Jule. It was impossible simply to tie the end of the creance to a stake because if the eagle did check off she would build up so much speed that when she came to the end of the creance the sudden shock would jerk her down and strain her legs. So when the bird did decide she was going too fast to make her landing and veer away, Jule had to run with her, gradually bringing the bird to ground as though playing kite. The strain was too much for Jule's arms so she had to tie the creance around her waist. This worked perfectly. Jule was just heavy enough to put a drag on the creance and by simply letting Águila pull her along the ground she brought the eagle down without injury—to the eagle, at any rate.

Finally Águila became such an expert flier I even attempted to fly her to a swinging lure as though she were a falcon. "Flying to the lure" is a standard means of exercising falcons. The falconer swings the lure around his head and the hawk makes repeated dives at it with the falconer jerking it away at the last second. A falcon in good condition can make 75 or 100 stoops to the swinging lure. Realizing what a huge bird Águila was, I doubted if she would be physically able to make the turns and twists necessary for "flying to the lure," but it was worth trying.

The first time I flew her to a swinging lure, Águila tried to bind to it in the air and when I pulled it away, she turned and came in from a different angle. She tried position after position, sometimes hanging almost motionless while she studied the situation and then swinging in after making a great turn. Some of these turns were tremendous, several hundred yards in diameter, and the twists she gave in midair trying to foot the lure obviously put a terrific strain on her. This trial-and-error technique was a regular habit with her and when flying free to my fist I often saw her, after missing the first time, circle around and come in again lower or against the wind, obviously having found out what was wrong.

Águila put in over a dozen stoops at the lure that first day and it was the most impressive exhibition of flying she had ever made. Seeing such a gigantic bird in action over your head is a breathtaking experience. But Águila was never to repeat the performance.

At first, the eagle had taken for granted it was her fault that she couldn't catch the swinging object. When she realized that she was being tricked, she did a wingover and came straight for me. I was so astonished that I continued to swing the lure but there was no mistaking Águila's fury. When I saw her feet come forward for the bind, I threw myself flat on my face. Águila whistled over my head, dropping sharply to grab me as she went by. Unable to pull out of her dive, she struck the ground sharply a few yards away, spun around and came running back at me on foot. I hurriedly tossed her the lure and she automatically grabbed it.

With the lure in one foot, she stood there for a few moments glaring at me and obviously contemplating further punitive measures. Finally she thought better of it and with a look that plainly implied "Don't try that again!" she began to tear off pieces of the meat.

After that day, Águila would never put in more than two or three stoops at the lure. Then she would simply alight beside me and wait until it was handed her. This was just another example of Águila's superior reasoning powers; very different from those of a falcon who will stoop at a lure indefinitely and never realize what is happening.

Unfortunately for me, Águila was not always as reasonable as I could have wished. In my efforts to make her stay in the air and exercise, I would often hide the lure so she couldn't see it. Águila soon caught on to this device, which she clearly regarded as a dirty trick. One day while she was circling about over my head trying to decide where I had hidden the lure, a rabbit bolted out from under my feet. Instantly Águila wheeled about and started after it. The rabbit dashed over a little hill and vanished down a hole. When Aguila couldn't find it, she flew back and attacked me in a rage, clearly thinking I had hidden it.

There is no denying the fact that Águila was lazy and a great believer in letting her head save her heels—or rather her wings. "Ringing up" was a hard task for her but after a few weeks she learned the location of the different up-drafts in the hills and she'd fly a quarter of a mile away to hit the sunny slope of a mountain where there was a thermal lift to carry her up. This made no difference when exercising her, but I knew that when we actually started to hunt, teaching Águila to "wait on" overhead would prove to be impossible.

Chon turned out to be an excellent assistant falconer. He quickly learned such important words in falconry jargon as *lure, yarak, creance,* and so on. That, however, was about the only English he ever did learn and he told me that he once tried his vocabulary on his schoolteacher and she told him I must be talking Russian. He wasn't strong enough to carry the eagle but often I would put Águila on the ground, give Chon the leash, and go off looking for a good place to lure-fly. Águila, who was impatient to get going, would occasionally go into a rage and attack the boy. Chon had gotten to know the bird so well that instead of being panic-stricken, he would expertly dodge each rush, calculating to the inch how fast the bird could turn. On the ground, Águila was quite clumsy; walking with a peculiar pigeon-toed gait and occasionally boasting herself along with her wings. Chon could easily avoid her charges and as long as he held the end of the leash, Águila couldn't get into the air to stoop on him. Chon considered this great sport, shouting *"Olé!"* after each charge as though at the bullring and slipping neatly under Águila's outstretched wing as she tried to turn with him. Once in the air, Águila never paid any attention to Chon—she was only annoyed because he wouldn't let her go.

During these daily expeditions with Águila, one fact became more and more painfully apparent. It would be a physical impossibility for anything except a gorilla to carry the eagle into the hills where the lizards lived and still have enough energy left to crawl around the rocks to start the game. So Jule and I decided to get a horse and train it and the eagle together. Then Águila could be flown from horseback. Hawks of all kinds were hunted from horseback during the Middle Ages and I saw no reason why an eagle couldn't be.

But the first few horses we tried saw every reason. The minute they saw Águila come rushing toward them, her enormous pinions outstretched, the wind whistling through her feathers, her long yellow feet thrown out before her for the landing, the horses bolted. Jule was an expert horsewoman and to her fell the questionable distinction of training the horses. She was plucky and skillful with the terrified animals, but after a while even she had to admit there were some things a horse wouldn't do and letting an eagle land on him was one of them.

When we were almost ready to give up, we acquired Teresa. Teresa was a wise old mare, formerly the property of a Mexican general. She had been in three revolutions, had three generals shot off her broad back and been stolen twice. Nothing could surprise her any more—nothing, that is, except having an eagle flown from her.

Teresa did not actually bolt when she saw Águila headed her way at some fifty miles per hour, but she showed the whites of her eyes and walked around on her hind legs, something she hadn't done for years. But at the end of a few days she and Águila had gotten used to each other and Jule announced that she was ready to try Teresa on the treacherous mountain trails. At last, after many weeks of hard work, we were ready to begin iguana-hunting.

Our first attempts were disappointing. I had not taken into consideration one of the best-shown characteristics of birds of prey. They cannot see a motionless object. I had often seen a pigeon escape a falcon by dropping into a field and remain motionless while the puzzled hawk beat the air above it. This is one of the principal reasons falconers use dogs in hawking: the dogs will keep the quarry in the air.

The first lizard we saw was a moderate-sized one, about as long as a small dog. We had seen him before and he always bolted up a long, gravelly slope that gave a pursuing bird a good chance at him. Jule was carrying Águila on Teresa while I followed on foot. She rode forward cautiously.

When we were still a long distance away the lizard rose on his deceptively short legs and began to show signs of apprehension.

His forked tongue flickered in and out as he tasted the breeze—lizards, like snakes, "hear" with their tongues. Apparently they are either able to pick up sound vibrations or else they are capable of tasting minute particles of scent carried by the wind. In either case, long before we were in proper flying distance, this lizard became alarmed. He began to slide off his rock, but he still moved slowly with frequent halts. This was the moment to cast off the eagle.

Jule held up the bird with the traditional falconer's cry, "Gaze Ho!" Águila crouched her head down between her hunched shoulders and turned her wonderful telescopic vision on the hills. She could have seen a rabbit two miles away—a moving rabbit. But she could not see the lizard in plain sight at two hundred yards.

There was nothing to do but ride forward. Jule touched Teresa with the spur and the mare trotted toward the iguana, picking her way daintily over the loose rocks. For a second the lizard squatted down like rabbit freezing. Then without warning he flashed up the slope.

Before Jule could throw her off, Águila had sprung off her fist. For a few precious seconds her great wings beat the air while she hung almost motionless. Then slowly she overcame the initial inertia and shot away after the lizard.

Unfortunately, the iguana had not waited patiently for the end of these maneuvers. He was speeding up the slope so fast his long body seemed to be a flickering shadow. But Águila had reached her full speed by now. Fast as the reptile was moving, he seemed to be standing still compared to the meteoric flight of the bird. But still he had a long lead.

Jule and I stopped breathing as the eagle swiftly overtook the fleeing lizard. The iguana was almost at the top of the slope now. Águila suddenly reversed her wing stroke and, flinging out her terrible yellow legs before her, shot in for the kill. Just as she did so, the lizard reached the top of the cliff.

Before him was a sheer drop of sixty feet onto merciless rock ledges. The iguana never paused. He rushed straight out into space, his speed actually carrying him a foot or so into midair before he began to fall. Águila cast up (zoomed up in a sharp curve), turning her head to watch the falling reptile. Then, keeping her wings rigid, she dropped sideways down the side of the cliff, cutting the air like a falling knife.

But she was too late. The iguana hit the rock, his feet beginning to move while he was still in the air, and darted into the mouth of a cave. When, after much climbing, I had reached the spot, Águila was standing on a boulder looking into the black pocket. The iguana was gone; our first attempt had failed.

For a week Jule and I carried Águila into the mountains every day, and every day the eagle continued to make futile attempts to catch the swift lizards. Finally it was through Wriggles that she succeeded.

Wriggles always hated to be left behind if we were going anywhere. If Jule so much as picked up the car keys, Wriggles rushed out and was sitting hopefully in the front seat of the station wagon when we arrived. Every day Wriggles would come prancing out when we mounted the horses, always sure that we would not desert her. At last, Jule broke down.

"This time I'm taking Wriggles too," she said. "She can play around the rocks while we hunt with the eagle."

Since we weren't catching anything anyhow, I consented. Wriggles rode triumphantly on the pommel of Jule's saddle while I carried Águila. Both Jule and I were a little worried about the puppy, but the two animals had grown accustomed to each other and I was sure Águila no longer regarded Wriggles as something edible.

Once on the mountainside, we left Wriggles to chase rabbits while we rode on to look for iguanas. We spotted one almost at once, and Jule took the eagle while I dismounted.

Jule held Águila while I crawled around behind the iguana and tried to make him run toward the eagle to escape me. In spite of my nervous protestations, Jule had taken to riding toward the lizards at full gallop, throwing off Águila at the last moment. This was so dangerous on the narrow mountain trails I never could watch it without my hair standing on end. But by this time the horse and eagle knew each other so perfectly that Jule did not even bother to rein Teresa in when Águila was flying back to her. If we were in a hurry to get to another ridge where an iguana had just been sighted, Jule would call to the eagle and the bird would fly to her fist while the horse swung along the trail at a canter. In fact, sometimes the eagle would come without being called, and if Jule was not ready for him would alight on Teresa. He did this once while the girl and the horse were picking their way along the edge of a cliff and for a moment I thought the startled mare would carry all three of them over the brink.

In this case I had to climb down a long slope in order to get below the lizard. It was not dangerous, but in slippery riding boots it took a long time. Meanwhile Wriggles came panting back to Jule, caught sight of me, and came cavorting down the slope.

The iguana saw her, but the little dog was actually smaller than the reptile and the big lizard simply half-rose and hissed at her. Wriggles was charmed. She approached closer to sniff. The iguana snapped and swung around, keeping his open jaws facing the dog. At this moment Jule had a stroke of genius and threw off the eagle.

Everything was in Águila's favor. She came whizzing down

the long slope and almost before the lizard knew what was happening, the great bird had him. Although we wanted the iguanas alive, I allowed Águila to kill and eat this first one to encourage her in future hunts.

For a while we optimistically thought that our troubles were over. But a week later we had a sharp reverse.

Águila had an unfortunate habit of using her beak instead of her talons to kill, a trait typical of the bald eagle and a most annoying trait for a trained bird. Even when Águila was completely manned she would sometimes strike at my face when she was excited. I honestly believe there was no real malice intended, but once she laid open my left cheek and I was afraid for my eyes. It is impossible to punish any bird of prey (they never forget a blow or injury), so there was nothing I could do about it. But this time it was Águila, not I, who suffered from this trick.

Wriggles had bayed an iguana on top of a rock. Counting his long, whippy tail, the lizard must have been six feet long and stood higher than the dog. Wriggles was prancing around screaming at the iguana to get off his rock and fight but once when the little dog got too close, the big lizard opened a mouth festooned with crooked, triangular teeth and hissed. Wriggles paused, retreated carefully about ten feet, and began barking louder than ever.

I saw Jule on the trail ahead of me, coming down the steep slope with Águila on her fist. She heard Wriggles giving tongue and looked up. Her mouth fell open.

"Wriggles caught a dinosaur!" she screamed.

Wriggles saw that reinforcements were arriving and began to dance in closer to the iguana. Suddenly the lizard's tail lashed out. Wriggles went rolling down the slope groggily and went off staggering, whining to herself.

Then Águila took off with one great sweep of her wings. She hadn't been able to see the iguana until he moved but down she swept toward him with open wings like a skimmed piece of slate. Wriggles saw the bird's shadow pass over him and ducked instinctively.

I suspect that Águila had been growing annoyed because we took the lizards away from her and substituted dead ones in their place as a reward. This had worked very well the first few times, but Águila had begun to catch on. Instead of coming in with a rush and seizing the iguana with her powerful talons, she lit beside it and tried to catch the reptile with her beak.

Instantly the iguana reared up, his blood-red mouth wide open. As Águila moved in, he struck out with his tail. The eagle was knocked sideways, but she struck back with her wing. The iguana rushed in under the blow and locked his jaws in the bird's breast feathers. Águila broke away, leaving a mouthful of feathers in the lizard's jaws. The iguana thought he still had the eagle and stood holding the plumes, momentarily bewildered. This gave Águila a chance to grab the lizard by the head, but the iguana rolled with her like an experienced wrestler. I saw Águila's white tail go flying up as she went over.

Then Wriggles came charging in from the sidelines. Keeping a wary eye on the lizard's tail, she nipped at his flank. The iguana spun around, snapping angrily. Águila managed to get on her feet and jumped over the lizard's back, the reptile's head following right at her toes. Águila alighted, turned, and reached out one foot to grab the iguana by the muzzle. She had learned to do this very neatly. She'd feint with one foot until she could maneuver an iguana into a convenient position, then grab him by the muzzle—holding his mouth shut with one foot and immediately grab him by the back of the neck with the other. To keep the lizard from rolling with her, she would next fling out her big wings like brakes on either side while bracing herself with her tail. No iguana had ever broken that hold.

But this time something went wrong. Águila missed her hold and I saw the lizard lunge forward. The eagle sprang back, then went up into the air and came down on the iguana's back. She promptly held his mouth shut with one foot while pinning his neck down with the other.

By that time I had come up. I tore my shirt into strips and with Jule's help, tied up the iguana. He later became quite tame and lived for many years in the Philadelphia Zoo.

When we came to examine the eagle, we found her standing in a pool of blood. At first I thought the blood had come from the iguana, but when I picked her up and began to wipe off her feet I saw that the iguana had bitten through one of her toes.

Jule took Águila in her arms and galloped back to Taxco. That night we drove Águila to Mexico City and had a surgeon examine the injury. He said the toe was almost completely bitten off and wanted to amputate it, but we decided to take a chance. The toe healed perfectly but the talon came off and never grew back again. Fortunately, it was one of the minor talons and did not affect her hunting ability, but for a long time afterward Águila would never fly iguanas.

Nine

We had been fortunate in our choice of a home in Taxco. Taxco has not changed greatly since the seventeenth century and many of the houses are virtually worlds of their own, surrounded by high walls, grilled windows, and little patios shaded by fig and mango trees. Our house and garden were caught up in a pocket of the great cliff on which the town is built and from our patio we could look down two thousand feet into the valley below.

A tiny, cobblestone street, overhung with jasmine that trailed from wrought-iron lamp posts, led to our house. There was only one door with an iron-barred wicket capable of withstanding a battering ram and equipped with a huge lock. Not that the lock was ever needed; Maria, our Indian housekeeper, slept on a cot across the doorway and no one could enter or leave the house without her knowledge. Maria took for granted that she could use the house as an overnight lodging for her relatives when they came in from the mountain villages to trade in the Taxco market, and often when we got up in the morning we would find half a dozen recumbent forms wrapped in their serapes lying around the fireplace. When they departed, they always left something as payment for their lodging—a bag of charcoal, some fresh mangos, or a basket of corn—which Maria scrupulously turned over to us.

We had a small staff of servants. Jesusita, Maria's cousin, who did most of the heavy housework; Chequita-Maria, Maria's niece, who was twelve and could only do light chores; Antonio, the houseboy who kept the grass in the patio clipped with a pair of shears until it was as fine as a golf green, and of course Chon, who helped with Águila and carried Jule's basket for her when she went shopping. Everyone helped with the animals.

Almost as soon as we arrived in Taxco, I let it be known that I was in the market for any kind of wild animal. So far as the local Indians were concerned, all wild animals were classified under two headings; those that were good to eat and those that were not—the latter being considered vermin. Therefore when the news got around that there was a crazy gringo in Taxco prepared to pay good money for any sort of creature regardless of its culinary qualifications, a panic struck the villages. Within a few days our little patio resembled a miniature zoo and you could hardly get across it without having stepped on an armadillo, a caracara, or a red-bellied squirrel.

When the patio overflowed, the animals moved into the house. We had a pair of fawns that slept on a pile of straw by the foot of our bed, partly to protect them from the other more aggressive animals and partly so Jule could give them their eleven o'clock nightly feeding from a bottle. To preserve our sanity and cut down on fights, several of the animals had to be tied to the legs of tables and chairs in the living room. This was especially true of the coatis.

The coatis were among the first animals we collected in Mexico. Coatis are relatives of the raccoons and look a little like long-nosed anteaters, a little like terriers—and mainly like nothing else on earth. They have very long, thin tails striped like a barber's pole and hands that can open any bottle or box. We got the coatis on our way to Taxco. We had stopped at a gas station and while the tank was being filled, I noticed what seemed to be a dead animal not much bigger than a rat tied by an old piece of string to the pump. On closer inspection, it turned out to be a baby coati—half-starved, mangy, and covered with dirt and lice. The station attendant told me the creature was named Poncho and belonged to his young son, but he would gladly sell the baby for a peso. I made the purchase—whereupon the attendant's little boy, who was watching the transaction, burst into tears.

I felt like a monster. In spite of the poor little creature's wretched condition, he was clearly a beloved pet. Jule was equally effected. Kneeling by the sobbing boy she asked, "Do you love Poncho very much?"

"Sí, señora," wept the boy. "And as soon as he got big enough I was going to skin him and make a cap of the hide."

That lovely sentiment cost the youngster exactly one small coati.

We found that Poncho had a brother who was being used as a doorstop by another villager and bought him too, naming him Pedro. Then we took the two babies on to Taxco.

Both babies were as vicious as any ill-treated, half-starved wild creature could be, and getting them washed and deloused was a painful process. The babies put up such a fight that I got the impression they'd rather have stayed where they were and be skinned. I'd have given up but Jule stuck with it to the end while the coatis screamed, bit, clawed, and fought each other when they couldn't get at us. But I have never seen any animals tame as quickly as they did. By the end of a week they were galloping around the house, rushing out in the patio to dig for worms and then cavorting back to wrestle with Wriggles.

We finally had to forbid them the house unless they were tied up. The coatis could climb like monkeys and one would get on a shelf and throw dishes at the other one who was trying to catch him. If I interfered, they'd gang up on me—and both could bite. They soon learned how to open the icebox and Maria lived in dread of them. Every day I took them for walks in the hills where they had a wonderful time catching bugs, investigating holes, and chasing field mice. Although they could kill a mouse or even a rat with one flick of their daggerlike teeth, they never bothered any of the other animals we had around the house and our caracara, a vulturine bird who doubled as a garbage-disposal unit, could chase them away from their dinners even though the coatis could have disposed of him with one quick nip.

Sometimes they would play tag with Reddy, a little red-bellied squirrel Jule had raised on an eyedropper, but always in fun. Reddy could be quite a biter herself although she never harmed us. She was, however, not above jumping on visitors unexpectedly and locking her teeth in their flesh. Visitors hated her because Reddy generally had to be cut out of them. But she was very cute and loved to play with us, bouncing up and down like a rubber ball and then rolling over to have her stomach tickled. As far as I was concerned, Reddy had only two bad habits: building nests inside my shirt when I was trying to type and eating the furniture. While I was at the typewriter, Reddy would rush busily back and forth collecting old bits of cloth and pieces of paper which she stuffed inside my shirt preparatory to climbing in herself for a snooze. If I got up to clean myself, Reddy would chatter with indignation, her tail going up and down all the time. Her habit of chewing the furniture was more serious. Soon none of the chairs had any backs and we had to lock her out of the bedroom as she had developed a fine taste for suitcases.

Naturally, there were occasional disputes among our family. The armadillo never caused any trouble and his coat of mail protected him. He spent most of the time sleeping behind the toilet and although he gave visitors shocks by darting out between their legs unexpectedly, they soon got used to him. Our white egret could look after himself, and when the coatis got too close he would give them a sharp rap on the head with his long beak that sent them scurrying. A few animals never did take to captivity. One was Jo-Jo, a boat-billed heron brought up by a friend from Acapulco. Jo-Jo was about the size of a chicken with a huge, flat bill nearly as big as he was that made him look lopsided. He refused to eat by himself so I had to cut up his fish and throw it down his throat when he opened his beak to bite me. He had a sore inside his beak which Jule and I had to paint daily with disinfectant. Jo-Jo hated it and I think this was the reason he never got tame, but we finally cured him. Poor Jo-Jo was very lonely; none of the other animals seemed to like him, but finally he took up with two tame pigeons who lived under the beams of our porch. We got him a duck, thinking a duck would be more his size and disposition than the pigeons, but Jo-Jo preferred his first friends. When we went down to Acapulco for a week end, we took Jo-Jo with us and let him go in the lagoons where he could find other herons.

Perhaps the most appealing pets we had were the kinkajous. We had two, a mother and daughter. The best way to describe a kinkajou is to imagine a teddy bear with a long, prehensile tail. The kinks were comparatively slow-moving but they got around and not even Snarlyeow had such a potent spare arm. The kinks would hang from the chandelier by their tails and grab food off trays as it passed below them. When they were tied up, which they had to be if we were all to live in the same house, and an object was out of reach of their arms, the kinks would turn around and lasso it with their tails. They were especially fond of lassoing Chequita-Maria around the ankle and tripping her as she went by, particularly if she was carrying a tray of food which they could grab before it could be cleaned up.

Actually, we seldom tied up the kinks except in the evenings and then only after the mother kink took to drink. When we had friends to supper, it had at first seemed a great joke to give the mother kink a cocktail, which she drank very neatly, holding the stem of the glass firmly with her tail. Unfortunately, she soon developed such a taste for liquor that she became a nuisance. Worse yet, she couldn't carry her liquor—after all, she weighed only about ten pounds—and like most alcoholics, nothing could persuade her that she was under the influence. Instead of lying down and sleeping it off, she would insist on doing a tightrope-walking act along the mantelpiece. Watching her weave her way along the narrow mantel was a horrifying experience; you never knew when she'd fall off and go crashing down on the hard tiles. As a result, we had to run around under her, ready to catch her in case she toppled off. We also had to watch the end of the mantelpiece as the kink not infrequently would keep right on going and fall off on her head. When she felt herself slipping she would make a wild snatch with her tail, generally roping a candlestick or a vase and then everything would come down together. The next morning she would lie on the bed holding her head and when Jule offered her a breakfast of nice hot oatmeal, the kink would scream and try to bite. Finally we had to limit her to a small glass of wine.

The kinks' great friend and companion was Chequita-Maria. She had a dolls' tea party in the patio under the mango tree every evening and the kinks were always invited; the coatis were barred as being too rough. The kinks sat decorously in chairs and drank their tea from cups with their forepaws, balancing themselves with their tails. Chequita-Maria treated them exactly like animated dolls, dressing them up in dolls' clothes and explaining all her troubles and problems to them. The kinks always listened politely, at least if she gave them something to eat.

Jule's shopping requirements were the wonder and awe of the market. Jo-Jo and the egret required fresh fish; Águila needed pigeons, the armadillo got eggs, milk, and hamburger; the kinks fruit and oatmeal; and the coatis raw meat. When to this list you add condensed milk for the fawns and nuts for Reddy, it is no wonder that the dietary habits of the Mannix household became a Taxco legend.

Occasionally we had to make a trip back to Pennsylvania for business reasons. Most of the animals we could leave in Taxco under the supervision of Maria, but even Maria drew the line at looking after the kinks and coatis. "Señora, you have no idea how difficult it is to cook meals with them grabbing dishes off the stove," she told us. "And when they are tied up, you can't dust the living room. They make a game of seizing the mop as you go by them." So we always had to take the kinks and coatis with us.

Driving with the animals loose in the car proved to be more of a problem than we'd realized. Not only did they climb all over us, but the kinks got frightened when we went around the curving mountain roads and grabbed us around the head, often covering our eyes at critical moments. While crossing the desert they all became dehydrated and when we stopped at a motel were half-mad with thirst. They soon discovered that there was always water in the toilet and learned to make a concerted dash for it, whereupon a fight invariably broke out. I remember vividly one puzzled motel proprietor who had come over to see if everything was all right, stopping aghast at the sounds issuing from the bathroom—and Jule's angry expostulation "Don't fight, there's a whole john full of it!" did nothing to clear up his bewilderment. We tried to solve this problem by giving them water en route, but they spilled so much of it we had to give up the idea.

On our first trip, we didn't know that it is necessary to have import permits plus a veterinarian's certificate before bringing animals into the United States. We soon found out.

Driving across the International Bridge at Laredo, we stopped at the U.S. Customs and Jule hopped out of the car followed by Poncho and Pedro. She had only taken a few steps before she was stopped by a custom officer.

"Look, lady, there's a couple of things with long noses following you. I don't know what they are but you'll have to get a permit from the United States Biological Survey to import them."

"How do I do that?"

"Write to Washington."

Sadly we drove back across the bridge. Here we were stopped by a Mexican custom inspector.

"Senor y señora, you cannot bring those animals back into Mexico without an import permit. For that, you must apply to the Game Department in Mexico City."

We were trapped in the center of the International Bridge with two coatis and two kinkajous. Then Jule got a brilliant idea.

"Dan, the Mexican inspectors don't look into packages carried by Mexicans, only at packages carried by Americans. Wait a minute."

She jumped out of the car and ran down the long bridge. A few minutes later she returned with two bewildered Indian women carrying large baskets full of groceries. A deal was quickly arranged resulting in the coatis being put in one basket and the kinks in the other. We took the groceries in our car and the women walked across without question.

We met the women a block away from the customs station. They agreed for five pesos a day to board our animals until the necessary papers arrived. We moved into a hotel in Laredo after frantically cabling Washington.

Our permits arrived and I got a Mexican veterinarian to examine our pets. I'd forgotten in the excitement that a peso a day was the standard wage for the average Indian and five pesos represented untold wealth. When we arrived at the little shack where the coatis were staying, we found them lying luxuriously on the one bed surrounded by the entire Indian family who were respectfully offering them dishes heaped high with all the delicacies of the season. The coatis were so full they could hardly move, but from time to time they would condescendingly pick up some tidbit and toy with it.

"Do you think they look all right?" I asked the vet.

"Look all right!" said the man in disgust. "Those creatures are living better than I ever have." He gave me the certificate and left in disgust. We crossed the border without further trouble.

We had a number of other animals while we lived in Mexico, each of whom had his own personality and his own place in our lives. We had a little cacomistle or ring-tailed cat brought in by some miners, that roamed the house like a domestic kitten. We also had a pair of fawns brought in by a hunter who had shot their mother, and Jule raised them on a bottle. We even had a jaguar cub for a short time, but he proved completely intractable and a danger to the other animals so we had to let him go. In fact, after two years in Mexico we thought we had kept virtually every sort of Mexican fauna but we were in for a surprise. That was the year we acquired several vampire bats.

I first heard about the vampires through Dr. Alfredo Tellez Giron, Chief of the Animal Pathology Laboratory in Mexico City. Dr. Giron had isolated "derriengue fever" in vampires and shown that they were causing the death of thousands of cattle. The vampires were also known to carry rabies. In 1936 there had been an epidemic of rabies on Trinidad; forty-seven people were attacked by the vampires. Most interesting to us was that possibly vampires had migrated north and crossed the Texas border. The skull of a vampire bat was reportedly found in a cave in the Big Bend area of Texas. Together with Charles Mohr, then with the Academy of Natural Sciences in Philadelphia, we decided to explore caves in northern Mexico and find how close the vampire colonies were to the border.

Charles Mohr's interest in the bats was purely scientific, but Jule and I determined to keep a few as pets and see if we could tame them. No one seemed to know much about the weird creatures. We couldn't understand why a sleeper attacked by a vampire never seemed to wake up, how the bats went about delivering their nocturnal raids, or how an animal as small as a bat could apparently show considerable intelligence in plotting his forays. Perhaps by keeping pet vampires we could answer some of these questions.

Vampires are comparatively small bats. Their bodies are only about three inches long and they have a wing-spread of little more than a foot. A single vampire can only drink about a tablespoon of blood, but a horde of them can cause a sleeper to lose enough blood to weaken him. They are found only in this hemisphere and were first reported by the conquistadores. European scientists thought these men were simply repeating a native legend until Charles Darwin proved the existence of the vampires by sleeping out in the jungle and letting himself be bitten. But not until it was discovered that the vampires could transmit disease was any real interest taken in them.

Although Jule was six months pregnant, she insisted on coming along. It seemed to me that crawling through a system of unexplored caves full of infuriated rabid vampires was not a good idea under the circumstances, but Jule assured me that

I'd need her. "You're very good with eagles and things like that, Dan," she explained. "But these poor little bats will be very upset when they're taken out of their caves and put in a cage and they'll need affection and proper care." So I let her come along.

We discovered our first vampires in the cave of Los Sabinos, about 200 miles south of the border. At the time this was the northernmost colony of vampires ever reported, although since then another colony has been found 50 miles closer to the United States. The village of Los Sabinos consisted of half a dozen thatched huts deep in the jungle, a few people, and several sheep, pigs, and goats. I spent some time talking to the Indians as I was curious to find out what sort of people would voluntarily live next to a community of vampire bats. The villagers discussed the bats as calmly as New Jerseyites would talk about mosquitoes. The bats came every night to feed on their stock—and on them. The villages retired to their huts as soon as the sun went down and carefully filled in every chink. If anyone forgot a chink, when he awoke the next morning he was dripping blood from half a dozen little wounds. When the animals got bitten so badly they became weak, the villagers took them into the huts too.

I asked if they'd ever thought of moving. They had, but this was a good, high spot in the jungle with a spring of excellent water. There were no ticks, mosquitoes, or polluted wells. What were a few vampires?

Two Indians, a father and a son, offered to act as guides to the cave. I noticed them calmly testing a 150-foot fiber rope of a type usually used by climbers preparing to ascend the Matterhorn.

"How high is the roof of this cave?" Jule asked.

"How high is the sky, señora?" the son replied carelessly.

The Indians insisted on taking along a double handful of the rough, home-dipped candles that hung in bunches from the ceilings of the huts.

"The candles don't give as much light as our miner's head-lamps," Charlie Mohr pointed out.

"The candles don't have batteries that go dead, either," said the old man stubbornly.

The Indians told us that no one knew how deep the cave might be. "Several people have tried to reach the end, señors," he explained. "Maybe some succeeded. Nobody knows because they never came out again."

It was several miles to the cave and part of the path led up the steep slope of a mountain. To spare Jule, I rented a horse for her. As Jule has always been an expert horsewoman and can ride much more easily than she can walk, this seemed a good idea at the time. But I hadn't counted on the path being nothing more than a faint game trail or the side of the mountain being practically perpendicular. As the slope grew increasingly steep and the trail more indistinct, I urged Jule to get off and walk, but both Jule and the horse's owner were indignant at the idea. "Why, señor, this is a magnificent road—a royal road!" the Indian protested. "People have been *known* to get across it!" Jule insisted that the horse was amazingly sure-footed—my experience with people who love horses is that every horse is amazingly something-or-other—and since we still had a long way to go, I said nothing more.

We were almost to the cave's entrance when I heard a crash behind me, mingled with cries from the Indian. Jule and the horse were rolling over and over down the slope. They crashed through a fringe of bushes and disappeared.

"Scratch one baby," I thought as I plunged down the slope after them, dreading what I'd see at the bottom. They'd gone over a ledge and when I reached it, there was nothing to be seen below but the waving tops of bushes.

"Jule, are you all right?" I shouted.

To my relief, Jule's voice came up from the bushes. "Of course I'm all right, but hurry. This poor horse is dreadfully frightened and I'm having trouble keeping his head up."

When we reached them the terrified horse was thrashing about in the undergrowth on his side while Jule was making a manful effort to get him to his feet. I grabbed for Jule while the Indian grabbed the horse. Both were unhurt, but I was a nervous wreck. To make matters worse, Jule insisted on riding the sweating, trembling animal the rest of the way to the cave.

The entrance to the cave was shrouded by a forest of curiously twisted trees that looked like the papier-mâché creation of a Hollywood murder-mystery set. Our guides led the way down a steep slope into a natural amphitheater, hung with jungle creepers as big as cables. Across from us a black slit like a giant, toothless mouth showed in the white limestone. Vines overhung it like a straggly mustache. The older guide pointed. "This is the vampire grotto."

Leaving the shaken horse to graze, we climbed through the opening into the great entrance hall, 70 feet high. The younger guide picked up some animal bones. "Sometimes animals are foolish enough to spend the night in the cave entrance," he remarked. "They never see daylight again."

As it would be extremely unlikely that any number of the little vampires could kill a large animal in a single night, the bones probably belonged to sick animals that had wandered into the cave to die, but they gave an uncanny touch to the place nonetheless.

We lighted our lamps in our miners' helmets and started downward into the cave. The entrance hall was filled with boulders, piled together like children's marbles. We stepped from one to another, descending deeper and deeper into the earth. The vast mouth of the cave diminished behind us until it looked no bigger than a rathole. Then it vanished completely. We began feeling our way down a great slope in complete darkness except for the puddles of light from our headlamps. At intervals the guides lit candles and left them sticking to the rocks to mark our path back. They showed in the intense darkness like tiny fireflies.

Then the slope ended in a steep drop, falling away into a vast black hole so deep that not even our powerful flashlights could reach the bottom of it. The guides started climbing down the sheer wall, working their way from handhold to handhold. As each of us climbed down the rock, the others held their flashlights so we could see the handholds. Bats began to pour out of the hole like clouds of black confetti but they were the little, insect-eating kind and although I could feel the wind of their leathery wings, none of them touched us.

Below us, the guides had stopped on a ledge. I could see them playing their lights back and forth along an overhang which projected over nothingness. One after another we landed on the ledge and looked over into the abyss. "This is where we use the rope, Señor," the old man explained.

They doubled the rope so we could use one strand as a safety line and climb down the other length. I wrapped my feet around the climbing rope and, gripping the safety line, slowly inched backward over the edge. I began to let myself down seventy feet, and then the rope ended. I hung there, knowing I could never climb up hand over hand, especially with a knapsack on my back containing sixty pounds of scientific equipment.

"I've come to the end of the rope. What shall I do?" I yelled.

"Just let go," the guides shouted.

"What do you mean by that?"

"There's a ledge right under you. Let go and you'll drop on it."

I turned my headlamp down and saw the ledge. As soon as I was off the rope, the rest came down one after another. We climbed down to the floor of the cave and Charlie Mohr held up his hand. "Hear them?"

I listened and heard a noise that sounded like the chittering call of ordinary bats combined with the whistle of steam from a teakettle. "That's the cry of the vampires," said Charlie.

We moved forward slowly into a big room with passages branching off on all sides. They were separated from the main hall by fringes of stalactites hanging like draperies around the openings. Getting down on our hands and knees we crawled under a strip of the stone teeth and ahead of us was a series of great, billowing terraces like monster fountains turned to stone.

We began to climb up the terraces. The rock was as smooth and as slippery as ice, but there were occasional hollows full of water where we could sit and rest. Suddenly on the wall ahead we saw little shapes running and leaping among the formations. The long shadows thrown by our lamps added to their height and looked exactly like little men rushing frantically about, trying to decide what to do. Every now and then one of them would crane himself up to peer down at us. They did not look in the least animal-like. They looked like goblins. An artist trying to illustrate a child's book of fairy stories could not have done better than to reproduce that scene.

These were the vampires. Running on their hind feet and the elbows of their wings, they could go as fast as a four-legged animal. They kept turning their enormous ears about as a rabbit would to pick up the noise we made. As we came closer several ran to the edge of the ledges and sprang into the air. Others stood their ground, baring their teeth and chattering fiercely. I grabbed one old warrior whose fur was a deep reddish-brown and as soft as moleskin. He fought savagely in my gloved hand, screaming with rage. As we put him into the collection box, he spit out two slivers of a brown substance we could not identify but later we found that he had sliced out two small pieces of leather from my glove. They were not bitten out; they were slashed out with his scalpel-sharp incisors. A razor could not have dug out those gouges in my glove as neatly.

Charlie tried to catch some with a net. The vampires seemed to understand perfectly what he was doing. Several of them leaped straight up in the air to avoid his strokes. Others bounced along the ledges like rubber balls and vanished into holes. Some vampires ran up the walls, lifting themselves with two long fingers growing out of the elbows of their wings. These fingers are amazing instruments; each ending in a curved nail like a squirrel's claw. Turning up our lights, we could see dozens of vampires hanging head down on the walls above us. They looked like miniature bearskin rugs, hung upside down with the open mouths and grinning teeth pointing downward.

We found three young vampires in a pocket of the rock, all huddled together with their weird little bulldog faces peering out at us anxiously. Every time they saw the net coming near them, two of the little devils would grab the third and shove him forward while they hid behind him. The victim would stare at us for a moment and then dive under his friends, shoving them back over his shoulder. Jule pulled them apart and lined all three up on a stalagmite but before I could get a picture one of them had kicked another and the fight started all over again.

When we got back to our hotel in Valles, the nearest town to Los Sabinos, and opened our collecting box we found our vampires in a state of shock. We had three adults—including the tough old fellow who'd bitten my glove—and two little ones. The old warrior was the only one who showed any animation, he was still willing to fight, but the others seemed paralyzed. Charlie added to our troubles by telling us that vampires have to eat their own weight in blood every twenty-four hours or they'll die. The Los Sabinos Indians had told us that the bats, in addition to feeding on humans and cattle, will also drink blood from a chicken, biting the bird in the leg (they can't get through the feathers). We had invested in a couple of chickens but these bats were obviously in no condition to feed on anything and we didn't know when they had last eaten.

"You may as well let me make skins of them," Charlie suggested callously and I felt the same way, but Jule wouldn't listen to either of us. "There must be some way to save them," she insisted. "If I could raise Reddy and Concha, I ought to be able to raise vampires. All they need to do is find out that we're their friends."

As usual, Jule went to work with her medicine dropper although now it was filled with fresh blood, contributed by the local butcher who frankly thought we were crazy. The only one she could work with was the old warrior who, we discovered, had only one eye. He had presumably lost the other in a fight with another vampire, possibly over a lady bat. The old fighter didn't take kindly to being force-fed. He bit, shrieked, whistled, and struggled in Jule's gloved hand. He positively refused to suck from the end of the dropper. The whole project seemed hopeless, but Jule refused to be discouraged. "Give him time, he'll have to quiet down a little first," she insisted. An hour later the old boy had quieted down enough so he'd sit crouched in Jule's palm, only snarling slightly when she scratched his head.

Then Jule tried the medicine dropper again. To make sure the blood was flowing easily, she pressed the bulb of the dropper slightly until a drop of blood appeared at the glass tip. An astonishing thing happened. The bat sat up, stretched out his neck, and with his curious pink, club-shaped tongue licked the drop off. Jule offered him another drop and he licked that away too. He was feeding.

The other bats were rigid from shock and Jule had to massage them gently until they came around. By two o'clock that morning, Jule had managed to feed them all. Her system was to put one of the bats next to the old warrior who was feeding readily. After a minute or so, the other bat would nudge over to get some and a fight would start. Then I'd decoy the old fellow away with another medicine dropper while Jule continued feeding the other bat.

Our main problem was keeping the blood from coagulating. Charlie Mohr solved that difficulty for us. By putting the fresh blood in a bottle with some marbles and shaking it up, the corpuscles of the blood were broken down and it would remain liquid for some time.

By the time we got back to Taxco, our bats were so used to us that we could feed them from a burro we rented for the purpose. The burro didn't mind the business—in fact, he was far more afraid of us than of the bats—and they took comparatively little blood. Most of the time, the burro didn't even know he was being bitten.

I wanted to see how vampires would attack a human being but here Jule unreasonably rebelled. "Dan, I've been willing to do almost anything with you in the animal line but I won't be eaten by vampire bats," she declared. "Maybe if I weren't going to have a baby I wouldn't mind." So I had to act as the subject while Jule took notes.

But the bats positively refused to bite me. They would crawl up and down my bare arm or over my legs and never offer to bite. Finally Jule broke down but they wouldn't bite her either. It was very discouraging.

At last we decided that they were still nervous about us. I would have to pretend to be asleep while Jule hid in our bathroom and watched through the curtains.

In spite of all our precautions, the bats still stubbornly refused to cooperate. I finally did fall asleep and Jule reported what happened.

As usual, it was the old fellow who proved the boldest. He was hanging with the others from the cornice of our bedroom. He woke up, licked his lips, and then stretched his wings, one after the other. Then he began to turn his little bulldog head from side to side, his nose twitching as though he were scenting the air.

Instead of flying over to the bed, he climbed down the wall using his hooks, hopping across the floor like a toad, and then bounded onto the bed covers. He sat there some time watching me and listening to my breathing. Then he quietly reared up on the tips of his wings and crawled up the covers toward my face, every motion elaborately cautious.

When he reached my face, he moved back and forth around the pillow, looking for a good place to bite. We later found that a vampire tries to get a spot with few nerves and plenty of blood so he seldom chooses the throat—not as dramatic as sinking his fangs into the jugular vein but far more practical. When he finally decided on a good spot, he approached cautiously and nipped the side of my neck gently. I tossed and he scuttled back hurriedly and waited until I was quiet again. Then he tried the lobe of my ear.

Here Jule interfered. "I just couldn't stand there and watch him drink your blood," she told me later. I must say that I was just as happy.

We did, however, watch the bats drink from the burro. When a vampire bites, he stretches his mouth open to the fullest extent and makes a single quick slash with his two long incisors. He does not stab but slashes out two small gouges and then instantly jumps back to watch the quarry's reaction.

If he has hit an insensitive spot, he then hurries in and begins to lap, not suck, the flowing blood. If the animal starts or shakes himself, the bat waits until he quiets down and then tries another spot. Once he has found a good spot, he will always return to that same place again. Each of our bats had a different spot where he fed on the burro. Indians told us that they can kill the bats by seeing where they've bitten an animal and then smearing poison on the scab. The bat will surely return to exactly the same spot.

A bite made by a vampire will continue to bleed long after the bat has left it, and more blood is lost this way than from the actual bite. Scientists have argued that the saliva of the bats must contain some chemical that prevents the blood from coagulating but apparently this is not so. The action of the tongue helps to keep the wound open while the bat is lapping but it seemed to us that the bats know enough to cut into a vein. The action of the victim's heart keeps pumping the blood out and this is why the wound continues to bleed. Our young vampires hadn't developed the approved technique and would bite the burro anywhere, but often they couldn't draw enough blood to satisfy them. Then they'd have to try somewhere else. But once they learned where a vein was, they never forgot the location.

I can't say the vampires made particularly good pets. They seemed to be highly specialized. Apart from their biting technique, they never showed any intelligence. They did learn to recognize Jule and would come to her for blood from the medicine dropper while they avoided me. Some even learned to lap from a saucer. Even when they became so tame that Jule could pick them up, stroke them, feed them, and then hang them up on the wall as though she were hanging up a scarf, they never responded to affection as did Reddy, our red-bellied squirrel, and never showed any interest in what was going on about them.

When it was time to leave Mexico, we let them go. As bats have an astonishing homing instinct, I've no doubt that their found their way back to their cave in Los Sabinos. They were interesting but hardly lovable.

Ten

We could live in Mexico for $50 a month, and I was able to make this much by writing for the old pulp-paper magazines like *Adventure* (which paid two cents a word) and an occasional piece in the aristocratic "slicks" like *Esquire* and *Collier's*, but the arrival of a baby would seriously disrupt our budget. Poor Jule felt herself solely responsible for this disaster in spite of a certain amount of cooperation on my part, and kept assuring me "A baby is just another kind of pet and perhaps may be even more fun." Unfortunately, babies are also expensive, and raising one in Taxco—even for Jule—would surely prove more complicated than raising a squirrel, coati, or even a vampire bat. Jule's family, the Junkers, generously offered to take us in during this trying period, plus any spare animals we felt that we couldn't do without. So in 1941 we left Mexico and returned to the Main Line, taking with us Águila, the coatis, the kinkajous, Concha, and of course Wriggles. The other animals we turned loose in the hills.

The baby turned out to be a little girl and we named her after Jule. Águila tried to eat her; it took Jule some time to persuade the bird that this new creature was part of the family, like Wriggles, and not a new kind of iguana. But the mother kinkajou took a violent dislike to the baby—sheer jealousy. The kink had fallen into the habit of climbing up into Jule's lap every day for her siesta and now she found her place pre-empted by this stranger. The kink conceived such a hatred of the baby that it was positively unsafe to have them in the same house together. Unfortunately, of all our animals the only one to fascinate baby Jule was the kink, which looked so much like a teddy bear. Jule tried hard to reconcile the kink to the baby and when little Jule was crawling around on the floor, she'd give the kink a banana to eat, hoping that in this way our pet would make up with the child. The kink always ate the banana sitting up on her hind legs, steadying herself with her tail, and peeling it with her forepaws. Baby Jule would crawl over hopefully and then hesitatingly put out a hand, only to be greeted with a savage snarl. She would then quietly crawl away backward, sit down, and burst into heartbroken tears. The coatis and Concha were perfectly willing to play with the baby but she didn't want them; she wanted the cuddly looking kinkajou. Finally Jule told me bluntly, "Dan, we're either going to have to get rid of the baby or the kinkajous and I want to keep the baby." I urged Jule to wait. After all, she could always have another baby while kinkajous were rare and valuable.

The coatis had the run of the house and made themselves a snug little nest in Mrs. Junker's box spring, from whence they would emerge unexpectedly at all hours of the day and night. Concha slept with us but liked to go for midnight forays to the icebox. She couldn't get the door open, but the coatis could and after Concha had cried for a while, they'd usually dart out of their box-spring home, run downstairs, and open it for her. Then the three of them would share whatever they found inside. We were afraid that after the warmth of Taxco, Águila might catch cold in a Pennsylvania winter, so the Junkers moved their car out of the garage and turned it over to the eagle.

It did seem to me that having a baby in the house was an imposition on the Junkers and I apologized to them several times for the inconvenience we were causing them. At last Mrs. Junker broke down and said, "Dan, the baby is really no trouble at all, but could you keep the animals under more control? I don't mind the coatis sleeping in my box spring during the day, but they have fights all night long underneath me and it keeps me awake." I was completely astonished; it had never occurred to me that anyone would object to animals around the house. After all, how many people have had the privilege of keeping coatis in their box springs? But Jule explained to me that her mother didn't understand animals as well as we did, so I moved the coatis up with us.

The Junkers grew so accustomed to the animals that often they forgot to warn people about them. All our animals were curious-looking creatures, so it was interesting to watch people's reaction to them. Even visitors who were cold sober were often reluctant to say they could see something hanging by its tail from the chandelier or complain that an anteater had come out of the woodwork and gone off with one of their overshoes. Jule had several sisters and one of them had a girl friend down from school over the week end. The guest was taking a bath when Poncho pushed open the door, trotted over, took a drink out of the tub, and then hurried out again. The girl said nothing to us but during dinner she seemed curiously distraught. At last she blurted out, "I know you'll think I'm crazy, but I could have sworn something with a long nose came into the bathroom while I was taking my bath and drank out of the tub. Am I losing my mind or what?" An old college friend of mine dropped in to see us and the Junkers most kindly offered to put him up for the night. I heard a little disturbance in his room and went in to see if he was all right. I found him sitting on the edge of his bed badly shaken with the baby kink snoring away on his pillow. He gasped out: "Thank heaven you've come. You've no idea what a weird sensation it is to be half-asleep and have something warm and furry climb in with you, wrap its tail about your neck, and then start to snore." We never meet but he repeats this story—and it gets better every time.

We'd only been back a few days when I wrote a story called "Hunting Dragons with an Eagle" and sent it to the *Saturday Evening Post*. They published it and it made a minor sensation. A few weeks after the story appeared, Universal Pictures asked me to make a technicolor picture based on the story and offered to supply a cameraman and a director. We were to go back to Taxco and make the picture on location, using our other animals as minor stars in the production.

Making this picture involved several problems, including baby Jule. The Junkers generously offered to take care of her while we were in Mexico, but there was also the problem of Águila. She had become very suspicious of iguanas ever since she had been bitten, and although she would chase them in fine style, when an iguana turned to fight, Águila would alight and march around him at a respectful distance until we came up and rewarded her with a piece of meat. This procedure worked very well as far as we were concerned because we wanted to catch the lizards uninjured, but for motion-picture purposes it wouldn't do.

As bald eagles were by then protected by a new and wise federal law, we decided to use a golden eagle. I was able to obtain one from Colorado; we named this new bird Tequila, after the fiery Mexican drink.

Tequila and Águila were as different as two birds could possibly be. Physically, Tequila was considerably larger. Águila weighed about 10 pounds and had a six-foot wingspread;

Tequila weighed over fifteen pounds and had an eight-foot spread. Tequila's hind talon was half again as big as Águila's and her grip was correspondingly more powerful. The ice-hockey glove I'd used with Águila wasn't thick enough to stand Tequila's grip and I reinforced the back with a piece of board, thinking I had the problem licked. The first time Tequila clamped down on my glove, her hind talon split the board and went deep into my hand. My hand was so swollen I couldn't use it for several days.

While I was laid up, Jule went out to feed Tequila. Because the two birds fought, we kept Tequila in the loft of the Junker garage and Jule had to open the door to toss in Tequila's food. One day while she was doing it, Tequila flung herself through the partly opened door and grabbed Jule by the shoulder.

Luckily, Jule was wearing a heavy winter coat so the eagle's talons didn't enter the flesh, but the bird was so powerful that Jule couldn't get her loose. With the bird still trying to throw her down, Jule managed to reach the open garage door and shouted for help. As soon as Tequila saw the open sky, she let go of Jule and was off.

I was lying in bed and saw the bird flap by. For a moment, I didn't realize what was happening and only thought "There goes a golden eagle. Don't see many of them in this part of the world." Then I did a sort of double take and leaped out of bed yelling "A golden eagle! Tequila's loose!" Still in my pajamas I ran for the back door, passing through the kitchen. By great good luck, the Junkers were having a roast that day and Mrs. Junker had it laid out on the table, preparatory to popping it into the oven. I grabbed the roast as I went. As I passed through the yard, I collected some clothesline. Luckily, we had put falcon bells on the bird and I could just hear them as I ran down the street.

Mrs. Junker told me later she would have made some comment about the roast as it was wartime and meat was strictly rationed.

The whole family had been saving up coupons for weeks to get that roast. But she forgot all about the roast as Jule reeled into the house sobbing "I've lost Dan's eagle and he'll never forgive me."

"I'm sure Dan loves you better than an eagle," Mrs. Junker reassured her.

"You don't know Dan," wept Jule, collapsing on a chair.

Tequila came down in a tree on the campus of Bryn Mawr College, the famous university for girls. Crawling on my belly through the underbrush, I was able to toss the roast, out where Tequila could see it, first tying it firmly to the clothesline. Then I settled down to wait.

I'd been there about half an hour when to my annoyance I saw two policemen crawling through the bushes toward me. Strange figures might easily make Tequila fly off, never to be seen again, and I shouted to them to go away. Instead, they rushed me.

"O.K., Buster, what are you doing in the girls' dorms wearing pajamas?" asked the biggest policeman.

"What do you think I'm doing, I'm catching eagles," I told him.

Even after they saw Tequila, they still seemed suspicious and at last I told them to call Mrs. Chadwick-Collins, then one of the college officials, who was an old friend of the family's. When she heard about it, she merely said, "Oh, that must be Dan Mannix. A very fine old Main Line family; they've been crazy for generations. He's probably after some sort of animal." The policemen left, muttering to themselves, and eventually Tequila came down and I was able to catch her.

As soon as my hand had healed, we left for Mexico taking the two eagles and the other animals with us. Mrs. Junker seemed almost relieved to have us go—especially Poncho and Pedro, who gave her a loving nip as we loaded them into the car. She assured us that baby Jule would be absolutely no trouble, which was nice of her as babies are a terrible nuisance. Although the car was rather crowded, we reached Taxco without trouble and were able to get our old home and our dear Maria as housekeeper. Chon was delighted with the new eagle and proved as skillful in working Tequila as he had with Águila.

As we had hoped, Tequila made a better hunter than Águila. Her usual method of attack was to knock an iguana down with a strafing attack—diving over him and delivering a terrible raking blow with her hind talons as she went past—and then, swooping back, pick up the unconscious reptile and carry it off to eat. Usually she did not go far but if by chance the iguana happened to be on the edge of a cliff, Tequila would occasionally pick up the lizard, set her wings and soar across the valley to the next ridge. This was easy enough for Tequila but as I had to go after her (Tequila, like all raptors, would not return after a full gorge) it was hard on me. Not being able to soar across valleys, I had to climb down one cliff, cross the intervening valley, climb the second ridge, get the bird, and bring her back on my fist. This trick of Tequila's once nearly cost the bird her life even though it also gave her a chance to demonstrate her phenomenal strength.

One afternoon Tequila had seized a small iguana and carried him off across a valley. Through the field glasses I could see her riding the air currents with open wings like a man riding a surfboard. She came down on a distant range a good mile away as the crow flies.

Unfortunately, I wasn't a crow so I had to climb down the mountain, cross the valley, and start up the far range. While I was sweating up the steep slope, I happened to look up. Silhouetted against the sky was a group of Indians with a yelping hound. One of the men carried an ancient flintlock rifle. They were obviously looking for the eagle.

I was tired but I climbed those last hundred yards at full speed. Crawling over the top of the ridge, I saw Tequila sitting not fifteen feet away with the dead iguana still in her foot. As I started toward her, the Indians' dog burst out of a thin stand of corn and rushed at the eagle, barking savagely.

Tequila turned her head slowly to stare at the yelping dog. Her contempt seemed to drive the hound crazy. He made a wild dash at the bird, snapping and growling.

Without letting go of the iguana, Tequila suddenly grabbed the hound by the muzzle with her other foot. With one twist she flung him down and held him helpless. Fifty feet away on the other side of the corn, the Indian hunters were calling to the dog but the hound was muzzled so completely by the eagle's foot that he could not cry out. I crawled over to them. The dog was rigid, paralyzed by the bird's crushing grip.

I tried to rip Tequila's foot loose but it was like trying to loosen welded steel. The dog was dying and obviously in great pain. The Indians were still searching for the dog, calling frequently, and it would be only a few minutes before they found us. I had no desire to face a group of armed mountain Indians whose hunting dog had just been killed by my eagle. It was a grisly business but there was nothing else to do.

I pulled out my heavy hunting knife and put the dying dog out of his pain. Then as Tequila still wouldn't let go, I was forced to decapitate the dead animal. I left a ten-peso note beside the body and with Tequila clutching the dead iguana in one foot and the head in the other, I worked my way hurriedly down the cliff.

When I was well away from the range, I sat down with Tequila in a cave and talked to her until she dropped the remains of the dog. Her long, curved hind talons had gone right through the skull.

We had one more accident while flying the eagles—this one of a far more serious nature.

Whenever we flew the eagles, a group of children from an Indian village in the hills would came out to watch us. Neither of the birds took the slightest notice of them, but we were naturally worried and I hired two of the older boys to make sure that none of the smaller children came too near the eagles. However, as weeks passed and the eagles would often fly directly over the children's heads without even glancing at them, we began to relax.

One afternoon I had Águila stationed on a rock and was trying to get an iguana to bolt from a pile of rocks where he had taken refuge. A crowd of the children had collected but were some distance off and I paid no attention to them. While I was working among the rocks, a small boy carrying a baby slung on his back papoose-style suddenly bolted out from behind the pile and started to run toward the other children. Apparently he had arrived late and didn't know what was going on.

Águila was poised on the edge of her boulder watching every move I made with fierce intensity, ready to launch into the air the moment anything moved. As the child darted out, Águila shot off the rock and came rushing down on him. Chon shouted to the boy in Spanish, "Fall down!" but the child was either too terrified to hear or did not see the bird. Jule and I both shouted to Águila but the eagle was too intent on the moving object to stop.

Just before Águila hit the boy, she evidently realized her mistake. She was going too fast to stop, but she threw her legs out in front of her as a man might throw out his arms to break an impact. As the baby was on the boy's back, Águila hit the baby. All three of them rolled on the ground together.

Jule and I rushed in. Jule grabbed the baby and I picked up Águila, who was sitting on the ground with open wings, clearly puzzled and uncertain what had happened. The boy lay on the ground, screaming with surprise and terror.

Jule hastily examined the baby, who was unhurt, having been protected by the heavy woolen serape the boy had used as a carrying sling. The boy had a slight scratch on his shoulder where the tip of one of Águila's talons had gone through the wool.

Jule took both children on Teresa and galloped with them to their village. As soon as we got back to Taxco, we sent a doctor to examine the children. The doctor told us that except for the talon scratch neither child had been injured but the parents had put the baby under the care of a local witch who had told them she could frighten the evil eagle spirit out of the children. When the doctor arrived, he had found the baby laid out on the floor while the witch sat beside him, beating him with a rattle and screaming.

Early the next morning Maria told us that a committee from the village headed by the children's parents were waiting outside. The mother told us that the baby was hysterical, crying constantly, and the witch wanted 50 pesos to effect a cure. We suggested that they rely on the doctor, but both parents indignantly refused. At last, we gave them the 50 pesos.

The next morning the whole group was back again. The witch's charm had failed. "She has done everything," the mother assured us. "Dropped snakes on him, let tarantulas crawl over his face, sat up all night blowing a flute in his ear but the child only cries the louder."

But, it seemed, all hope was not lost. The witch knew of an even stronger charm which was certain to cure but this charm cost 500 pesos.

Jule had a brilliant idea. She suggested asking the priest to see the baby and report on the case. The mother refused. "I am grateful to the priest for much that he does but he is very narrow-minded about a useful practice like witchcraft," she explained.

We refused to give the witch any more money unless the priest approved so the committee trudged sadly back to the village.

A week or so later, Jule happened to ride past the village and saw the boy who had been hit by Águila playing beside the house. In a hammock near him lay the sleeping baby looking very healthy. Jule rode on and passed the witch. The witch glowered at her and Jule saw the woman slip around the corner of the house where the children were. A moment later came a terrible yell from the baby, much as if someone had just stuck a pin in him. The witch came hurrying back after Jule.

"You see, the baby is still sick from the eagle spirit!" she screamed. "If you had only given me the five hundred pesos, everything would be all right now."

The witch never did get the 500 pesos, but even with the 50 she probably still regards it as her biggest case.

We made the picture for Universal without incident except that Águila took a violent dislike to our director. It was typical of Águila to take these strong likes and dislikes while Tequila was perfectly indifferent to everyone. Águila was now an expert flier; in fact, rather too expert. The moment she was released in the mountains she would go soaring off, gliding from one thermal draft to another, constantly rising higher and higher until she was only a tiny dot in the blue sky. At first it was often difficult to bring her down for the pictures—but we soon solved that difficulty. The director had only to show himself and instantly the tiny dot would begin to grow. We could see the bird dropping, her wings folded tight against her body, her feet folded up under her ready for the strike. The director would wait as long as he dared and then race for his car. Promptly Águila would unfold her wings, banking in the air currents as she came around to take after him. Giving a few quick, hard wingbeats, she would increase her speed as she flashed in. Several times she almost caught him as he dived into his coupé, slamming the door behind him. Then Águila would circle around the car, screaming with fury, until I called her down.

After a few of these attacks she realized she couldn't fly the director down. On the next attempt, she circled the car as usual, screaming lustily. Then she suddenly quieted and landed gently on the top of the coupé. She tiptoed softly across the roof until she was just above the door. There she waited, without a sound, cocking her head on one side exactly like a robin listening to a worm. After a few seconds, the director cautiously opened the door, stuck his head out and asked "Is she gone?" In a flash, Águila had him by the back of the neck. It took three of us to pry her loose. This was quite the cleverest thing Águila ever did.

After the motion picture crew left, Jule and I decided to take a vacation in Acapulco. Acapulco was then little more than an Indian village with only one good hotel, the Mirador. Leaving the animals in charge of Marie and Chon, we drove down to the seacoast.

The Mirador turned out to be built on the side of a cliff overlooking a marvelously blue Pacific. The architect who designed the hotel had taken advantage of the various nooks and crannies of the cliff and, as a result, nearly every room gave the impression of being a little cottage all to itself. We spent the first few days swimming and resting. Then we took a boat cruise up a lagoon some twelve miles north of Acapulco called Pie de la Cuesta. Here I decided to do some bird photography—the lagoon was full of magnificent tropical birds: white egrets, black-capped night herons, pink spoonbills, even a pair of storks.

There were also the black, hooked-beak cormorants sitting on mangrove stumps. Although they were not colorful, to me they were the most interesting of all the birds because I knew they could be trained to fish, much as hawks are trained to hunt. Fishing with trained cormorants was a great sport in Europe some three hundred years ago. Charles I even had a "Master of the Royal Cormorants" and used to fish with them from a barge while floating with his court on the Thames. Although I'd never trained cormorants and never supposed that I'd ever have the opportunity to try, I had read quite a bit on the subject and knew something about it.

No one knows when cormorant fishing began, but it probably originated in the uplands of China because the narrow streams and fast currents there make the use of nets impractical. There are records of it going back to 1000 B.C., and it was probably old then. The first white man to witness this sport was Father Odoric, who went to China thirty years after Marco Polo and described what he called "fishing with trained water crows." The French took him literally and later called the birds *corbeau marin,* which the English turned into *cormorant.*

The Chinese made quite an art of the business. They wouldn't use wild birds, but developed their own breed of cormorants, raising the birds in big hatcheries like chickens. According to Friar Odoric, the mother cormorant was allowed to sit on the eggs "until she turned red in the face," when the eggs were put under a hen. The young birds were fed eels' blood until they were "hard summed." Then their training began.

The youngsters were tethered near the edge of a lake by long strings and small dead fish were tossed into the shallow water. As the fish were thrown, the trainer whistled the "dive" call. When the bird had got its fish, it was pulled by the string while the trainer whistled the "retrieve" signal. Then the bird was rewarded. Eventually bigger fish were used and a loose-fitting ring put around the bird's neck so it couldn't swallow its catch.

According to these early missionaries, a flock of trained cormorants operated in a way that would put a well-trained pack of foxhounds to shame. Once they had located a school of fish, they would spread out and form a ring around it. Then they would begin working in, grabbing fish as they went. When one bird swam back to the boat to disgorge his catch, the two cormorants on either side closed in to take its place. If one bird got out of formation, the whole flock would scream and beat with their wings until the miscreant got back into place. There was always a head cormorant, who operated as a kind of top sergeant; the Japanese (who also went in for cormorant fishing) called him *Ichi* (the boss). Ichi was the last bird to be put in the water and the first to be taken out. If any of the others did anything it shouldn't, Ichi beat up the offender. Ichi always sat on the boat's bow and the rest were lined up according to rank—the best birds next to Ichi, the boots down by the stern. If a bird got in the wrong place, the rest bit him until he found his proper spot.

Cormorant fishing is apparently rare in modern China but is still quite common in Japan. The Japanese do not bother to train the birds so elaborately as did the Chinese. The Chinese were able to dispense with the collar and creance; the Japanese cormorants always wear both. When a bird gets a fish, it's dragged back to the boat and choked until it coughs up the fish. One fisherman can handle the strings of a dozen birds (although how he does it without getting himself and the cormorants tied into a knot is beyond me). In Japan, cormorant fishing is usually done at night by torchlight, which dazzles the fish and makes the whole affair much easier.

During the middle of the last century, cormorant fishing was quite a fad with French and British sportsmen, people even going to the lengths of dressing up like Chinese mandarins for the process. A head cormorant called North Pole was sold for $500. The birds were taught to fly to their owners' fists like trained hawks, and during the training period their beaks were covered with straw scabbards (an excellent idea, as I discovered). They were worked without strings but wore their collars. They did not retrieve; the owner had to wade over and take the fish away.

I decided to adopt the European technique. I practiced first with anhingas—a fishing bird that is smaller and more delicately built than a cormorant and can only catch small fish. Although I almost lost my right eye when one struck at me with his long, needle-sharp beak, I succeeded in training them reasonably well. Two years later when we returned to Acapulco on another trip, I started on cormorants.

There were still many questions I had about these diving birds, and I couldn't find the answer either in books on the history of cormorant training or works on natural history. How long can a cormorant stay under water? Can a bird actually swim down a fish, or are they able to catch them only by a sudden dive (equivalent to a falcon's swoop) or by a fluke of some kind (the anhingas caught nearly all their minnows by driving them into shallow water)? How can they see under water? How intelligent are they in their fishing? Not being able to find the answer to any of these questions, I decided to find out for myself.

European cormorant trainers preferred adult birds for the same reason falconers prefer adult hawks; they were experienced fliers and hunters. But I decided to use eyesses. There was a small island in the lagoon where a number of cormorants were nesting among the mangrove trees. Jule and I set out with a native fisherman paddling the canoe.

I climbed a tree that held several of the stick-platform nests, whitewashed with droppings, each containing a couple of young birds with their throat pouches going like delirious balloons. Hanging some 30 feet above the ground, I stuck my head over the edge of a nest.

Instantly one of the young cormorants lunged at me with his daggerlike beak. The blow was as quick as the strike of a rattlesnake and the hooked beak sliced the lobe of my ear as neatly as a razor.

"Look out for your eyes!" Jule shouted from below.

Holding on with one hand, I grabbed the bird with the other. He had a two-and-a-half-foot wingspread, a neck as long as his body, and claws on the ends of his webbed feet. I felt as though I'd tackled a combination eagle, snake, and wildcat. The cormorant beat me over the head with his wings, tore at me with his claws, and tried to put out my eyes with his beak. At last both of us fell out of the tree into the mud. Jule grabbed the bird and shoved him into a bag. After another struggle, I managed to secure the second youngster.

That night I put on the diving mask I used when skin-diving to protect my eyes and tried to get the eyesses to eat. Neither bird would take the fish I offered; they were more interested in trying to maim me. They folded up their necks like lazy tongs and then struck at my face so swiftly that I couldn't follow the movement. They evidently regarded the mask as a cowardly device, for after stubbing their beak on it a few times they gave up and concentrated on the fish. Anything up to a pound or so vanished in a flash. If it were bigger than that, they required a couple of gulps to get it down.

Later, I put hawk jesses on them and carried them around. The birds tamed fairly quickly but when I tried getting them to retrieve dead fish from the lagoon with creances tied to the jesses, they rebelled. Cormorants have specially hooked beaks designed to hold onto a slippery fish—and the hooks can also hold onto the trainer. Worse yet, the bites always infected.

How the Orientals overcome this problem I don't know, but after several days I decided I was doing more harm than good with the creances. The birds had begun to hate me; they baited off their perches whenever I came near and fought whenever I tried to carry them. I abandoned the whole system. Instead, I started training them to fly to my fist like hawks, rewarding them with a small piece of fish for each successful flight. This method worked far better and we became friends again. They would even follow me around when I went for a walk, paddling along flat-footed like ducks and gobbling eagerly. If I got too far away, they would stop to rest but I had only to turn and call and both birds would take to the air instantly, zooming toward me and then lighting on my gloved arm by backing with their wings and throwing out their webbed feet with exactly the motion a duck uses when lighting on water. If they started to slip off they'd grab my shirt with their beaks to steady themselves.

One bird was slightly larger than the other so I considered him to be a male and the other a female, although I don't think there's any real way to distinguish the sexes among cormorants. The "male" was quick, nervous, and unpredictable. One moment he'd be climbing up my knee, hooking himself up with his beak like a parrot, and begging for fish. Then without any warning he'd let me have it with his beak. The "female" was slower to approach, but she finally made up her mind to come over and she made no attempt to bite.

I named them Ichi and Mrs. Ichi. They weighed about 7 pounds each and would eat four pounds of fish a day. I never saw anything eat the way those birds did, although in Europe there is a saying, "he eats like a cormorant." Their gluttony is the real reason they make such good fishers—they'll keep going long after any other bird would have gotten tired and stopped.

Our picture with Universal had proved so successful that Jule and I had been able to buy a small farm in Pennsylvania; when we returned, we took Mr. and Mrs. Ichi with us. We had a pond on the farm and I threw in some live bait, expecting the birds to dive after it. They paid no attention to the live fish, not connecting them with the dead fish they had been eating. I should have foreseen this difficulty, but like most people I still had the belief that all predators instinctively recognized their natural prey. Experience should have taught me that nothing could be further from the truth.

Young predators are taught what to kill by their parents, and soon become "wedded" to one particular type of quarry, much as children who are used to one particular type of food find it difficult to switch to another. On one of our Mexican trips, Jule brought her twelve-year-old-brother with her and the boy nearly starved to death because he refused to eat tortillas and frijoles instead of bread and potatoes. Anyone who has tried to introduce children to a new type of cooking has encountered this problem. The same is true of wild animals. In the first place, they simply do not recognize the new food as edible. The principal reason there are not more "chicken hawks" is that hawks seldom realize the chickens are good to eat. A farmer once told me he had seen a red-tailed hawk make repeated raids on his barnyard and waited for the bird with a shotgun. Sure enough, he saw the hawk plunge down among the chickens but when the bird rose he was carrying a rat. The farmer found that the red-tail was catching the rats that came to eat at the feeding troughs and never disturbed the chickens. The hawk was not showing any morality; he simply did not recognize the chickens as edible. If he had once killed one by chance and happened to eat it, he would never have bothered with rats again but would have become a confirmed "chicken hawk."

It is rare that lions or tigers attack humans, but once one of the big cats does by chance kill a human and discovers these strange two-legged creatures are not only easy to kill but also good to eat, he becomes a man-eater. Such an animal has been known to charge through a herd of cattle to get at the herdboy. The famous "man-eaters of Tsavo," two young male lions who stopped the building of the Mombasa-Uganda railway in 1898 because of their constant attacks on the Indian laborers, refused to come to any bait set out for them and finally live humans had to be exhibited in cages. These two lions probably developed their abnormal tendencies because the corpses of laborers who died from fever and other causes were left in the bush instead of being buried and the lions, acting as scavengers, found and ate them—thus developing a taste for human flesh.

Man-eaters often become amazingly selective in their choice of food. Jim Corbett tells of a man-eating tiger in India who would attack only women. While in India myself, I heard of a tiger who would attack only postmen. This animal had killed a postman by chance and after that haunted the mail routes but, not realizing that other humans were equally good to eat, would only attack individuals in the correct uniform. This tiger was finally shot by a game ranger who disguised himself as a postman to provoke the attack. On a far less dramatic basis, I once lost a fine pair of green jays we had brought back from Mexico because neither bird would eat anything but a special sort of grain. They had been taken from the nest and raised on this grain from fledglings. I took a supply of it with me but had no idea that the jays were so wedded to this one diet that they would eat nothing else. When I ran out of the grain, the birds died.

I was luckier with the cormorants, although for a long while it seemed as though neither would even bother to stick his head under water to look for fish. Instead, they swam about gobbling happily and watching me. I had to put the dead fish on the bank, then half in the water, and then just under the surface. It was several days before the birds would dive after them. As they still refused to catch live fish, I had to throw dead and living fish in together. In their excitement, the birds would grab both. By slowly eliminating the dead fish, I taught them to fish. Since then I have seen wild cormorants teach their young to fish by first dropping dead fish into the water and later live fish regurgitated from their throat pouches.

When the birds were used to live prey, I took them to a stream where there were plenty of small brook trout. But here the Ichis showed more adaptability than I'd foreseen. They'd learned that anything which moved was potential food—and this included frogs, small snakes, crawfish, and even field mice. For the next few days the couple behaved like setter pups turned loose in a field who'd rather chase rabbits than find a covey of pheasants.

In my opinion, most predators—instead of being blood-thirsty killers—are lazy and would far rather pick up food the easy way than go to the trouble of hunting it. Also, young predators lack the skill and confidence to know how to tackle difficult quarry and need a long apprenticeship under the tutelage of their parents. It is surprisingly difficult for a predator to catch quarry; many of them rely on teamwork, either between a pair hunting together or an entire group, as with wild dogs. From what I have read about trained-cormorant fishing, the birds work together as a group. It would be interesting to find out if wild cormorants also use this technique. I can only say that until the Ichis learned to work together, they never caught anything but small fish and these mainly by luck. A single bird had almost no chance against a trout; the fish doubled too fast for him. But with both birds working together, the odds were with the cormorants.

The first time I saw the birds exhibit any evidence of teamwork was in pursuit of an old trout that lived in a pool under a bridge. I usually worked the birds upstream so the silt they kicked up wouldn't muddy the water ahead and make it hard for them to see. The trout got to know this and kept a careful watch downstream. As soon as he saw the birds coming, he'd vanish like magic.

One afternoon while we were still a hundred feet from the bridge, the birds stopped and regarded it thoughtfully. Ichi, always the more enterprising, took off and flew to the upstream side of the bridge to try his luck there. Naturally, the fish promptly bolted downstream, where it had to dive under Mrs. Ichi. She turned a complete somersault trying to get it, and the trout was driven into the shallow water. Ichi was right behind, but at the last moment the fish gave a sudden jump and landed on a mud flat, flopping desperately. The birds, swimming underwater, didn't know what had happened. I tried to pick up the fish but it managed to flop back into the water— where Mrs. Ichi promptly grabbed him. After that, the birds would split up when coming to a pool, Ichi going upstream and Mrs. Ichi keeping below.

They learned a number of other tricks as time went on. If there was white sand on the bottom of a pool, a fish would be frightened by the shadows of the cormorants below it and often would shoot right up into their beaks. The birds learned to wait for this. If one bird got a fish too big to swallow, the other would come to help. Both birds would sink their hooked beaks into the catch and tow it ashore. Cormorants have to swallow a fish whole; they can't bite off pieces, so in the wild state I doubt if they ever catch a large fish. I'd cut off the head and tail for them and if I didn't get there fast enough, the birds would start honking for me to hurry.

Cormorants live to be about thirty years old and keep learning all the time, so my birds were just pups even after six months' fishing. An experienced old bird will often catch four or five small fish out of a school and hold them in his neck and throat pouch before returning to shore but mine, once they had a fish, would swim to me at once, letting the rest of the school go. Also, being young, they spent much of their time playing. Cormorants can stay underwater for an astonishing length of time; they have air sacs within the body which they apparently can use as a supply of oxygen. My birds often stayed under for five or six minutes. This ability to stay underwater is very handy when they're after a fish, but often the birds would become fascinated by a shiny pebble or an old tin can at the bottom of a deep pool and spend a minute or so looking it over. I could beat the water, yell, throw in bait—the birds paid no attention to me.

There was not the slightest doubt that the birds could see underwater. Diving birds have a special transparent membrane like an extra eyelid which they shut into place when swimming under the surface. This membrane, called the nictitating membrane, serves exactly the same purpose as a skindiver's goggles—it protects the eyes from the water but, being transparent, enables the bird to see. I would often go swimming with the birds, wearing a skin-diver's outfit and the tympanic membrane could be clearly seen underwater. It is white and translucent.

It is hard to believe that anything can outswim a fish, but actually several birds and mammals can do so quite easily. In fact, it seemed to me that the fish depended more on being able to outwit the birds than on mere speed. Unless you're a fisherman and know how wary fish can be, you probably don't regard fish as being smart—until I started hunting pigeons and rabbits with hawks I didn't regard them as being smart either. All animals show remarkable ability in avoiding their natural enemies, and no fish grows old unless he knows plenty about the habits of fishing birds and can outwit them. I discovered that most fresh-water fish can only swim hard for a short time; then the fish becomes so tired that a man can reach into the water and scoop him out by hand. An old fish knows that it can't rely on speed alone and has as many tricks as a fox, which it will use one after another to fool its pursuers.

The most elaborate hunt the birds ever made was in an old quarry after a large-mouth bass. It lasted forty-five minutes, although the fish wasn't in action all that time.

The bass usually stayed near the mouth of a little inlet choked with water lilies, but on this occasion the birds succeeded in driving him from his sanctuary. The bass tried to lose them by dodging in and out between the stalks but the birds followed every move he made: their long necks outstretched, their webbed feet kicking behind like outboard motors, their torpedo-shaped bodies cutting through the water like projectiles. Their bigger bodies made a cloud of silt rise from the bottom and the bass whirled and dove into this smoke screen like a fighter pilot taking refuge in a cloud. Ichi plunged in after him while Mrs. Ichi wisely swam around the outside.

The fish exploded out of the cloud, saw Mrs. Ichi, and ducked under a log. Not even her long beak could dislodge him, although she must have stayed under water for six or seven minutes probing around. When she finally had to come up for air, Ichi took her place, standing on the bottom and using his beak as a lever in an attempt to turn the log over. Then Mrs. Ichi came down and spelled him. This went on for twenty minutes until the bass decided it had had enough. While the birds were changing guard, it suddenly shot out, headed for the safety of the deepest hole. In a moment the birds were under the fish, forcing him toward the surface. For an instant, the bass broke water, tail-walking like a hooked sailfish, and then dived straight down while Mrs. Ichi, taken by surprise, surfaced and swam around desperately, trying to see what had happened.

Ichi saw the bass going down and followed. Neither fish nor bird seemed able to swim straight downward. The bass was descending as though following the path of an invisible cork-screw and, being larger, the cormorant could not make such tight turns. He followed in a series of great circles. The whole business was much like a pigeon's "ringing up" to get above a falcon. As the fish neared the green tangle of plants at the bottom, the bird put on a sudden burst of speed. Although he could not reach his twisting prey, he came down so fast that the suction made by his body threw the fish off balance. Steering with his long tail, Ichi made the water swirl until the fish was spun over on its side. Then the cormorant struck. For an instant the silver belly of the bass flashed deep in the brown water. Then Ichi came shooting upward with a full throat pouch.

The Ichis lacked the dignity and impressive mien of hawks—both of them were natural clowns—but they were friendly and smart. It is impossible to allow an adult hawk to fly free and expect him to return, but the Ichis were tame as pet ducks. Several times when I had them on their perches, they managed to break their jesses (being in water so much rotted the leather, although I kept it constantly coated with dubbing) but they never tried to escape. They'd come waddling to the back door and stand there honking for me to take them fishing. If I wasn't home, they'd go fishing on their own, flying back at sunset.

At last, I decided to turn them loose on our pond. They stayed there several weeks, always flying over to me for food, but finally one day in late autumn Ichi checked off before lighting on my hand and Mrs. Ichi followed him. To my surprise, instead of returning or flying back to their beloved pond they began to mount in the air like falcons, rising higher and higher until they were lost to sight. They never returned. I believe they headed south for the winter and trust that, wherever they are, they are well and happy and have raised many families of baby Ichis.

Eleven

Our picture, *Eagle versus Dragon,* won the Featurette Award and proved so popular that it is still being occasionally shown. Editors began writing me asking for articles, the Lee Keedick Agency booked us for a lecture tour, and *Coronet* magazine listed *Águila* as one of the twelve biggest animal money-makers of all time. I had become established as a writer and it seemed remarkably unfair that a war should be on. Several million other young men unquestionably felt the same way, but there didn't seem to be much any of us could do about it. I entered the Navy in the photographic branch of the service while Jule handled the lectures. The marvelous Junkers, as usual, helped us out with baby Jule but mutinied when it came to the animals. We had freed most of them in Taxco before returning, but of course we kept Águila. She had to go to the Philadelphia Zoo.

Águila didn't like the zoo. They put her in a cage, and Águila hadn't been in a cage since the days of the chicken coop in Salem, New Jersey. True, it was a very nice, roomy, outdoor cage—but it was still a cage, and Águila was a lady of determined likes and dislikes. The first time a keeper entered the cage to clean it, Águila went for him. The man fled, dropping his broom, with Águila after him. After chasing the keeper around the cage a few times, Águila took off in the direction of Fairmount Park and vanished.

When Roger Conant, then curator of the Philadelphia Zoo, heard the news he set out immediately with head keeper Regan to find the bird. After driving around the park for several hours, they finally located Águila sitting in a tree. The two men got out of the car to look the situation over. Roger explained that the bird was trained to come to the fist when called. Regan, a keeper of many years' experience, snorted with disgust.

"You mean if I hold out my hand—like this—and shouted 'Come, Águila,' that darned eagle would. . . . Run for your life, Mr. Conant! Here she comes!"

Regan dove for the car just as Águila swooped down, but Roger knew how much Águila meant to us and received the bird on his bare arm—something I certainly wouldn't have cared to do myself. He managed to get her back to her cage, but Águila clearly wasn't happy in a zoo. She beat herself against the bars, refused to eat, and finally Jule had to drive up from Washington, D.C., where I was stationed and get her.

We rented a small house in Georgetown and Águila moved in with us. Since Jule couldn't take care of Águila and go on lecture tours also, the tours had to be abandoned. Also, Jule was going to have another baby. This baby turned out to be a boy and we named him Dan. Baby Julie was retrieved from the Junkers and we lived together as a family, the first lesson both children having to learn was not to tweak Águila's tail feathers; Águila did not take kindly to having her tail feathers tweaked. Wriggles proved more adaptable and put up with the children with the same philosophical good nature she had always shown toward our other strange pets.

After the war I felt I had to take writing more seriously. With two children to support, playing with cormorants, exploring bat caves, and raising baby squirrels must stop. There seemed to be one, and only one, aspect of man's relationship with wild animals in which there was a constant and unfailing interest— killing them. The newsstands were plastered with sportsmen's magazines and publishers always seemed ready to accept manuscripts with such titles as "Through Rumblebellypore with Rod and Gun." I determined to become a chronicler of big-game hunting.

My first effort along these lines involved a trip to Kodiak Island in the Aleutians to describe the hunt of the great Kodiak bears, the largest carnivorous land animal in the world today. These monsters weigh up to 1600 pounds and are the descendants of the prehistoric cave bears our ancestors once dreaded. I made the trip, but it took endless rewrites before the article was finally sold. I was far more interested in the bears than the hunters. Seeing one of the big brownies happily sliding down the side of a glacier like a kid on a sled was a delight to behold. Shooting one did not seem to me particularly difficult or important—possibly because knowing nothing of firearms I could not appreciate the problems involved. It still appears to me that photographing wild animals is infinitely harder, and more rewarding, than shooting them, although experienced sportsmen have assured me that this is not the case.

Then I got a lucky break. In 1951, my agent received a bulky manuscript from John A. Hunter, a professional white hunter in Kenya, telling of his experiences in a lifetime of big-game hunting. The manuscript had already been submitted to a number of publishers without being able to get away from "and so I dropped the charging lion with one well-directed shot" style of writing which seems inherent in books on hunting. But after reading the manuscript, my agent got the impression that here was a man who knew and even loved animals although he had devoted his life to killing them. He suggested that I go to Kenya and spend several months with John Hunter working on the book. As I'd have rather have gone to Africa than ascended into heaven, Jule and I left for Nairobi. As usual, the Junkers took the children and even allowed Águila to move back into the garage. Águila didn't mind the garage and John, the Junkers' Japanese houseman, got along with the bird very well. John was one of the few people Águila wouldn't attack.

Hunter turned out to be a stocky, soft-spoken man of sixty-four who, although as a government "control man" he had shot large numbers of animals, was also an excellent field naturalist and knew wild creatures intimately. We got along well together and the resulting book, *Hunter,* was a best-seller. I tried to do other books about big-game hunting, but I have never been able to capture the sportsman's thrill of the hunt and these attempts were a failure. My interest in animals has always been as personalities rather than targets and this showed in my writing. But while we were in Kenya, I met Raymond Hook.

Hook was an old-time Kenyan who lived on the slopes of Mount Kenya completely alone except for his native boys. Hook made a living trapping wild animals for zoos, but his specialty was obtaining cheetahs for Indian rajahs. A cheetah is a big, spotted cat (the word *cheetah* means "spotted" in Hindi) and is often called the "hunting leopard." Physically and psychologically they are an almost perfect blend of dog and cat. They have doglike paws with blunt, nonretractable claws and long, slender, greyhound bodies. They cannot climb (although they can run up a sloping tree, as a dog can), have a poor sense of smell and remarkable eyesight. They rely on running down their quarry and are famous as the fastest of all mammals. They probably can do 70 miles per hour for a short spurt. In spite of their doglike qualities, they are definitely members of the cat family—but are the only members that can be perfectly tamed. Because of this trait and their phenomenal speed, they have been used since time immemorial for coursing game, mainly in India and the Middle East.

Hook had several freshly caught adult cheetahs waiting to be shipped out. "The Maharaja of Kolhapur has thirty-five cheetahs and the Maharaja of Bhavnager has thirty," he told me. "For some reason or other, cheetahs seldom breed in captivity, so they all have to be wild-caught."

After seeing Hook's pets, I decided that life wouldn't be worth living without a cheetah. So when we returned to the United States, we made arrangements with Warren Buck, an experienced animal dealer in Camden, New Jersey, to get us a cheetah kitten. After several weeks of delay, Mr. Buck called to say that the cheetah had arrived.

Jule and I instantly drove to Mr. Buck's establishment a few miles outside the city. The cheetah was considerably bigger than we'd expected; easily six feet long including his tail and weighing about 70 pounds. Although scrawny and undernourished after his long trip, he bounced around his cage like a spotted rubber ball, ricocheting off the sides and running his paw out hopefully through the feeding slot. Thinking he was a female, we named him Rani, and the name stuck.

When we returned to the Junkers with Rani, Mrs. Junker took one look at our new acquisition and then said quietly "Oh no!" While I was manhandling Rani's shipping crate up to our bedroom, I heard her say anxiously to Jule, "Dear, don't you think buying a tiger is unwise?"

Looking back, the elaborate precautions I took before letting Rani out of his crate seem ridiculous. He was by far the largest mammal I'd ever tried to tame, and I expected the worst. I put on hip boots in case he grabbed me by the leg, brandished a chair and a prod pole in imitation of lion-tamers, and wore a heavy leather jacket. I'm glad no one was around to witness what happened after all these preparations. Rani came romping out of the crate, gyrated around the room in delight, and then rolled over on his back with all four feet in the air, begging to have his stomach rubbed. In half a minute, instead of disciplining him I was playing with him.

Even so, there was nearly one accident that made me glad for the jacket. Once Rani reared up on his hind legs and threw out his forepaws against my chest. He was plainly only playing, but there was a slashing sound and when he dropped down again there were two diagonal cuts in the heavy leather. Since a cheetah's claws are no sharper than those of a domestic dog, I could not imagine what had happened. It was several days before we discovered the answer.

All cats have a special claw, called a dewclaw, on the inside of the foreleg a few inches above the paw, which corresponds to our thumb. This dewclaw is generally kept folded in against the leg; to find it you have to run your hand through the cat's fur. But when necessary, the cat can project it outward almost at a 90-degree angle. This dew-claw is as useful to the big cats as her rear talon is to a falcon; it is their principle killing tool. When a lion or a tiger springs on quarry, the cat hooks these dewclaws into the animal and holds him as effectively as though he were caught by curved tongs. The American puma or mountain lion also has these dewclaws and almost invariably uses them in pulling down deer. Lion-tamers have told me that they are more afraid of these dewclaws than of the cats' teeth or talons.

When Rani had sprung up against me, he had felt his paws slipping off my leather jacket. An ordinary cat would have shot out his talons to get a better grip, but with his blunt, doglike claws, Rani had instinctively used his dewclaws. The dewclaws had slashed like miniature knives. As pet-lovers always say at a time like this, "he didn't *mean* any harm"—and of course he didn't, but this is a good example of the difficulties in handling dangerous animals who may not intend to hurt their owners but have no idea of their own potentialities.

The day we got him we were able to take Rani out for a walk on a lead. He behaved exactly like a big dog being taken out for the first time in months: rolling delightedly on the grass, trying to chase every bird he saw, stopping at every tree. He began purring like a contented Diesel engine. Rani had a tremendously loud purr. Later, when we let him sleep on the same bed with us, because of his purring we couldn't get to sleep until Rani had dozed off.

A motion-picture company had asked me to make another short subject with Águila so we left for California with Wriggles, Águila, and Rani, Rani riding between us on the front seat. We planned to rent a house on the coast and Mrs. Junker kindly agreed to fly out later, bringing the children with her. Rani was no trouble, but he nearly got us involved in a series of accidents. A car would start to pass us and the driver would suddenly shout, "Say, they've got a lion in that car!" Then he'd drive alongside us, often so fascinated that we'd nearly have a collision. We finally had to put Rani in his cage when passing through towns or in heavy traffic.

I was interested to see if Rani had any hunting instincts. Because he was still only a pup, I decided to enter him on jackrabbits. These rabbits are regarded as a pest so there are no restrictions on hunting them. They are fast, keep to the open country, and seemed the perfect quarry. We had found several dead on the highway and Rani had eaten them readily so, knowing the cheetah's phenomenal speed, I had no doubts about the outcome.

We saw our first live jackrabbit just at dawn while crossing the plains of Nebraska. A big, white-tailed jack with black-and-white squares like signal flags on his long ears bolted across the road. He ran parallel to the car and then ducked into a culvert. It was a wonderful opportunity to see what Rani could do.

We stopped the car and piled out with Rani. Jule stood at one end of the culvert holding the cat on a slip as though he were a greyhound while I went about to the other end with Wriggles to shoo the rabbit out. Wriggles snuffed at the hole and began to bark. Instantly the rabbit burst out of the other side.

Jule didn't slip Rani, although the cat was going mad with excitement. She later explained that she was too afraid of losing him. I shouted at her, Wriggles barked, and at last she let the cat go. Rani went flashing away, gathering speed at every bound.

The jack wasn't going at full speed; he had slowed down to see what was going on. Every fifty feet or so he'd give a high bound so he could look back over the sagebrush and watch what was happening. But when he saw Rani speeding toward him, he really started running. The jack drifted over the flats like a blown bit of fluff, but compared to the cheetah he seemed to be standing still. The cat was nearly on top of him when the rabbit doubled back, Rani whirling with him, the cat's long tail thrown out at right angles to balance himself as he skidded around. For the first time, I realized the purpose of the cheetah's abnormally long tail; it serves as a counterweight to his body when making a sharp turn. A single greyhound finds it almost impossible to double fast enough to get a jack, but a cheetah can do it easily.

Rani tried to grab the jack in his mouth but the action of bending over took too long and the jack got a few yards' advantage. He came racing back toward the road with the cheetah gaining at every bound, but instead of ducking into the culvert a second time as we expected, he turned sharply and ran alongside a drainage ditch beside the road. Rani was just behind him. At the last instant, the rabbit jumped sideways across the ditch. Rani turned to follow and plunged head-first into the excavation. The cheetah turned a complete somersault and landed on the bottom with all the breath knocked out of him while the smart jack vanished over the fiats.

As we had taken a tent along, we were able to spend the next ten days in Nebraska hunting jackrabbits with Rani. We had plenty of cooperation from the local farmers who hate the jacks because of the damage they do to crops. The farmers, after their first shock on meeting Rani, were generally willing to go out with us in the early morning or late afternoon when the rabbits are out. The most likely spots were usually along the edges of grainfields where the jacks come to feed. We would drive along the edge of the fields in our car with Rini hanging out the window until a jack was sighted. Then Rani would vault out the open window and the chase was on.

We had taken for granted that Rani would have no trouble getting jacks, but we soon found that the rabbits, like all wild animals, are astonishingly skillful at defending themselves against a natural enemy. The most deadly trick jacks have learned is to dive through a barbed-wire fence. They would deliberately wait until Rani was just behind them before pulling this trick. Twice Rani hit the wire so hard that he bounced back a foot or more, and once he was nearly knocked out. By a miracle, he missed getting hung up on the barbs, but we finally stopped running him in districts where wire was strung. The farmers told us that dogs are often mutilated and even killed by jacks decoying them into barbed wire.

The jacks had another trick. They would let Rani nearly catch them and then suddenly leap straight up in the air. Rani would go rushing past and then have to stop and look around to see what had happened to his quarry. Meanwhile the jack would have landed and be running off in another direction. By the time Rani had located the rabbit, the cat would have lost all his momentum and it would take him several yards to build up speed again.

Although the jacks were smart, Rani was no fool either. When a jack bounded into the air, Rani learned to slam on his brakes and slide head-up, watching for the rabbit to come down. Sometimes he managed to be there when the rabbit hit the earth. But Rani's most important discovery in rabbit-catching was not to try to grab the jack in his mouth; the rabbit could double too quickly for that. Rani learned to reach out with his forepaw when he was almost on top of the rabbit and knock him over. Rani's forelegs were very long and dexterous, and a blow from his paw was enough to knock the rabbit off balance. That was all Rani needed.

Motels have a certain prejudice against taking in cheetahs, so we got into the habit of stocking up with provisions at a general store and then camping out in our tent in the hills or forests for a week at a time. The first week we camped out with Rani, I awoke in the middle of the night half-frozen. Rani had gotten cold and quietly collected my blankets. He was curled up in them, contentedly purring away. When I tried to get them back, Rani hung on with teeth and dewclaws and I had to cuff him to make him let go. Rather surprisingly, Rani always accepted punishment very well, but no sooner had I begun to doze off when I felt him stealing the blankets again. This time I let him have them and Jule and I shared a sleeping bag. This worked very well for several nights until Rani discovered the principle of the sleeping bag. Then he tried to get in with us. We had to keep the bag zippered shut all the way to hold him out.

Rani hated to be chained, so when we were in an isolated area we allowed him to run loose around the camp. In southern Utah we camped in what seemed to us a completely deserted area and let Rani run free, but there was a dirt road running through the sagebrush we hadn't noticed. While we were putting up the tent, we heard the sound of a motorcycle. A man was buzzing along the road and we saw, to our horror, that Rani had stopped and was regarding him with delighted interest.

I shouted to the cat but he paid no attention; probably he couldn't hear me above the noise of the cycle. Then I saw him crouch down, preparatory to making a charge. I started running but it was too late. Rani burst from the sage and dashed after the cycle, obviously thinking it some new sort of animal.

The rider glanced over his shoulder, did a double-take, and then stepped on the gas. The cycle shot ahead at 50 miles per hour. The man obviously considered himself safe, but he didn't know cheetahs. Rani easily overtook him and loped alongside the cycle. Rani wasn't being aggressive; he was merely curious and would reach out from time to time to make a pass at the man's leg to see what he was made of, while the rider desperately tried to coax a little more speed out of his machine. At last Rani got tired of the game and trotted back to me while the cyclist vanished over a little rise, bent double over the handlebars and going for all he was worth. We immediately broke camp and left Utah before the cyclist could get to a town and report what he'd seen, although I doubt if anyone would have believed him.

We also had trouble letting Rani run loose in Wyoming. One evening Rani didn't come to my whistle so I started out to look for him. We were camped by the shore of a mountain lake almost completely encircled by pine forests, the bright green trees coming almost to the water's edge. At the far side of the lake the trees ended and the open prairie stretched away to the horizon. I followed Rani's tracks in the sand along the lake shore and found that he had headed out across the flats. This was annoying but not alarming; Rani often went rabbit-hunting on his own, but I was always afraid that he might meet a man with a gun.

I started out through the sage, whistling and calling. Topping a little rise, I saw below me a herd of pronghorn antelope, the fastest animals in this hemisphere. The wind was blowing toward me and the brown-and-white animals were feeding peacefully among the sage. They were about a quarter of a mile away. The herd seemed to be under the command of a beautiful pronghorn buck and while I watched, the leader suddenly raised his head and gazed intently in my direction.

For what seemed an interminable period the old buck stood stone-still. Then he left his herd and came slowly toward me. I could see now that he was looking at something below me and, following his gaze, I saw Rani crouched at the foot of the rise where I was standing. The cat was rigid as a statue, his big eyes fixed on the antelope with an almost-hypnotic intensity. The setting sun, dropping low on the horizon, had begun to reflect from the cat's golden-brown coat, and this reflection had apparently attracted the buck's attention.

The antelope leader stared at Rani a long time, but he could not see the crouching cat clearly because of the knee-high sage. Suddenly he turned and trotted to the top of a little hill where he could get a better view. There he stopped and from this superior elevation he studied the cat again.

Now that he was discovered, Rani seemed to lose all interest in the hunt. He rolled over and began to play with his tail. The other antelope saw him and became curious. The whole herd came over to investigate. Step by step they wandered over until they were within a hundred yards of Rani.

Suddenly the guardian buck on the hill gave a shrill whistle and trotted off. The other antelope whirled and followed him. Rani was lying on his back, batting at the air with his paws, but as soon as the antelope began to move away he spun over, landing on his feet. Instantly he dashed away after the herd, seeming to reach his top speed in half a dozen bounds.

The antelope stopped trotting and began to run, bounding over the ground like enormous rabbits. Rani streaked along, rapidly closing the gap between them, but I could tell he was still not going full out. The antelope seemed to realize this also, for as Rani got closer they suddenly unloosed a tremendous burst of speed that they had been keeping in reserve. But Rani had also been saving himself for a special effort and I could see him draw on his reserve power for the last rush.

Like a brown blur of light, Rani came speeding up behind a young buck. The buck zigzagged from side to side, very much as the rabbits had done, and Rani swayed with him in perfect unison. The two animals were going at such a tremendous speed that I could not see clearly what happened but suddenly Rani pulled up beside the antelope. Leaping up, he threw himself against the antelope's flank, striking out stiff-legged with both front paws. The antelope staggered but kept going. Rani jumped again, hitting the buck with his full weight. The buck tripped and then fell heavily on his side. At once, Rani sprang for the antelope's throat but the buck's thrashing hoofs kept him away. The cat circled, trying to come in again, but the antelope leaped to his feet and made another dash for freedom. This time Rani let him go.

I was astonished that my terrible "killer cat" had been beaten off. Not until years later did I realize that cheetahs are delicate creatures, built solely for speed, and in the wild state never take anything but gazelles and small antelope; our pronghorn weighs over a hundred pounds. I had, however, seen Rani display two typical cheetah characteristics, both purely instinctive. While in Africa, I saw a wild cheetah lure Thompson's gazelles within charging distance by playing with his tail and arousing the Tommies' curiosity. Cheetahs also usually try to knock over gazelles by "straight-arming" them on the flank with stiff forelegs. Rani was a pup when I got him, so both these acts must have been purely instinctive. He was surely never trained by his mother.

After that experience, I put in some intensive work trying to teach Rani to stop on command, heel, and stay. Here Rani showed his strange dog-cat psychology. A well-trained dog will trot along by his master's side for miles but Rani, being a cat, worked by fits and starts. He would heel nicely for a hundred yards, then lie down for a two-minute rest and nothing, could budge him. By using a long training leash, I taught him to stop on command, but as soon as I took the leash off Rani would pay no attention to me. Finally I discovered that if I left a short length of line dangling from his collar, Rani thought he was still on the lead and would obey reasonably well.

Much to my surprise, I found that it was comparatively easy to teach Rani to retrieve, a trick almost impossible to teach most big cats. Rani had no great desire to devour his kills and would carry his quarry around in his mouth, exhibiting it proudly like a housecat with a mouse. After learning to retrieve a ball, he didn't object to retrieving game. However, Rani would never have made a good bird dog; he had a poor sense of smell—for an animal, at least—and locating game birds by scent was completely beyond him.

But Rani worked out a system of his own for hunting prairie chickens. While looking for jacks, Rani would occasionally run across a covey of the plump gray birds. At first he simply chased them as an untrained dog would do, and naturally the chickens flew off. Then he tried stalking the coveys. Rani didn't stalk like a housecat; instead, he stood almost erect watching the prey with his curious, intent expression. Then he would take a single, stiff-legged step forward, keeping his body rigid as a ramrod. As he got nearer his quarry, his tenseness increased until he was as taut as an overdrawn violin string and his motions grew slower. It took him a full minute to raise one of his rigid legs and put it down again. Meanwhile, the chickens were running around a few yards in front of him, picking up seeds and totally unconscious of the slow motion toward them. Suddenly, and without the slightest warning, Rani would charge.

For a fatal instant the chickens would hesitate before exploding skyward. In that moment, Rani was among them. As the chickens flushed, Rani would spring into the air, making a quick clutch with his forepaws and snapping with his jaws at the same time. Usually he got nothing but a mouthful of feathers, but by sheer luck he managed to nab a chicken the first time he tried this system. After that, he conscientiously stalked every covey he found.

Strangers were always astonished that we could take Rani's kills away from him without any trouble. "Someday that cat is going to turn on you when you try to take food away from him" we were constantly warned. Actually, after Rani had made a kill, he would bring his prey over to me and cry until I cut it open for him.

Once, and only once, we thought we'd lost Rani. We were camping on the Navajo Reservation and I'd taken Rani for a walk in the early morning. He refused to go back to the car with me. Rani had done this before, but when I got in the car and drove a few hundred yards, Rani would always come loping after me, fearful of being left behind. I tried this trick but even after half a mile there was still no sign of Rani so I went back.

Rani had disappeared—gone off hunting on his own. For a while I was able to follow his tracks in the sandy soil, but I soon lost them and had to go to Keams Canyon for an Indian tracker. He followed Rani until two o'clock that afternoon. Then he stopped and said, "He's backtracking." True enough, Rani was heading back to where he'd last seen the car, his foreprints over his old tracks.

We hurried back. We had almost reached the car when we saw a Navajo on horseback following the trail. Before my tracker could hail the man, Rani burst out of a clump of sagebrush and charged the horse. The mounted Indian did not panic. Instead, he simply spun his horse around and pulling his blanket from his shoulder, flapped it in Rani's face. Rani instantly veered off and then lay down panting. When we came up, the mounted Indian remarked calmly, "I was wondering what sort of an animal made those tracks. They look something like a mountain lion's, but I knew it must be a foreign creature of some sort." For an Indian living deep in the heart of the reservation, that man was the coolest, most sophisticated individual I've ever met.

In Los Angeles, we moved in with Henry Dreyfus, the famous industrial designer, and his wife, Doris. We had met the Dreyfuses some time before in New York and they were probably the only family in America who would have allowed comparative strangers to arrive unannounced accompanied by an eagle and a cheetah. The Dreyfus children were delighted with Rani—Águila, as usual, stood on her dignity—and played with him by the hour. But we finally decided that even the Dreyfuses were beginning to show signs of cracking under the strain; besides, Jule missed the children, so we rented a house at Malibu. There I was able to take Rani for a run every day in the hills and fly Águila with freedom almost as complete as we'd had in Taxco.

Mrs. Junker came out with the children as she'd promised. Danny was still only a baby and Julie accepted the animals as casually as she accepted the fact that we owned a car. When her little friends came to call and showed surprise at the sight of Rani sprawled out on our living room sofa, Julie would say impatiently, "Oh, that's only a cheetah. Now come and look at my new doll." We made our picture for RKO, called *The Boy and the Eagle,* with Dickie Moore, the famous child star. The year we spent at Malibu was comparatively peaceful except for the time we nearly killed Elizabeth Taylor with a rattlesnake.

The Taylors lived a few houses away from us and we probably would never have met them if Elizabeth's pet poodle hadn't made the mistake of coming around to call when Rani was taking his walk. I still don't think Rani meant to hurt the poodle—he just wanted to see what it was made of—but after one look at what was bounding toward him, the poodle fled for home, letting out a terrified yelp at every bound. Rani chased the poodle under the Taylors' house and while I was trying to get a leash on the cat, Mr. Taylor came to the door and inquired gently what was going on. I explained and he was very nice about the whole thing. Later that day, Elizabeth came over to see Rani. She was a little girl then and loved animals. She was also extraordinarily good with them; better than anyone I've ever seen except Jule. Elizabeth was absolutely fearless and it was only by dint of great persuasion I was able to keep her from trying to play with Águila, who definitely did not like strangers. Elizabeth used to drop over frequently and often when I came back from the hills after flying Águila, I'd find her sprawled out on the living room carpet playing with Rani and Wriggles.

I have always been interested in snakes, and while we were in Malibu a friend sent me a very fine Mexican green rattler nearly six feet long. I kept him in a cage in the sunporch and our own children were told never to go near him. I showed him once to Elizabeth, who seemed only mildly interested and as she was a teen-ager it never occurred to me to warn her to leave the snake alone. One afternoon I returned from the hills to find Elizabeth and two other girls giggling delightedly while Liz seemed to be admiring herself in the mirror. I asked what the joke was.

"Oh, I was trying to take the rattlesnake out to show my friends and he struck at me," Liz casually explained. "He missed and struck the wire on the side of his cage. The venom sprayed all over my face, see?"

Unless she had a cut on her cheek, the venom couldn't have hurt her, but I've seldom had such a shock. I called for Jule and together we washed the famous Taylor face. Liz regarded the whole affair as hilariously funny and explained that she was sure the snake hadn't meant to hurt her. After that I kept the snake locked up, thus doubtless making the production of *Cleopatra* possible—Liz was perfectly capable of trying again. Even in those days she was a beautiful, delightful, and completely reckless young lady.

It was through my interest in snakes that while in California Jule and I had the most terrible experience of our career.

Twelve

I had first heard of Grace Wiley some years before when Dr. William Mann, then director of the National Zoological Park in Washington, D.C., handed me a picture of a tiny woman with a gigantic king cobra draped over her shoulders like a garden hose. The snake had partly spread his hood and was looking intently into the camera while his mistress stroked his head to quiet him. Dr. Mann told me: "Grace lives in a little house full of poisonous snakes, imported from all over the world. She lets them wander around like cats. There's been more nonsense written about 'snake charming' than nearly any other subject. Grace is probably the only non-Oriental who knows the real secrets of this curious business."

Looking at the picture of that deadly creature I knew what Ruskin meant when he described a snake as a "running brook of horror." Still, I like snakes and when Jule and I moved into our Malibu house, I made it a point to call on Grace Wiley.

Grace wasn't at the address Dr. Mann had given me. The neighbors had seen some of her pets in the yard and called the police. Grace finally settled outside Los Angeles near the little town of Cypress. After a phone call, I drove out to see her. She was living in a small three-room cottage, surrounded by open fields. Behind the cottage was a big, ramshackle barn where the snakes were kept. Grace was cleaning snake boxes with a hose when I arrived. She was a surprisingly little lady, scarcely over five feet and probably weighed less than a hundred pounds. Although Grace was sixty-four years old, she was as active as a boy and worked with smooth dexterity. When she saw me, she hurriedly picked up the four-foot rattlesnake who had been sunning himself while his box was cleaned and poured him into his cage. The snake raised his head but made no attempt to strike or even to rattle. I was impressed but not astonished. In captivity, rattlers often grow sluggish and can be handled with comparative impunity.

Grace came forward, drying her hands on her apron. "Oh dear, I meant to get dressed up for you," she said, trying to smooth down her thatch of brown hair. "But I haven't anybody here to help me with the snakes except Mother—and she's eighty-four years old. Don't trip over an alligator," she added as I came forward. I noticed for the first time in the high grass a dozen or so alligators and crocodiles. They ranged from a three-foot Chinese croc to a big Florida 'gator more than twelve feet long. I threaded my way among them without mishap, although several opened their huge jaws to hiss at me.

"They don't mean anything by that, any more than a dog barking," Grace explained fondly. "They're very tame and most of them know their names. Now come in and meet my little family of snakes."

We entered the barn. The walls were lined with cages of all sizes and shapes containing snakes. Grace stopped at each cage, casually lifting the occupant and pointing out his fine points while she stroked and examined him. Grace unquestionably had one of the world's finest collection of reptiles. I watched her handle diamondback rattlesnakes from Texas, vipers from

Italy, fer-de-lance from the West Indies, a little Egyptian cobra (the "asp" that killed Cleopatra), and the deadly karait from India. Then I saw Grace perform a feat I would have believed impossible.

We had stopped in front of a large, glass-fronted cage containing apparently nothing but newspaper. "These little fellows arrived only a short time ago, so they're very wild," explained Grace indulgently. She quietly lifted the paper. Instantly a forest of heads sprang up in the cage. Grace moved the paper slightly. At the movement, the heads seemed to spread and flatten. Then I saw that they were not heads but hoods. I was looking at the world's most deadly creature—the Indian cobra.

Man-eating tigers are said to kill 600 natives a year but cobras kill 25,000 people a year in India alone. Hunters have been mauled by wounded elephants and lived to tell about it, but no one survives a body bite from a big cobra. I have caught rattlesnakes with a forked stick and my bare hands, but I'm not ashamed to say I jumped back from that cage as though the devil were inside—as indeed he was.

Grace advanced her hand toward the nearest cobra. The snake swayed like a reed in the wind, feinting for the strike. Grace raised her hand above the snake's head, the reptile twisting around to watch her. As the woman slowly lowered her hand, the snake gave that most terrible of all animal noises—the unearthly hiss of a deadly snake. I have seen children laugh with excitement at the roar of a lion, but I have never seen anyone who did not cringe at that cold, uncanny sound. Grace deliberately tried to touch the rigid, quivering hood. The cobra struck at her hand. He missed. Quietly, Grace presented her open palm. The cobra hesitated a split second, his reared body quivering like a plucked banjo string. Then he struck.

I felt sick as I saw his head hit Grace's hand, but the cobra did not bite. He struck with his mouth closed. As rapidly as an expert boxer drumming on a punching bag, the snake struck three times against Grace's palm, always for some incredible reason with his mouth shut. Then Grace slid her open hand over his head and stroked his hood. The snake hissed again and struggled violently under her touch. Grace continued to caress him. Suddenly the snake went limp and his hood began to close. Grace slipped her other hand under the snake's body and lifted him out of the cage. She held the reptile in her arms as though he were a baby. The cobra raised his head to look Grace in the face; his dancing tongue was less than a foot from her mouth. Grace braced her hand against the curve of his body and talked calmly to him until he folded his hood. He curled up in her arms quietly until I made a slight movement; then he instantly reared up again, threatening me.

I had never seen anything to match this performance. Later, Grace opened the cobra's mouth to show me that the fangs were still intact. The yellow venom was slowly oozing over their tips.

If Grace Wiley had wished to make a mystery out of her amazing ability I am certain she could have made a fortune by posing as a woman with supernatural power. There isn't a zoologist alive who could have debunked her. But Grace was a perfectly honest person who was happy to explain in detail exactly how she could handle these terrible creatures. I spent several weeks with her studying her technique and now that I understand it I'm even more impressed than I was before.

Although I had kept snakes for many years, I was probably more astonished by Grace's performance than someone who knew nothing about reptiles. My mistake lay in supposing that all snakes are more or less alike. I knew rattlesnakes but I knew nothing about cobras. Although the cobra is intrinsically a far more dangerous snake than the rattlesnake, Grace would never have attempted to handle a diamondback rattler in the manner she handled this cobra. To understand why, you have to know the physical and psychological differences between the two reptiles.

A rattler has two "coils." When he is resting, he lies coiled up like a length of rope with his head lying on the topmost coil and his rattle sticking up in the center of the heap. When he is angry, he rears the upper third of his body a foot or more off the ground, coiling it into an S-shaped design and sounding his rattle continuously. Snake men call this position the "business coil." The rattler is like a coiled spring. He can strike out the full length of the S, inject his venom, and return into position for another strike literally faster than the eye can follow. He cannot strike farther than the raised S, nor will he attack. To attack, he would have to come out of coil and lose his advantageous position. He is like a boxer with his bent arm drawn back for a haymaker. As soon as his opponent comes close enough, he can let him have it.

A cobra, on the other hand, rears straight upward. If you put your elbow on a table, cup your hand to represent the open hood, and sway your forearm back and forth, you will have a good idea of the fighting stance of a cobra. Your index finger represents the tiny, mouselike head that does the business. You will see at once that you cannot strike out as far as you could with your arm drawn back. Your range is limited to the length of your forearm. Here is a large part of the secret in handling cobras.

Because of the deceptively coiled S, no one can tell exactly how far a rattler can strike. But with a little practice, you can tell a cobra's range to the inch. Also, the blow of a cobra is comparatively slow. A man with steady nerves can jerk away in time to avoid being bitten. This is exactly what a mongoose does. The mongoose keeps just outside the cobra's range and when he does dart in for a bite, he can jump clear of the blow. A mongoose would stand no chance at all against a rattlesnake.

Another vital difference lies in the method of striking. The rattler does not bite. He stabs with his fangs. A rattler's fangs are very long, so long that they would pierce his lower jaw if he did not keep them folded back against the roof of his mouth. When he strikes, the rattler opens his mouth to its fullest extent, the fangs snap down into place, and the snake stabs. The fangs are hollow and connect directly with the poison glands in either side of the snake's head. When the snake feels his fangs go home, he instantly discharges his venom deep into the wound. The fangs operate like miniature hypodermic needles and are extremely efficient.

The cobra has no such elaborate apparatus. His fangs are short and do not fold back. Instead of stabbing like the rattler, he must actually bite. He grabs his victims and then deliberately chews while the venom runs down into the wound he is making. These apparently minor distinctions mean the difference between life and death to anyone working with snakes.

When Grace approached a wild cobra, she moved her hand back and forth just outside the snake's range. The cobra would then strike angrily until he became tired. Then he was reluctant to strike again. Grace's next move was to raise her hand over the snake's hood and bring it down slowly. Because of his method of rearing, a cobra cannot strike directly upward (a rattler can strike up as easily as in any other direction), and Grace could actually touch the top of the snake's head. The snake became puzzled and frustrated. He felt that he was fighting an invulnerable opponent who, after all, didn't seem to mean him any harm. Then came the final touch. Grace would put her open palm toward the snake. At last the cobra was able to hit her.

But he had to bite and he could not get a grip on the flat surface of the palm. If he could get a finger or a loose fold of skin he could fasten his teeth in it and start chewing. But his strike is sufficiently slow that Grace could meet each blow with the flat of her palm. At last Grace would be able to get her hand over the snake's head and stroke his hood. This seemed to relax the reptile and from then on Grace could handle him with some degree of confidence.

I don't mean to suggest that this is a cut-and-dried procedure. Grace knew snakes perfectly and could tell by tiny, subtle indications what the reptile would probably do next. She had been bitten many times—she would never tell me just how many—but never by a cobra. You're only bitten once by a cobra.

"Now I'll show you what I know you're waiting to see," said Grace as she put the snake away. "My mated pair of king cobras." Dropping her voice reverently, she added "I call the big male 'The King of Kings.'" She led the way to a large enclosure and for the first time in my life I was looking into the eyes of that dread reptile, the king cobra—or hamadryad.

The common cobra is rarely more than five feet long. Even so, he has enough venom in his poison glands to kill fifty men. Grace's king cobras were more than fifteen feet long—longer than a boa constrictor. The two hamadryads contained enough venom, if injected drop by drop, to kill nearly a thousand human beings. That wasn't all. The hamadryad is the only snake known to attack without any provocation. These fearful creatures have been reported to trail a man through a jungle for the express purpose of biting him. They are so aggressive that they have closed roads in India by driving away all traffic. This is probably because the hamadryads, unlike other snakes, guard their eggs and young, and if a pair sets up housekeeping in a district, every other living thing must get out—including elephants. When a king cobra rears up, he stands higher than the head of a kneeling man. They are unquestionably the most dangerous animal in the world today.

When Grace first got these monsters, she was unable to handle them as she would ordinary cobras; so she had to devise an entirely new method of working with them. When the kings first arrived, they were completely unapproachable. They reared up more than four feet, snorting and hissing, their lower jaws open to expose the poison fangs. "A very threatening look, indeed," Grace called it. She put them in a large cage with a sliding partition. Unlike other snakes, hamadryads are knowing enough to notice that when their keeper opens the door in the side of the cage to put in fresh water, he must expose his hand for a fraction of a second. These cobras soon learned to lie against the side of the cage and wait for Grace to open the door. She outwitted them by waiting until both of the hamadryads were on one side of the cage and then sliding in the partition before changing water pans. She did not dare to go near them with her bare hands; she used a padded stick to stroke them. Yet she was able to touch them four days after their arrival. "I petted the kings on their tails when their heads were far away," she told me. "Later in the day I had a little visit with them and told them how perfectly lovely they were; that I liked them and was sure we were going to be good friends."

A few weeks later, the King of Kings began shedding his skin. Snakes are irritable and nervous while shedding, and the hamadryad had trouble sloughing off the thin membrane covering his eyes. Grace wrote in her diary "I stroked his head and then pulled off the eyelids with eyebrow forceps. He flinched a little but was unafraid. He put out his tongue in such a knowing manner! I mounted the eyelids and they looked just like pearls. What a pity that there have been nothing but unfriendly, aggressive accounts about this sweet snake. Really, the intelligence of these creatures is unbelievable."

The King of Kings was so heavy that Grace was unable to lift him by herself. Jule offered to help her carry the snake outside for a picture. While Jule and Grace were staggering out the door with the monster reptile between them, the king suddenly reared and rapped Jule several times on her forehead with his closed mouth. "He's trying to tell you something!" exclaimed Grace. He was indeed. I saw that the Chinese crocodile had rushed out from under a table and grabbed the hamadryad by the tail. Jule relaxed her grip and the king dropped his head and gave a single hiss. The croc promptly let go and the ladies bore the cobra out into the sunlight. I was the only person who seemed upset by the incident.

Out of curiosity, I asked Grace if she ever used music in taming her snakes. She laughed and told me what I already knew: all snakes are deaf. Grace assured me that the Hindu fakir uses his flute only to attract a crowd and by swaying his own body back and forth the fakir keeps the snake swaying as the cobra is feinting to strike. The man times his music to correspond to the snake's movements and it appears to dance to the tune. The fakir naturally keeps well outside of the cobra's striking range. Years later when I was in India, I discovered that this is exactly what happens. I never saw any Oriental snake-charmer even approximate Grace's marvelous powers over reptiles.

Grace's only source of income was to exhibit her snakes to tourists, although she was occasionally able to rent a snake to a studio (she always went along to make sure the reptile wasn't frightened or injured) and sometimes she bought ailing snakes from dealers, cured them, and resold them for a small profit to zoos. While I was with her, a dusty car stopped and discharged a plump couple with three noisy children who had seen her modest sign *Grace Wiley—Reptiles*. Grace explained that she would show them her collection, handle the poisonous snakes, call over the tame alligators, and let the children play with Rocky, an eighteen-foot Indian Rock python which she had raised from a baby. The charge was twenty-five cents. "That's too much," the woman said to her husband, and they went back to the car. Grace sighed. "No one seems interested in my snakes. No one really cares about them. And they're so wonderful."

One day Grace telephoned me to say that she had gotten in a new shipment of snakes, including some Indian cobras from Siam. "One of them has markings that form a complete G on the back of his hood," she told me. "Isn't it curious that the snake and I have the same initial! I call him My Snake." We laughed about this, and then Jule and I went out to Cypress to take a last set of pictures of Grace and her snakes for an article I was doing about this remarkable woman.

When we arrived Grace was talking to a couple of kids who had brought a pet turtle to show her. We set up our photographic apparatus and after a while I began to grow restless. "Couldn't we go ahead with our pictures?" I hinted. Grace replied gently, "These boys have come for miles on their bicycles to show me this turtle. They really seem to love reptiles and I can't send them away." We waited for more than an hour before the boys departed with their remarkable turtle.

We took several pictures and then I asked Grace to let me get a picture of the cobra with the G on the hood. "I didn't look very well in those other pictures," said Grace anxiously. "I'll comb my hair and put on another blouse." She was back in a few minutes. Jule and I had set up our cameras in the yard behind the barn, first removing several alligators and a big monitor lizard named Slinky to avoid any possibility of accidents. I wanted a shot of the cobra with spread hood, and Grace brought him out cradled in her arms. Before allowing me to take the picture, she removed her glasses as she felt that she looked better without them. The cobra refused to spread and Grace put him down on the ground and extended her flat palm toward him to make him rear—something I had often seen her do before, but never without her glasses.

I was watching through the finder of my camera. I saw the cobra spread and strike as I clicked the shutter. As the image disappeared from the ground glass of my Graflex, I looked up and saw the snake had seized Grace by the middle finger. She said in her usual quiet voice, "Oh, he's bitten me."

I dropped the camera and ran toward her, feeling an almost paralyzing sense of shock for I knew that Grace Wiley was a dead woman. At the same time I thought, "Good Lord, it's just like the book," for the cobra was behaving exactly as textbooks on cobras say they behave; he was deliberately chewing on the wound to make the venom run out of his glands. It was a terrible sight.

Quietly and expertly, Grace took hold of the snake on either side of his jaws and gently forced his mouth open. I knew that her only chance for life was to put a tourniquet around the finger instantly and slash open the wound to allow the venom to run out. Seconds counted. I reached out my hand to take the snake above the hood so she could immediately start squeezing out the venom, but Grace motioned me away. She stood up, still holding the cobra and walked into the barn. Carefully, she put the snake into his cage and closed the door.

This must have taken a couple of minutes and I knew that the venom was spreading through her system each moment. "Jule," said Grace, "call Wesley Dickinson. He's a herpetologist and a friend of mine. He'll know what to do." Calmly and distinctly she gave Jule the telephone number and Jule ran to the phone.

Then Grace turned to me. Suddenly she said, "He didn't really bite me, did he?" It was the only emotion I saw her show. I could only say, "Grace, where's your snake-bite kit?" We both knew that nothing except immediate amputation of her arm could save her, but anything was worth a chance.

She pointed to a cabinet. There was a tremendous collection of the surgical aids used for snake bite but I don't believe any of the stuff had been touched for twenty years. I pulled out a rubber tourniquet and tried to twist it around her finger. The old rubber snapped in my hands. Grace didn't seem to notice. I pulled out my handkerchief and tried that. It was too thick to go around her finger and I twisted it around her wrist. "I'll faint in a few minutes," said Grace. "I want to show you where every-thing is before I lose consciousness."

Cobra venom, unlike rattlesnake, affects the nervous system. In a few minutes the victim becomes paralyzed and the heart stops beating. I knew Grace was thinking of this. She said, "You must give me strychnine injections to keep my heart going when I begin to pass out. I'll show you where the strychnine is kept. You may have to give me caffeine also."

She walked to the other end of the room and I ran alongside trying to keep the tourniquet in place. She got out the tiny glass vials of strychnine and caffeine and also a hypodermic syringe with several needles. I saw some razor blades with the outfit and picked one up, intending to make a deep incision to let out as much of the venom as possible. Grace shook her head. "That won't do any good," she told me. Cobra venom travels along the nerves, so making the wound bleed wouldn't be very effective but it was all I could think of to do.

Jule came back with a Mr. Tanner, Grace's cousin who lived next door. Tanner immediately got out his jackknife, intending to cut open the wound, but Grace stopped him. "Wait until

Wesley comes," she said. Tanner told me afterward that he was convinced that if he had amputated the finger Grace might have lived. This is doubtful. Probably nothing except amputation of her arm would have saved her then, and we had nothing but a jackknife. She probably would have died of shock and loss of blood.

Grace lay on the floor to keep as quiet as possible and slow the absorption of the venom. "You'd better give me the strychnine now, dear," she told Jule. Jule snapped off the tip of one of the glass vials but the cylinder broke in her hands. She opened another tube and tried to fill the syringe; the needle was rusted shut. Jule selected another needle, tested it, and filled the syringe. "I'm afraid it will hurt," she told Grace. "Now don't worry, dear," said Grace comfortingly. "I know you'll do it very well."

After the injection, Grace asked Jule to put a newspaper under her head to keep her hair from getting dirty. A few minutes later, the ambulance with Wesley Dickinson following in his own car, arrived. Wesley had telephoned the hospital and arranged for blood transfusions and an iron lung. As Grace was lifted into the ambulance, she called back to Tanner, "Remember to cut up the meat for my frogs very fine and take good care of my snakes." That was the last we ever saw of her.

Grace died in the hospital half an hour later. She lived about ninety minutes after being bitten. In the hospital, Wesley directed the doctors to drain the blood out of her arm and pump in fresh blood. When her heart began to fail she was put into the lung. She had become unconscious. Then her heart stopped. Stimulants were given. The slow beating began again but grew steadily weaker. Each time stimulants were given, the heart responded less strongly and finally stopped forever.

We waited with Mr. and Mrs. Tanner at the snake barn, calling the hospital at intervals. When we heard that Grace was dead,

Mrs. Tanner burst into tears. "Grace was such a beautiful young girl—and so talented," she moaned. "There wasn't anything she couldn't do. Why did she ever want to mess around with those awful snakes?"

"I guess that's something none of us will ever understand," said her husband sadly.

Grace was born in Kansas in 1884. She studied entomology at the University of Kansas and during field trips to collect insects it was a great joke among Grace's fellow students that she was terrified of even harmless garter snakes. When she was still young, Grace married a big, handsome man very popular with women who was attracted by the girl's shy loveliness. Grace was deeply in love. Her hearty, confident husband seemed to her the personification of masculinity, but the delicately formed girl was unable to hold the full-blooded man's love and they separated. Grace turned with a passionate interest to the creatures she had so long feared. In 1923 she became curator of the Museum of Natural History at the Minneapolis Public Library but quarreled with the directors, who felt that her reckless handling of poisonous snakes endangered not only her own life but that of others. She went to the Brookfield Zoo in Chicago; here the same difficulty arose. Finaly Grace moved to California where she could work with reptiles as she wished.

An attempt was made by several of Grace's friends to keep her collection together for a Grace Wiley Memorial Reptile House, but this failed. The snakes were auctioned off and the snake that had killed Grace was purchased by a roadside zoo in Arizona; huge signboards bearing an artist's conception of the incident were erected for miles along the highways. So passed one of the most remarkable people I have ever known.

Thirteen

For the next few years we traveled extensively, taking the children with us and leaving the animals with the longsuffering Junkers. We spent a year on Capri, some time in England and France, and even managed to work in a trip to India, where I did several articles. But in 1950 we decided that the children were getting too big to be dragged around the surface of the globe so we settled in our small farm near Valley Forge, Pennsylvania. My old family home had long been sold and the surrounding area turned into a park. My grandparents and my mother were dead and Father had married a Russian countess, a survivor of the Revolution, and moved to Switzerland, so there was nothing to hold me to what had once been my home.

Our farm was completely isolated and the locality had not changed since Revolutionary times. Near us ran the old Conestoga Trail, where ox teams had pulled the famous Conestoga wagons on the trek westward; now our children rode their horses there nearly every day. Sometimes in the evenings Jule and I would go to the old General Warren Inn where the Hessians had plotted the Paoli Massacre during the Revolution, and twice a week during the winter the Whiteland Hunt met at the corner of our property. The first time they met there, Rani had a field day chasing the hounds around the countryside and I think I may say that it was the most unusual fox hunt on record—the hounds and the huntsmen racing for their lives across country pursued by Rani. Luckily, Rani didn't hurt the hounds even when he caught up with them—just knocked them over left and right as he went through the pack on his way to the huntsmen. Next to motorcycles, Rani was most fascinated by horses and liked to lope alongside one, patting him on the flank when he showed signs of slackening his speed to urge him on to fresh exertions. The horse recovered from the experience very well but even after we'd brought the huntsman back to our home and poured half a bottle of whiskey down him, he still kept shaking convulsively and talking a lot of nonsense about man-eating tigers.

Like everyone living in the country we had a servant problem, and it must be admitted that ours was of a special nature. The average domestic took a dim view of Rani and Águila, especially as Rani was a great tease and liked to chase maids up trees. At last we decided to import a girl from Europe and after considerable negotiations, managed to persuade a young French girl named Cecile to come over. As Cecile seemed a somewhat timid type from her letters—she labored under the illusion that the United States was full of Indians, gangsters, and wild animals—we said nothing about our pets, deciding that it was better to let them come as something of a surprise to her. They certainly did. When the taxi dropped Cecile off we forgot that we'd left Águila on her perch at one side of the garden gate and Rani on his leash at the other. We saw the taxi and Julie hurried to the front door to greet our new friend, but there was no one there. Jule went out to see what had happened and was astonished to find the girl already far down the driveway running like a jackrabbit. When we finally overtook her, it turned out that as she'd walked through the gate, Rani had jumped, at her from one side and Águila from the other. This little incident gave Cecile a false impression of our great democracy which persisted for several days, but at the end of a week she was perfectly capable of slapping Rani off the bed or retrieving a furious Águila from the branch of a tree. She stayed with us for several years and we've never found anyone who could replace her.

Naturally, we were constantly acquiring new pets—including a ten-foot Indian rock python I named Peter, after Peter Ryhiner, the famous wild animal collector who had presented him to me. Curiously enough, of all our pets it was Peter (who seldom left the house and never caused anyone any trouble) that most frightened visitors.

I think it is the appearance of the great serpents rather than any potential harm they can do that so terrifies people. The lidless, unwinking eyes, the flowing current of the long body, each part moving in a different direction but all with the same will and in the same way. The constantly changing patterns made of moving coils, so like an enormous pile of cable yet so unlike, for the coils are alive and directed by an intelligence. The black flame of the flickering tongue and the terrible, unknown potential of the great muscles flexing under the smooth scales. It has been claimed that this instinctive terror is inherited from our apelike ancestors, to whom the great tree-climbing serpents were the most terrible of all adversaries.

I doubt this theory because children, especially boys, feel none of this dread. In fact, probably no animal so appeals to children as a snake. The reptile house at the zoo is always full of children. Our son Danny, then twelve, had never before shown any particular interest in our animals but he was fascinated by Peter.

Handling a big snake is an unforgettable experience. There

is the gentle touch of the soft lips and delicate tongue, together with the strange feeling that you are holding a living electric current swathed in smooth scales. You seem to have an animated stream of water in your hands, piloted by a mind completely alien to your own.

While the neighborhood children were beating on the front door to be allowed to see Peter, their frantic parents were telephoning begging us not to let the children near him. They were perfectly willing to let the children play with Rani, who was potentially far more dangerous. On one occasion a mother brought her small son on the place without bothering to ask our permission and Rani, while trying to play with the child, knocked him down. The child was not unnaturally terrified and set up such a screaming that Jule and I rushed out to see what was the matter, The mother took the whole affair most calmly, merely remarking, "I'm sorry that happened as it may give the child a dislike of leopards"—surely the most understandable of all phobias. Yet this same woman refused to come into the house so the hysterical child could lie down for a few minutes because "of that terrible snake you have."

Most people think that all snakes are poisonous and this, at least, was the usual explanation given for being afraid of Peter. Peter, like all constrictors, isn't poisonous and kills by wrapping his coils around his victim, usually a chicken or rabbit. The constricting powers of even the biggest snakes are not nearly so great as people suppose; no snake, for example, is powerful enough to crush the bones of his prey. The pressure of the coils simply keeps the lungs from expanding and the victim dies from asphyxiation. So although pythons have occasionally killed animals as large and powerful as leopards, they have seldom killed human beings. A man has hands and can generally unwrap a snake before he loses consciousness.

Danny insisted on letting Peter crawl around his bedroom. This was all right as long as Danny kept his door shut, but Danny often forgot. It seems impossible to convince a twelve-year old that a python once placed with loving care on a bed will not necessarily still be there after you have returned from a game of catch with a friend. As a result, Peter was always turning up in odd places around the house. Jule complained more about poor Peter than she had about any other animal we'd ever had. "After all, he isn't really friendly," she protested. "And he doesn't do anything but sleep all the time and try to bite you if you trip over him in the dark."

I must admit that Peter could be a problem. Pythons are semi-aquatic, and Peter loved to get into the tank of the water closet where he lay coiled around the plumbing. Once he got himself braced there, it was impossible to get him out. People who didn't know about him got a decided shock when they used the toilet; Peter strongly disliked having it flushed while he was inside, rearing up unexpectedly with a blood-curdling hiss. We tried filling up the bathtub for him, but he preferred the water closet. He didn't spend all his time there by any means and when hurrying through the house, you always ran the chance of coming suddenly on Peter while rounding a chair or sofa. Although usually quite tame, Peter didn't like to be stepped on and his bite, even if not poisonous, was unpleasant. Peter's teeth curve inward and once he had a grip on something he couldn't let go. Snakes can't bite off chunks of their quarry as does a mammal; anything they swallow must be swallowed whole, so this tooth arrangement is to aid a snake in swallowing his food. But trying to release yourself from Peter's jaws was like trying to pull against a score of inch-long fishhooks.

Danny was always careful to look for Peter when going through the house, but the rest of us sometimes forgot. Another disadvantage of Peter as a domestic pet was that any room in which he was loose soon became a wreck, for Peter, a very good climber, cased every inch of it. He crawled behind books in the bookcases, knocking them out as he went along. He hung from lamps and examined the mantelpiece, brushing a few stray vases to the floor with his nose as he slid along. Julie, our then-fifteen-year-old daughter, disliked Peter intensely. She wasn't afraid of him; she just considered him a nuisance. In fact, Julie didn't like any of the animals. This was partly because she was a dainty little person and regarded animals as dirty and smelly but mainly because she was a rigid conformist and none of her friends kept pythons, cheetahs, or eagles.

Danny couldn't understand why anyone should object to Peter, Like all children, he adopted a strictly anthropomorphic attitude toward any animal he liked. I once overheard him protesting to Cecile that she had been cruel to Peter.

"But I assure you that I have not been," Cecile protested. "I would not get close enough to that serpent to be cruel to him."

"Well, you looked at him as though you didn't like him," Danny insisted. "And Peter's a very sensitive snake."

Peter may have been sensitive mentally but he certainly wasn't physically. One day I walked into the living room and smelled burning flesh. There was Peter curled up on a hot radiator apparently happy as a clam, but the smell was coming from him. Grabbing him back of the neck with one hand and about halfway down the body with the other, I lifted him—but trying to handle Peter when he didn't want to be handled was like trying to control a fire hose with a full force of water pouring through it. I had to yell for help and Danny ran in and gave me a hand. Together, we got Peter spread out on the floor. His belly was badly burned. He'd just sat there and allowed himself to be fried.

Snakes have very little feeling. There have been plenty of cases of keepers in zoos putting live rats into a snake's cage for food and discovering later that the rats had eaten the snake. The snake seemingly was unconscious of pain. Their nervous systems apparently don't function under certain conditions.

We were able to cure Peter by keeping his belly well rubbed with olive oil, but later he managed to tear himself badly on a nail. This was more serious. The cut refused to heal and we couldn't find a vet who would go near Peter. Finally, we found a talented and courageous young graduate student at the School of Veterinary Medicine at the University of Pennsylvania named Leonard Marcus who cut away the infected flesh and took five stitches in the wound while Danny and I wrestled with Peter. It was quite an evening, especially since—while Dr. Marcus and I were resting after the operation—Danny fed Peter a large rabbit to console him. The rabbit was so big that in going down it stretched Peter's neck and tore out the stitches so the whole thing had to be done over again.

Incidentally, it is unnecessary to feed snakes live quarry. The flickering tongue of a snake picks up minute particles of scent in the air and transfers them to a cavity in the roof of the mouth called the Jacobson's organ. This organ does for the snake what our noses do for us—identifies the various scent particles so the snake knows what's around. As a result, snakes are often said to "smell with their tongues." As long as the quarry is still warm and giving off scent, the snake will eat it.

Peter's two accidents made Danny more careful about letting him roam around. Danny didn't care how many vases Peter broke or what a scare he gave Julie's friends when they used our bathroom facilities but the realization that Peter could hurt himself came as a great shock and Danny reluctantly agreed to let us keep Peter in a large, thermostatically controlled cage kindly proved by Mr. Carl Kauffeld of the Station Island Zoo, only letting Peter out to take his bath and then keeping him under strict chaperonage.

Danny also learned through painful experience not to go near Peter after he'd been handling rabbits or chickens because Peter would strike at him. Like all snakes, Peter was very short-sighted and trusted to his Jacobson's organ to locate food. If something was warm and smelled right, he tried to eat it. When Danny told me thoughtfully, "You know, Father, snakes don't think like human beings," I knew he was making progress.

Like me, Danny had always been a solitary kid who had difficulty making friends, but unlike me he did not enjoy being lonely. Partly because of Peter, so many of the local kids became interested in reptiles that the Chester County Aquarium (which had formerly carried an uninspiring line of fish, canaries, and guinea pigs) found it necessary to include snakes. Mel Venti, the proprietor and an enthusiastic amateur zoologist, organized a club called the Junior Aquarium Society and the youngsters met once a week to discuss fish and reptiles. Danny joined and met a number of boys with interests similar to his own. The manual training instructor at the school told me happily that for the first time Danny was showing a marked aptitude in shop; previously he had hardly been able to hammer a nail. "For a long while he was so clumsy that he broke all the tools and ruined all the wood we gave him," the instructor explained. "But it must have been just an adolescent phase. Now he's become quite a good little carpenter and is always making something." I asked him what Danny was making. "Snake cages," the instructor explained.

All youngsters are fascinated by poisonous snakes simply because of the element of danger. As there are no poisonous snakes in our vicinity, I had never warned Danny about them and he once returned from a week end in Virginia with three baby copperheads in a paper bag. He was delighted and so was I, but Jule ordered them out of the house. "You know how he takes Peter to bed with him," she warned me. "And he's still careless about letting him escape sometimes. He can't have poisonous snakes until he's learned how to take care of them." I was forced to agree.

In my youth, I had often gone collecting rattlesnakes, so when spring came, I took Danny rattlesnaking in New Jersey. The snake-hunting season is in early spring, when the rattlers are just beginning to emerge from their winter hibernation. Rattlesnakes "den up" for the winter in rock ledges, crawling into the deep, narrow cracks well below the frost line. There they sleep the winter through, lying in huge heaps like giant spaghetti until the warmth of the rocks tells them that summer has come. For the first few days they lie about on the warm rocks, soaking up sunshine until their cold blood begins to circulate freely and they are ready to set out on the search for food. Snake-hunters try to catch them while they are still in the vicinity of the dens and semi-torpid.

Danny and I started out one morning in early May to try our luck at a famous rattlesnake den called, appropriately enough, Mount Misery. The den is on the property of a former cranberry farmer named Asa Pitman. As a young man, Pitman had bought the property because of a bog which made it ideal for cranberry farming, wondering at the extraordinarily low price. He moved into the abandoned house near the mount with his young wife and set out his cranberry plants. When spring came, he found he was living on top of a rattlesnake den. Pickers refused to work in the bog and Pitman was ruined. Then, with amazing resourcefulness, he decided to harvest the rattlesnakes. Rattlers have a commercial value; their venom is used by laboratories in the making of antivenin and is also used in the treatment of certain diseases. The snakes themselves are sold to zoos, carnivals, and circuses.

Pitman is now dead and a summer camp has flooded the site of the old den for a swimming pool, but then the den was still in existence. After skidding and stalling on the sandy roads through the pine barrens, we came to the old Pitman house. Here we left the car and started out for the mount, taking with us our snake-catching equipment, consisting of burlap bags and poles with running nooses at the ends.

We plunged into the woods, following a narrow trail covered with moss so thick that I felt as though we were walking on a Persian carpet. The interlocking branches of the pines shut out the direct glare of the sun and we moved in a soft twilight, the air heavy with the sweet, tangy odor of the trees. Then we came out of the pines into the yellow sunlight. In front of us was a marshy bowl covered with the curved fiddleheads of new ferns and on the other side of the bog stood Mount Misery, really only a small hill some thirty feet high—its slopes covered with great slabs of shag rock. From under the rocks flows a tiny, gin-clear stream that feeds the bog. It is because of this stream that the snakes den up under the shag. The stream remains the same temperature winter and summer, never freezing, and thus serves as a thermostat for the rock piles. In autumn the snakes follow the course of the stream deep into the rock recesses and lie there near the water until spring calls them out to wander through the pine barrens.

We crossed the bog as silently as possible; although snakes are deaf, they can feel the vibrations of footsteps through the ground. There were no snakes out sunning themselves and I began to be afraid that we had come too early in the year. For some time we tapped on rocks and poked our sticks under them without luck. Then a loud, angry humming broke out under one of the slabs of shag. Although I had been expecting the noise for the last hour, I jumped when I heard it. The buzz of an infuriated rattlesnake is a more alarming sound than the whine of a bullet.

I told Danny to stand back while I turned the stone over. Once, many years before, I turned over a flat stone and a whole nest of rattlers fell over my feet. I had to stand still until they crawled away and they were very slow about doing it. This time I stood well above the stone before turning it over.

There was a big yellow rattler lying in flat coils. Timber rattlesnakes come in a surprising variety of shades: black, brown, yellow, and even lavender. For a second this fellow lay still except for his rattle, which moaned like a hive of restless bees. Then as Dan pressed nearer with his noose-pole, the rattler, reared himself upright, his head a good foot clear of the ground, his forked tongue slipping slowly in and out as he tasted the air.

I got the bag and held the mouth open while Dan cautiously approached with his noose. The snake avoided the open noose with great skill but on the fourth attempt, Danny got him. As soon as the snake felt himself a prisoner he began to thrash against the stones so violently that Danny could hardly hold him. Letting go of the stick with one hand, he grabbed the flailing body with the other. I held the sack close to him but the reptile managed to get a turn around Danny's arm with his body and using this purchase nearly tore his head free of the noose. The rattle was going madly, several times striking against Dan's face. The snake's mouth had gapped open and I could see the fangs slip out of their sheaths of soft, white flesh. Curved, white, and semi-transparent, they looked like long fingernail clippings.

Dan managed to maneuver the snake over the mouth of the sack and lowered him in. At the last moment, he released the noose and the snake fell into the bag but as he did so he slashed sideways, missing the back of my hand by a fraction of an inch. I quickly twisted the mouth of the bag and later we tied it securely with string.

We got two more snakes that morning. I nearly stepped on one for in spite of all my care, the mottled dark brown pattern of the snake's body matched perfectly the dead ferns on which he was lying. Luckily for me, he was still sluggish from his long winter's sleep and lay motionless while I quietly moved away. But when Danny slipped the noose around his neck, he was suddenly galvanized into action, flinging himself back and forth among the bracken while the air was full of the heavy, musky odor peculiar to rattlesnakes and overripe cantaloupes. It took both of us to get him in the bag and I took the pole from Danny and dropped this one myself.

Our last snake was crawling among the rocks and before we could get to him, he was halfway down a hole. I had to pull him out by the tail while Dan stood ready with his noose when the snake's head would appear. This is one time when the old-fashioned forked stick would have been better than the noose-pole. With a forked stick, you pin down the snake just back of his broad head shaped like the pip of a club card. Then you grab him by the neck with one hand while holding his body with the other. The great trouble with the forked stick is that when the stick is removed there is a little space between the snake's head and your fingers, sometimes just enough to enable the snake to twist around and fasten his fangs in your hand. But here it would have been ideal for when the snake's head came out, Danny wasn't able to catch it in time with the noose and the rattler doubled with terrible speed on me. I dropped him and he slithered off. Danny stopped him and he reared up into the business coil, a giant spring above the bracken. He hung there swaying in a strangely unnatural manner like a coil of rope suspended by an invisible thread. The sound of his Tattle seemed to set off several other snakes under the rocks who burst into humming as though connected to him by an electrical current, although it must have been the vibrations of our feet on the rocks that they felt as we ran toward him. Danny noosed him without too much trouble and we added him to the bag.

"Won't Mother be surprised when she sees all the snakes we got?" said Danny proudly as we started back toward the car. Mother was indeed surprised, but as she said after Dan had gone to bed that night, "I think Danny's gaining more confidence in himself. After all, it isn't every twelve-year-old who could handle live rattlesnakes." I agreed that Danny was definitely coming along.

Fourteen

In spite of his interest in snakes, Danny paid no more attention to the other animals than did his sister Julie who, at fourteen, continued to detest the whole lot. This attitude was as mysterious to me as my lack of interest in the Navy had been to my father; I simply couldn't conceive of any normal boy not being fascinated by an eagle, a hunting leopard, and a pet 'coon. But the arrival of Ottie changed all that.

During a trip to Florida, Jule and I acquired a baby otter we named Ottie. Ottie didn't weigh more than five pounds wringing wet and was no bigger than an undersized dachshund, but he was even livelier than the coatis. On the trip north in our car, Ottie worked out an uproarious game consisting of taking a wild leap from the rear seat and landing on top of my head. He wriggled under seats like a snake, managed to get himself caught, and then cried until we stopped and extricated him. His hind feet were webbed but his forepaws weren't and he took apart everything he could find. Finally we had to buy a cage and put Ottie inside it, whereupon he screamed and wailed all the way to Pennsylvania.

When we reached our farm, Jule and I reeled out of the wrecked car and collapsed while Ottie tore around the grounds at his curious, humpbacked gait that made him look like a delirious inchworm. When we let him in the house he raced through it on a lightning tour of inspection, took a refreshing bath in the toilet, and then went to sleep on our bed—first carefully drying himself on the pillow.

Perhaps the best description of an otter was made by Friar Odoric who saw the Chinese fishing with trained otters in 1513. He wrote, "The Chinese fish by the aid of another fish called a diver. It has a muzzle and neck like a fox, forepaws like a dog, hind feet like a duck and the body of a snake. It dives into water and I swear in less than two hours it had filled two big baskets, always depositing the fish in the baskets."

Sometime in the sixteenth century, the art of training otters was introduced into Europe. It soon became the rage, especially in Sweden. Whole families were supported by a trained otter. Fishermen sold their nets and tackle, depending on two or three otters for their catch. Olaus Magnus reported in 1555, "The cook in our inn has an otter that sleeps by the fire. When the cook gives him a sign, the otter runs to the fishpond, catches a fish and brings it to him for cooking."

I tried to train Ottie following the directions left by Captain Salvin, a Victorian gentleman who had several trained otters and gives such helpful hints as "if an otter persists in eating the fish he catches, give him a red-hot one." Ottie and I never reached that point in his training, however. Being a member of the weasel family, he took a dim view of any attempt at discipline. Just getting a collar on Ottie turned out to be a major operation. He could twist like a snake and had the strength of a coiled steel spring. His teeth were not only needle-sharp, but he could both bite and slash with them. I'll say this for Ottie, though, he never carried a grudge. No matter how badly he bit me, he was always willing to climb up in my lap afterward and sit there happily sucking the end of his tail like a baby sucking his thumb. If I stopped petting him, he pulled his tail out of his mouth long enough to give a little querulous cry of complaint and to nudge me with his nose. Once the petting started again, he contentedly put his tail back and lay there making comfortable chuckling noises.

When I was younger, I didn't mind particularly being bitten or scratched by animals, but now I frankly don't like it. The bites seem to hurt more and infect more readily. Also, I have other things to do. So I kept Ottie in a large, outdoor cage where he could run around and only took him out for a short run in the afternoon, mainly down to our pond and back. I'd pretty much given up any idea of training him and kept him simply as another pet. Since he was completely undisciplined I did not let him into the house and, of course, did not attempt to take him fishing, as I had no control over him once he was free.

As long as I had been working with Ottie, Danny paid no attention to him, but when I more or less ignored him, I would often come out to find Danny in the cage playing with him. Ottie loved to roughhouse. He would crouch down, watching Danny with his bright brown eyes, and then suddenly charge. He was so quick that he seemed to be in five places at once; on Danny's neck, down his back, in his lap, up his trouser leg, and in his shirt. Danny would grab him and sling him about in a way that would have dislocated the spine of anything less supple than an otter but, after a wild dash around his pen, Ottie would come shooting back for more. Danny was willing to keep this game up for hours—which was more than I could do, especially as Ottie frequently used his needle-like teeth in moments of excitement. He never bit hard but he bit hard enough to draw blood and after an hour or so of this sport, Danny's hands were badly scratched. Yet he never seemed to mind.

One day I stopped to watch the fun and Danny looked up beamingly exclaiming "Isn't he cool?" I went in to join the fun and Ottie jumped on me in the same way, but after a bite or two I cuffed him to make him stop. Ottie retired, his feelings greatly hurt. Dan looked at me thoughtfully and said "You're afraid of him, aren't you?" I wouldn't have put it quite that way but I had to admit that I didn't want to lose a finger. Ottie was young, but an adult otter can be a dangerous animal. There is at least one case on record of an otter's having killed a man. In 1887, a trapper in the Yukon tried to take an otter out of a trap and the otter managed to get the man by the throat and punctured the jugular vein.

After that, Danny took Ottie over completely. I suppose it was the first time he had ever found anything he could do that I couldn't and it gave him confidence. He brought Ottie into the house and up to his room. The first few times, Ottie would go rampaging around in his usual way—Danny called it "ramming around"—but he soon learned to follow Danny up the stairs to his room immediately. Danny learned little tricks to keep Ottie amused such as giving him stuffed toys, which Ottie loved and would wrestle with indefinitely. They would sit together watching TV, Ottie busily engaged in sucking his tail during the programs. Otters are supposed to be nocturnal, but Ottie preferred to sleep with Danny, merely rising two or three times during the night to take a bath in the toilet before climbing back into bed and luxuriously drying himself off on the sheets before dozing off. Occasionally he would go wandering around the house and we would be awakened by the patter of little feet, followed by the sight of Ottie's head appearing over the edge of the bed. But as soon as Ottie saw he was in the wrong room, he'd leave hastily and we'd hear him gallumping upstairs to Danny's bed.

We tried to persuade Danny to housebreak him. Dan went so far as to put a box of sand by his door and introduce Ottie to it. Ottie was delighted with this new toy and after digging out all the sand, went to sleep in the box. But after a few days he got the idea—almost. No matter where he was, inside or outside, when he felt the urge he would tear to the box, put his feet on the edge, and let go. Then he would run to Danny for approval, which he always received even though he invariably missed the box. Jules finally solved this problem by spreading newspaper around the box.

Even apart from his reluctance to be housebroken, Ottie could hardly be considered the perfect house pet. Danny would often bring him in when we had guests—he was proud of his wonderful pet, but Dan had no control over him when Ottie saw food. If we had canapés, Ottie would take a flying leap into the center of the dish, grab as many as he could in his mouth, and hold onto the rest with his forepaws while chewing. If any guest had a highball, Ottie promptly dove into it head first. He wasn't interested in the liquor; he wanted to fish out the ice, which he loved to crack between his white teeth. Danny thought all this very humorous. The guests didn't.

The two spent most of their time during the summer swimming in our pond or playing on the bank. When they went in the water together, Ottie would frolic like a porpoise. His favorite game was to wrap himself around Dan's neck like an animated furpiece and ride grandly around the pool. If Danny tried to dislodge him, he'd scream with indignation. Ottie also learned to retrieve small objects like sticks and a celluloid boat even though he was fairly erratic about it. Sometimes he'd bring back anything Danny threw into the pond; other times he'd ignore it until Danny dove in after it. Then Ottie would drop whatever he was doing, swim desperately past Danny and grab the prize.

When spring came and the baby ducks began to arrive, Ottie had to be gotten out of the pond and kept locked up in the house while the mother ducks took their broods down for a swim. Danny developed a number of tricks to get Ottie out of the water. Sometimes he would run around the shore trailing a spool on the end of a piece of string, sometimes he would pretend to play with Wriggles or—and this was the most effective of all—he would suddenly lose all interest in Ottie and start running as hard as he could go toward the house. Ottie would almost invariably leave the water to chase him. The trouble was that Ottie could run faster than Danny and when the otter overtook the boy, he would nip at his ankles. At first these nips were only in play and did not break the skin but then Ottie started biting in earnest.

Ottie was growing fast and remembering my childhood experiences with Wayatcha, I urged Danny to carry a switch for if Ottie were to remain a pet he would have to learn discipline. I think Dan attributed my warning to my own fear of being bitten and ignored me. Ottie grew increasingly aggressive week by week and I knew that sooner or later there would have to be a showdown.

Ottie had become Danny's pet and Danny was very proud of his ability to work with him so I didn't like to interfere, but it was painful to stand by and watch Dan repeating mistakes I had made thirty years earlier. It is hard to know what to do in such cases, for training animals is an art rather than a science; you must know the animal and he must know you. Ottie regarded Danny as his friend and was indifferent to me. Danny was sure he could win him over by kindness. I was equally sure he could not. Although Ottie wasn't vicious, he was getting into the biting habit that becomes increasingly difficult to break as an animal gets older. I was afraid that Ottie would become a confirmed biter and then we would have to dispose of him and Danny would lose his beloved pet. I wanted to prevent this tragedy but that meant taking Ottie over myself and, after all, Danny would have to learn by experience.

One day while I was typing, I heard the back door slam. There was a moment's pause, and then came terrible, blood-curdling screams. They were not the screams of someone simply in pain; they were screams of awful agony and hysterical panic. As I jumped up, I heard Danny running wildly through the house. Then he began screaming again. I bolted into the living room and saw Danny running frantically around the couch. After him came Ottie, but such an Ottie as neither of us had ever dreamed could exist. The otter was leaping up to rip at the boy's legs and arms. He seemed completely demented—like a mad dog in a blind frenzy of killing. Danny was panicstricken, not only by the pain of the bites but from the fury of the attack.

I tried to grab the otter but he was in such a paroxysm of blood lust and moved so quickly I could not reach him. When I finally got him by the tail, he turned on me. I hit him with all my strength. He fell half-senseless and then began to drag himself away, trailing his hind legs. I thought that in my rage I had broken his back, but otters are tough and in a few seconds he had recovered the use of his hindquarters, crawling away to hide under the couch.

So far as I was concerned, that was the end of Ottie. He would have to go to a zoo. Danny, I was sure, would never go near him again. But Danny, still sobbing hysterically, went over to the couch and called "Here Ottie, poor Ottie!" and Ottie slowly emerged. He stood up on Danny's leg, rubbed his chin against his knee, and looked up at him imploringly. Weasels can go into a delirium of killing, as many a farmer who has had a weasel get into his chicken-house has found out. Originally, Ottie had only been playing with Danny when he chased and bit him. He had no idea how those bites could hurt. Then as the bites grew more and more severe, something had snapped in his mind and he had gone temporarily mad. Now he was asking forgiveness.

Danny continued to take Ottie swimming and for weeks afterward, Ottie was perfect—chasing the boy but never offering to bite. But religiously once a month Ottie would make another attack, although never in the same homicidal manner, apparently just to see if he could get away with it. Danny learned always to carry a switch and if Ottie went for him to give him a light cut over the back. That was all Ottie needed for another few weeks—but then he'd try again. Seemingly like some children he needed the feeling of security that comes from being disciplined occasionally.

Once Ottie realized that Dan was not like the rubber ball he used as a teething ring, they became even better friends. As Ottie was completely amphibious they would often go for walks together, sometimes traveling four or five miles with Ottie seldom more than two or three feet from Dan's heels. Sometimes Ottie would stop to investigate a woodchuck hole or a rabbit form and Danny would go on without him. But before long he was sure to hear a furious whistle and there would be Ottie, standing up on his hind legs and looking around to see what had become of him. As soon as Danny called, Ottie would come humping himself along and take up his usual position behind Dan.

After reading Friar Odoric's account of otters trained to fish in China, both Danny and I were eager to see what Ottie could do along this line when he grew older. As long as there was other game available (frogs, crayfish, or tadpoles), Ottie paid little attention to fish. When he did see one, he would stalk it, gliding along so slowly that he hardly seemed to move, pushing himself along with his tail and an occasional motion of his forepaws.

When he was within a few feet of his quarry, he would suddenly arch his back and snap himself forward with a motion so swift and unexpected I could hardly follow it. He was rarely able to swim a fish down, but sometimes he could pin one against the bank, holding it with his paws and then killing it with a quick bite in the head.

The biggest fish Ottie ever caught was an 8-pound bass. He had been creeping around the edge of the pool, pausing to stare intently into the water whenever he came to a likely spot, and not even bothering to raise his head when Danny called. He stayed so long in one spot that we'd decided he must have gone to sleep when suddenly Ottie dove. An otter makes absolutely no splash when he dives; it's like a jet of oil squirted into a bucket of syrup. A little chain of bubbles from his nostrils went up, two by two, and then came a sudden swirl on the surface. One minute went by, then two, and I began to get worried—Ottie had never before stayed down more than a minute or so.

Suddenly a bass broke the surface with Ottie clinging to his back, riding him like a horse. The otter's teeth were locked in the fish's head but the bass was still fighting. As they came up, Ottie let go long enough to get a gasp of air and instantly the fish shook him off and went down. Ottie circled the spot, looping up and down, his long, lean body hardly distinguishable from the brown, oily ripples around him. Finally he must have sighted his badly injured quarry, for he went down so straight that for a second his tail stuck up perpendicular to the surface like a periscope. Another pause and then Ottie appeared near the bank, swimming on his side and towing the dead fish along. He was so exhausted that he accepted without protest our help in getting the fish ashore.

Julie had never liked any of the animals and actually hated Ottie. "I don't particularly like getting bitten" she explained when, during a swimming party she was giving, Ottie had rushed down and taken a good-natured nip out of the calf of her leg. Although I could understand Julie's point of view, I think her resentment of our pets would have been defined by a psychologist as sibling rivalry. Julie was ten years old by the time we decided to settle down on the farm and until that time she had been shuttled from California to Capri or left with her grandparents. Jule and I had always worked closely together as a team and when Julie did see us we were always either training cheetahs, getting Águila ready for another lecture tour, or turning the house upside down over some new pet. Julie had not unnaturally come to feel that the animals were first in our affections.

Danny had finally been won over to our way of life, first by Peter and then by Ottie, but Julie had a feminine dislike of snakes and regarded Ottie as a wet, biting menace. When she became a teen-ager and discovered that boys coming to call often spent more time looking at Rani, watching Águila fly, or playing with Ottie than they did talking to her, her resentment increased. Often photographers would ask to have pictures taken of her with the animals, but Julie refused. "If they want pictures of the animals, they don't need me," she'd say resentfully. And once, pitifully, "No one ever wants to take my picture."

So I was dumfounded when Jule came to me one afternoon and said that Julie wanted to buy a baby monkey she'd seen in a pet store. I flatly refused. Monkeys make most unsatisfactory pets. They are highly susceptible to human diseases and have no natural immunity to them; an ordinary head cold develops quickly into pneumonia in a monkey. They are so human that keeping one locked up perpetually in a cage is a real cruelty, but allowing a monkey to run loose in a house is practically impossible. I told Jule this was nothing but a passing fancy with our daughter—and besides, pet-store wild animals are all too frequently diseased.

Jule demurred. "Dan, she's been saving up for this particular monkey for weeks. She saw it coming home from school one day and fell in love with it. You must let her get it."

I agreed to go down to the pet store and look at the monk. It turned out to be a baby female spider monkey, not much bigger than my fist. When the little thing saw Julie, it held out its hands, crying plaintively and as Julie gathered it to her bosom, the baby put both hands and its tail around her neck and snuggled down contentedly. "It's only a baby and it needs me," said Julie with a break in her voice. "Nothing you ever had needed me. Please, may I buy her?"

Naturally, we returned with the monkey. She had violent diarrhea and a cold. We have a small sunroom and I plugged in an electric heater which brought the temperature up to over 90 degrees. Julie insisted on staying with the baby, so we moved a cot in for her. The pet-store proprietor had been feeding the baby a steady diet of fruit, but I called Fred Ulmer, curator of mammals at the Philadelphia Zoological Gardens, for advice. Fred recommended a diet of "marmoset cake." In case anyone thinks that raising a baby monkey is easy, here's the recipe for marmoset cake:

Commercial baby cereal (62%), whole-milk powder (35%), wheat-germ meal (2%), and multi-vitamin preparation (1%). This is supplemented by a meat ration consisting of raw ground meat (86%), cod-liver oil (2%), and "Mineral Mixture C-I" (12%). This mixture is oystershell flour (40%), powdered skim milk (30%), Ledinac (25%), and iodized salt (5%).

Julie named the baby Jupo, a combination of her own name and that of her current most intimate friend, Poppy Mull. Jupo refused to eat her formula but Julie, while playing with her, managed to get the baby to suck some from her fingers. Although Fred had warned us to give the baby fruit as sparingly as we would candy to an infant, Julie rubbed some of the formula on grapes until Jupo got used to the strange taste of it.

Jupo did well on her diet. It seemed to me that one day she was a helpless baby and the next she was tearing books out of the bookcases, swinging by her tail from the chandelier, and going through the house like an unguided missile. In spite of Julie's tearful protests, we did try putting her in a cage. It's easy enough to put babies in cribs or playpens; they don't hold out entreating little hands to you and then, when you turn them down, crawl off into a corner, cover their heads with their arms, and sit rocking back and forth crying bitterly. We finally had to move everything out of the sunroom and keep her confined there.

Frankly, I was looking forward to spring when Jupo could be turned loose in the garden. So it was a memorable day for the Mannix household when the thermometer hit 70 and Julie carried Jupo out to the apple orchard. We were all afraid that Jupo might not come back after she had once had a taste of freedom but, as it turned out, Jupo had different ideas. She clung to Julie with hands and feet as well as her tail and screamed with terror. Jupo was suffering from agoraphobia, the reverse of claustrophobia. The great open spaces scared her to death. She wanted to get back to the friendly old sunroom.

It took two weeks of bribery, coaxing, and physical force before Jupo would even consent to sit on the grass beside Julie. Even then, she kept her tail tightly wound around Julie's arm as a safety line. She chattered nervously and hid her face in her hands if a leaf rustled. It was another fortnight before she'd turn loose her tail and make short runs away from her foster mother. Nothing would induce her to get anywhere near a tree. She regarded them as dangerous.

One day while I was pounding at the typewriter, Julie rushed in, crying hysterically: "Jupo's up a tree and can't get down." It turned out that Julie had finally managed to persuade Jupo to climb a tree by climbing it herself. Jupo had trustingly followed her for about 20 feet and then the monkey happened to look down. That did it. Jupo clung to the branch with a death grip and refused to be dislodged.

By the time I got out, Jupo had decided that although she didn't dare go down, she could still go up. She was now at the top of the tree with her tail wrapped around a slender twig and screaming for help.

As the upper branches couldn't sustain my weight, the only way we got Jupo down was to cut off the top of the tree and lower it from hand to hand with Jupo still clinging to the topmost branch. For a while we were afraid that she'd let go and fall, for when Jupo saw what was happening, she let go with her tail and used it to cover her eyes. But she made the trip down in safety.

Jupo refused to leave the house for the rest of the summer. If Julie tried to carry her out, Jupo would lasso the doorknob with her tail as she went by, meanwhile making a noise like a siren being murdered. It wasn't until the next year that we could get her out again. She was bigger and braver then and would even sit on the porch steps by herself, only giving a call every now and then to make sure somebody was around. If nobody answered her, Jupo would start pounding on the door, yelling like a banshee until she was let in.

One day, Jupo suddenly started screaming in what was clearly stark terror. We hadn't learned to understand Jupo's vocabulary at that time (she later turned out to have quite an extensive one) but there was no mistaking that noise. The whole family made a rush for the door.

Jupo was spreadeagled up against the side of the porch, gibbering with fear. A few feet away sat a squirrel staring at her. The squirrel was obviously fascinated by this queer-looking creature and wanted to play. It began to bounce up and down like a rubber ball and at every bounce Jupo let out another scream, at the same time doing her best to go backward through the woodwork. Jupo had never seen a squirrel before, but she instantly identified it as a bloodthirsty wild beast that ate baby monkeys.

Julie chased off the squirrel and carried Jupo into the house. The monkey was chattering with terror. When she recovered, she told us all about it. Charlie Chaplin was supposedly the king of pantomime, but he was nothing compared to Jupo. The monkey talked to us fluently for five minutes, running to the window and indicating where the attack had taken place, backing up against the wall to show her own terror, and then running out to the middle of the floor and jumping up and down to illustrate how the squirrel had behaved. At the end, she lay down on the floor with her hands over her face moaning to show what a terrible experience it had been. This was by far the most human performance Jupo ever put on. I've never experienced a better piece of dramatization.

As a result of the squirrel incident, Jupo again refused to leave the house. She spent her time looking out the windows at the garden, watching for any more savage beasts that might be lurking in the shrubbery. As far as Jupo was concerned, Pennsylvania was far too dangerous a place for a self-respecting monkey.

Except when she was angry, Jupo was so jolly and friendly that it was hard to think of her as a potentially dangerous wild animal. By the time she was three years old, she'd lost all her fear of heights and spent the summer swinging through the trees around our house in the approved spider-monkey fashion. She seldom went down on the ground except to play with Wriggles, so the open fields around our farmhouse formed a more effectual barrier for keeping her at home than any fence could have done. In the evening, she'd come and knock at the window to be let in for the night.

One afternoon, Julie and Danny were wrestling together and Julie was getting the worst of it. In what Julie considered the spirit of good, clean fun she shouted, "Jupo, come and help me!" Jupo was sitting on the roof of the house watching the children and had made no effort to interfere but when she heard Julie's voice, the monkey reached the lawn in two great bounds and rushed at Danny. Grabbing him with her long arms, she slashed open his forearm with her fangs. Julie screamed and grabbed Jupo in her arms but the damage had been done. Danny went to the hospital and it took seven stitches to close the cut.

A family council was held that evening, with Julie in tears and Danny pleading for Jupo because he said that it was all Julie's fault. This was true enough, but there was no use pretending that Jupo wasn't getting to be a serious problem. We put her back in the sunroom and, much to our surprise, Jupo accepted the confinement fairly philosophically. During the day we still let her play outside most of the time even in winter, except on extremely cold days. If Jupo got too cold, she'd open the window and go back to her room.

Even outside, Jupo was able to make things lively around the old homestead. When we decided to paint the corncrib green, Jupo came to help. Did you ever see a green monkey? Did you every try to get a paintbrush down from the top of a 60-foot oak tree? Did you ever try to get clothes in from the line while a monkey was wiping herself off with them? If the answer to these questions is *no*, you haven't lived.

Most of the tradesmen were very good about Jupo, but the man who delivered the beverages really got to dislike our pet. Jupo was fond of all bottled drinks—beer, Coca-Cola, ginger ale, soda water—it was all one to Jupo. She learned to open a bottle by dropping it from a tree and lapping up the fluid. When the beverage man arrived, he'd stick his head out of the car window and look around for Jupo. At first, Jupo used to jump on top of the car and wait for the man to come out carrying a case of bottles but the beverage dealer could hear her land, so Jupo had to give up that trick. Instead, she hid in the rain gutter running under the eaves and waited until the man came to the back door. He always carried the case of beverages on his shoulder and while he was knocking, Jupo would hang by her tail from the gutter, quietly lift a bottle out and run off with it before the delivery man knew what had happened.

Now Jupo really had become a serious problem. When we let her outside that spring, the family moved into a state of siege. Jupo spent hours testing every door and window to see if we'd left any unlocked. If you opened a door, even for a second, Jupo was in before it could be slammed shut. We finally worked out a system of signals so people could get in and out of the house. Someone stood by a window and watched until Jupo was spotted. If she was hanging by her tail from the rainspout over the back door, one whistle was sounded and it was safe to make a dash out the front door. When Jupo tore over the eaves to block that exit, the signal was two whistles (back door free). Then Jupo took to tearing off the shingles and throwing them at us as we dashed by.

In spite of everything, we managed to keep Jupo several months longer. Then she bit two children who had come to see the animals, so seriously that they had to be hospitalized. There was nothing for us to do except to keep her permanently locked up or send her to a zoo. Jule and I were convinced either solution would break Julie's heart.

Then one day Julie came to us with a suggestion. "I've been going around to the different zoos and there's a very nice one at Norristown where they have a male spider monkey named Butch who seems lonely. I think Jupo would be happy there."

"Won't you miss her?" Jule asked.

Julie said slowly, "Of course I will. But Jupo's grown up and she doesn't need me any more. Everyone grows up, you know. She has to marry and have a family someday. I can go and see her often and bring her presents."

So Jupo went to Norristown. She's expecting a baby this spring—and I must say that Butch is the only thing short of a gorilla who can handle Jupo. Not only is he considerably bigger than Jupo, he can also bite much harder.

This year Julie became seventeen and we decided to give her a coming-out party. On one matter Jule was determined. "Dan, this is to be Julie's party and her great day. Absolutely no animals. For this one day let's hide the animals away so there'll be no distractions. Let her rule supreme for this one night."

I agreed. We called Julie in to tell her the good news.

To our surprise, Julie demurred. "You know, I think people like to see the animals. Danny's old enough to come to the party and he'd be heartbroken if he wasn't allowed to show off his snakes. Anyhow, when people come to the Mannixes' they expect to see animals."

"But what about you, dear?" Jule asked.

"I've been talking things over with Poppy Mull. She's coming out this year too and we thought we might give a combined party. What about a circus party with all the animals?"

We stared in astonishment. "But you've always hated the animals," I protested.

"Well, ever since Jupo I've felt differently about them. I can understand now how attached you can get to an animal. What we really need are more animals. Could you get Bill Green and Mrs. Ray to come?"

Bill Green owns a traveling circus, consisting of trained llamas, a performing zebra, baboons, horses, dogs, tiny donkeys, and featuring Queenie, a wonderfully talented elephant. Mrs. Ray works as Bill's assistant. A few years before, they had stopped off at our farm for a few days en route to Florida for the winter.

"I think it could be arranged," said Jule gravely.

Bill Green agreed to stop off at our place on his way back to his summer quarters in Vermont. Due to the combined efforts of the Mannix family and the Mulls, we rented a tent which, it seemed to me, would have done credit to Barnum & Bailey at their prime. An orchestra was hired and arrangements were made to provide enough liquor to float the USS *United States*. All seemed rosy except for Daddy's checkbook.

Then we began to get advice from friends who had given coming-out parties for their daughters. To our horror we learned that a coming-out party seemed largely a military operation. "For heaven's sake, have the State Troopers on hand," one distracted matron urged us. "When we gave a party, the boys wrecked the house, started driving around the countryside blind drunk, and when the police did finally arrive at two in the morning, the situation had gotten entirely out of hand." Another lady told us that at her daughter's party, several drunken debutantes had fallen into the swimming pool and two had nearly drowned. My nephew gave me an account of a party he'd attended that sounded like the Battle of the Bulge. "When the cops arrived," he began as though this was the normal climax to a social affair, "they seemed sort of dumb, slow types but friendly. They just asked us to take it easy. Then one guy hit the sergeant over the head with a gin bottle. Uncle Dan," he went on impressively, "I never knew a bunch of cops could move so fast. They threw us all into the patrol wagon and we were twenty-four hours in the pokey until Mother came down and got us out."

After a few such accounts, Jule and I were prepared to call the whole thing off but Julie seemed strangely untroubled. "Oh, I know things like that happen at other parties," she told us lightly. "But Poppy and I have talked the whole thing over and nothing will go wrong. Just relax."

It was all very well for Julie to tell us to relax but when the day of the party dawned, Jule and I felt as though we were preparing for the Normandy landings.

Bill Green and Mrs. Ray had arrived and, with their usual brisk efficiency, had everything in order. Queenie, the elephant, was strolling around our pasture, pausing at intervals to pull up a particularly succulent bunch of grass and dust it off against her forelegs before chewing it meditatively. At first, our horses didn't get along too well with Queenie. Every time they winded her, they had conniption fits. Finally we had to lock them up in the barn. Even then when we took Queenie out of the pasture so they could have a run, the horses could smell where she had been and when they passed her droppings would suddenly bound into the air with a terrified snort. Curiously enough, they didn't mind the zebra colt a bit, recognizing the little fellow as a horse of a different color.

The horses weren't the only people disturbed by Queenie. We kept getting 'phone calls from people asking "Do you know that there's an elephant walking around your pasture?" But an old-time farmer who brings our milk every morning rose superior even to Queenie. She was grazing near our back door when he arrived. He walked within a few yards of her, handed me the milk, and started back toward his truck. Thinking he hadn't seen her, I said, "Elwood, do you mind taking a look at the barn gate? It seems a little loose on its hinges." As Queenie was within a few feet of the gate, I waited for his reaction. Elwood walked over to the gate, almost brushing against Queenie as he went, tested the hinges, and said "Seems all right to me." I asked wonderingly, "Don't you notice anything Standing beside you?" Elwood glanced up at Queenie, who was now smelling him with her trunk. "You mean that thing? Looks a mite bigger than most of the stock we got around here," and left without further comment. Elwood is a hard man to surprise.

Bill Green's trailer was so big we had to leave it parked in the driveway and deliverymen were forced to leave their cars and walk around it, threading their way through the llamas, miniature donkeys, ponies, and baboons all staked out on the front lawn. A bulldozer had to be called in to open a path through the shrubbery so the trucks bearing the tent and tent poles could reach the pasture. John Vanderherchen, supervising the pitching of the tent, had to work amid a crowd of children who had arrived under the not unnatural impression that a circus had come to town and the distracted Mrs. Thompson, social directress of the affair, hurried about trying not to trip over stray animals. As Mrs. Thompson seemed to grow increasingly nervous, Jule asked her, "But you've directed thousands of parties, haven't you?" "None like this," retorted Mrs. Thompson, removing her foot from the grasp of an inquisitive baboon.

But the party went off without a hitch. There were over 500 guests but no one got drunk; the astonished caterer remarked, "I never saw a party where youngsters drank so little." They never got the chance. Although there were two bars in constant operation, at half-hour intervals Bill Green and Mrs. Ray brought on the animals. The kids were delighted. It gradually became apparent that even the hardened sophisticates of the Main Line would rather watch Queenie go through her routine than drink.

Boys and girls alike crowded around the llamas to feed them peanuts and ask Bill about their habits. The girls were especially impressed by the llamas. A llama has a way of wrinkling its lower lip and looking down at you like a dowager examining a beetle through her lorgnette that would impress anyone. As Mrs. Thompson commented, "Those llamas are the only things I've ever seen who could snub a Main Line debutante."

The older guests enjoyed the animals too. We had meant to have only a few older people but once the word got around that we were going to have performing elephants, friends we hadn't seen in years called up to mention tactfully that they would be free that night. In fact, the children had to fight their way through the adults to pat the zebra colt and stroke the miniature donkeys. The baboons, who rode the ponies around the ring and did an act with Bill's dogs, were even more popular than Queenie. Jule, mystified, said to Julie, "Why, all your friends love animals!" and Julie replied somewhat impatiently, "Of course they do. After all, they're only children." An accurate, if slightly unflattering description of the usual guests at a deb party.

No one enjoyed the evening more than our own animals. Wriggles and Dennis, a new cairn terrier we had acquired, wandered around stuffing themselves with handouts from the guests and Macho, the gentle little squirrel monkey who was Jupo's successor, ate until he could eat no more.

The newspapers described it as one of the most successful parties on record. Partly as a result of the party, Julie, who like many young girls has ambitions to be an actress, received a call from the Valley Forge Music Fair to try out for a part in *Gypsy*. Greatly excited she departed in her car, taking along Wriggles and Dennis, who love motoring.

When she returned from the audition, she looked rather serious. We asked anxiously, "Did you get a part?"

"No," said Julie gravely. "But Dennis did. They said he was just the dog they needed to play opposite Vivian Blaine."

We looked at her, stunned. Then suddenly Julie began to laugh. She laughed until she had to sit down and finally we started to laugh too. "Well, Mr. Lester Tapper, who's one of the top men at the Music Fair asked me to come back next summer after I've had a year's dramatic study at the Neighborhood Playhouse in New York. And Dennis is a natural-born actor; he took to the part right away."

We decided then that we didn't need to worry about Julie. She had overcome her animal complex and had learned to regard them as friends rather than rivals.

We are still collecting wild-animal pets and I am still writing about them, traveling from Patagonia to Assam to get my material. I've written on many other subjects, but everyone seems to like the animals best of all. So do I. We have acquired an ocelot, given us by a Marine sergeant after she had clawed a Boy Scout, and a raven named Grip who has just wrecked our little English convertible by tearing off the canvas roof. Julie is now living in New York and Danny, with the prospect of college in the near future, hasn't much time for animals. Few people do when they grow up. But there will always be a new generation of children. One afternoon recently I came out to find three little boys chasing our peafowl—a peacock and peahen—around the barn. When I asked them what they thought they were doing, they explained, "These are Mr. Williams' birds. They sit on his roof every morning and he lets us come over and watch them." I explained that although I was happy to allow Mr. Williams to borrow the birds, they belonged to me. I also pointed out that it wasn't nice to chase birds, especially as the hen was sitting on a nest of eggs and only left them temporarily to sun herself on Mr. Williams' roof. I showed them the nest, and while we were talking the hen returned and began to brood the eggs. The kids were more astonished at this phenomenon than they would have been at a successful moon landing. One kid asked curiously, "What's she doing that for?" I told him the baby peafowl would come out of the eggs in a month's time. Although the youngsters were from the city and had only recently moved out to the country, two of them accepted this statement without question, but the third said contemptuously, "Oh, you're kidding us. Them things is nothing but eggs."

I told him to come back in two weeks and the eggs would be hatched. They were back on time and were lucky enough to watch the actual hatching. I broke the shell to get out one baby but the skeptic was still not convinced. "You put it in there," he said suspiciously as the downy baby was revealed. "Anyhow, they ain't got long tails so they ain't fer real."

These children had been brought up in a completely mechanical world. Yet when they turned on television they didn't want to see rockets or planes, they wanted to see Westerns where men rode horses. Our school board has put up a new 2½-million-dollar school equipped with every possible modern luxury and a faculty trained to lead the children in instructive group play, but a little five-year-old lady comes over daily to stand in silent admiration of the peacock as he struts around with extended train, shivering with the ecstasy of his own beauty. Once I asked my guest if she'd like one of the long train feathers. She hurriedly shook her head. "It would hurt him to pull it out." I told her the cock molted every autumn and I could give her a dropped feather. She accepted it wonderingly. "My, it's so soft!" she whispered, stroking the fine web. "And look how the colors change when you turn it!" Then she added, awestruck, "I'll bet it's the most beautiful thing in the whole world!" I assured her that artists had come to the same conclusion thousands of years ago.

So at least as long as there are children, there will always be someone who loves animals.

Image Gallery

In Mexico with my Golden Eagle, Tequila.

Chiquita Maria, our little maid, in our patio in Taxco,
Mexico, giving a tea party for the kinkajous.

Jule on Teresa with our bald eagle, Águila.

Jule and I with Águila.

Águila coming down on an iguana.

Águila's head.

"Poncho," our coati-mundi in Taxco. We had two of these little fellows.

Jule with the baby kinkajou.

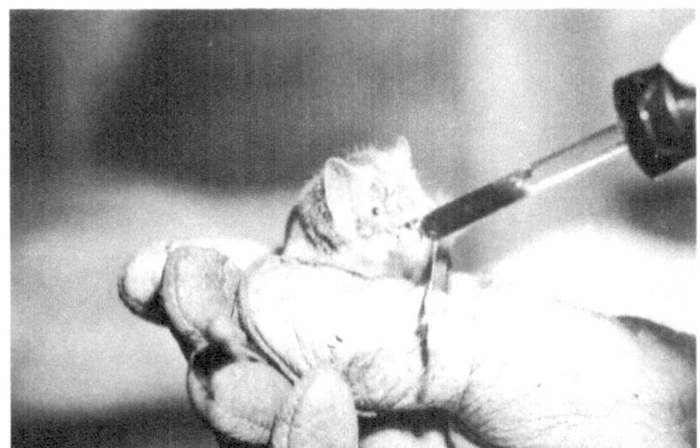

Vampire bat being fed blood from eyedropper by Jule.

Tequila flying to me in Mexico.

Antonio, our houseboy, with the caracara . . . the bird perched on his shoulder.

Cormorant bringing back fish, as they were trained to do.

Jule examining a big iguana.

My peregrine falcon, "Tara," on my fist when I was a youngster.

Wayatcha, my pet raccoon, when I was a boy.

Claude, the porcupine I had when I was a child.

My goshawk on a kill when I was a boy.

Mother opossum with her babies.

My pet skunk, Nikki, and Rags, our little dog.

Our daughter, Julie, some years ago, with a pet skunk.

Rani, the cheetah, jumping out of the car window and starting after a jack rabbit.

Rani moving in on a jack rabbit.

Jule and Rani in our tent in Wyoming.

Julie, her little cousin, Jules Loos, and Rani the cheetah at Malibu, California.

Mealtime for a baby squirrel.

Águila and Julie.

Jule with Concha, the ringtailed cat, in Taxco.

Jupo the spider monkey with Julie at Malvern.

Jule with one of our pet fawns in Taxco.

Jupo, the spider monkey, raiding the refrigerator.

Our pet otter, Ottie, enjoying a freshly caught fish.

Julie's debutante party, given in a circus tent with William Green's performing animals. *(Photo credit: Tom McCaffrey)*

Julie is at left and her co-debutante, Poppy Mull, at right. *(Photo credit: Tom McCaffrey)*

Julie's debutante party. *(Photo credit: The Philadelphia Evening Bulletin)*

Danny and Julie with their favorite rock python.

About the Author

Daniel P. Mannix was an award-winning American author and journalist, as well as a magician and filmmaker. Mannix's magazine articles about his experiences in the carnival, where he performed under the stage name "The Great Zadma," became popular in the mid-1940s and were compiled with the assistance of his wife in the book *Step Right Up!* His dozens of books and extensive essays range in subject from children's animal stories, environmental issues, and hunting accounts to historical examinations of the Hellfire Club, the Atlantic slave trade, and the Roman gladiatorial games. Mannix was particularly interested in the Wizard of Oz canon and composed a biography of L. Frank Baum for *American Heritage* magazine in the 1960s.

DANIEL P. MANNIX

FROM OPEN ROAD MEDIA